THE
2000s
MADE ME
GAY

THE 2000s MADE ME GAY

Essays on
Pop Culture

GRACE PERRY

ST. MARTIN'S GRIFFIN
NEW YORK

First published in the United States by St. Martin's Griffin, an imprint of
St. Martin's Publishing Group

www.stmartins.com

Designed by Devan Norman

Library of Congress Cataloging-in-Publication Data

Names: Perry, Grace, 1989– author.
Title: The 2000s made me gay : essays on pop culture / Grace Perry.
Description: First edition. | New York : St. Martin's Griffin, 2021. | Includes
    bibliographical references.
Identifiers: LCCN 2020056339 | ISBN 9781250760142 (trade paperback) |
    ISBN 9781250760159 (ebook)
Subjects: LCSH: Perry, Grace, 1989– | Lesbians—United States—Anecdotes. |
    Popular culture—United States—21st century.
Classification: LCC HQ75.5 .P44 2021 | DDC 306.7663092—dc23
LC record available at https://lccn.loc.gov/2020056339

Our books may be purchased in bulk for promotional, educational, or business
use. Please contact your local bookseller or the Macmillan Corporate and
Premium Sales Department at 1-800-221-7945, extension 5442, or by email at
MacmillanSpecialMarkets@macmillan.com.

First Edition: 2021

10 9 8 7 6 5 4 3 2 1

—

In loving memory of the Gchat era

—

CONTENTS

INTRODUCTION: SOME NOTES ON ESCAPISM   1

REAL-WORLD GAYS AND *REAL WORLD* GAYS   14

HARRY POTTER AND THE HALF-ASSED GAY CHARACTER   33

THE GOSPEL ACCORDING TO *MEAN GIRLS*   49

CHERRY CHAPSTICK   67

BE THE PR TEAM YOU WISH TO SEE IN THE WORLD   82

BLAIR WALDORF HAS NOTES ON MY SEX LIFE   102

BANTER BOYS: CHRISTIAN, SETH, JIM, AND ME   120

DISNEY CHANNEL PRESENTS: SAPPHIC OVERTONES   142

AMERICAN BITCH / AMERICAN BUTCH   159

TALKING / LAUGHING / LOVING / BREATHING   181

TAYLOR SWIFT MADE ME A U-HAUL DYKE   195

THE *GLEE* BUBBLE   214

ACKNOWLEDGMENTS   229

NOTES   231

THE
2000s
MADE ME
GAY

INTRODUCTION

SOME NOTES ON ESCAPISM

An iPhone blared the sound of an old-timey newsroom telephone, and the bedside lamp flicked on. My mom sat on the edge of the other queen bed and mostly listened. "Okay... okay...." She had to be talking to my dad. "And you're at the hospital now?" My eyes fluttered open, and I took in the hotel room. It was a Route 66–themed Best Western in Missouri. Staying on theme, the walls were dotted with black-and-white photos of road trippers posing with their big, bulky Fords—an homage to those who'd done the route from Chicago to Los Angeles before my mom and I had started eighteen hours prior. I bet those people made it more than one night on the route, though. I sat up, silent and disoriented, hoping this was a very vivid, very bad dream. After a few minutes, she hung up.

Zach had fallen, Mom said, but he was okay—*okay* being a euphemism for *alive*—conscious and responsive, but he had passed out and busted his face on the bathroom floor. An ambulance came to our house, to our childhood bathroom, where my thirty-year-old brother had fainted around midnight. They rushed him to the closest hospital. The ER doctors thought it must've been related to the headaches Zach had been having in the days leading up to our departure. His oncologists at Northwestern, who had been treating his leukemia on and off for four years, believed the headaches were a side effect of the new trial drug he was on. In the emergency room, my mother continued, he had a temporary catheter drilled into the side of his head in the middle of the night. That had relieved the symptoms nearly immediately. He was resting now. He showed no signs of permanent brain damage. He was "okay."

"Oh, and Dad said something else," my mom added. "Before the procedure, Zach's mental state started to . . . well, deteriorate. Apparently he wasn't making any sense. He was just . . . spelling out words and speaking in numbers?" My heart pounded. "And at one point, I guess he just started speaking only in Spanish? Like, he was saying, 'No más!' and 'Vámonos!' 'cause he wanted to get out of there."

I replied with an absurd line I'd find myself repeating a lot over the next week: "Oh, yeah, that's a thing with brain injuries. I saw that on an episode of *Grey's Anatomy*." My mom burst out laughing.

It was true, though! In early season fourteen, Dr. Amelia Shepherd (Dr. McDreamy's sister—McDreamy died in a botched surgery two seasons prior. Catch up.) is diagnosed with a massive brain tumor. She's a neurosurgeon, too, which makes the diagnosis extra wild. Anyway, she gets the tumor removed, and two days post-op, she finally speaks for the first time. Meredith and the others get word that Amelia's up and talking, and they rush to her room. And yes, she's speaking, but she's speaking French: "Un verre d'eau, s'il te plaît," she croaks, "J'ai soif." The Grey-Sloan Memorial Hospital (formally Seattle Grace Mercy West, née Seattle Grace Hospital. Catch! Up!) gang is confused. Amelia doesn't speak French, she speaks German! But Meredith, a Shepherd in-law, recalls that the Shepherd kids all went to French preschool, so that language must be somewhere in the recesses of her brain. "It reverses on its own . . . it's still good, it's progress," Dr. Grey explains. My *Grey's* knowledge served me well. I didn't have to google *speaking foreign language brain injury* to figure out what was going on with Zach.

I didn't have to subject myself to the limitless permutations of diagnoses WebMD would offer. I didn't wonder whether Zach had entirely forgotten the English language. I'd heard of this before. It happened to Amelia Shepherd, and she was more or less fine in the next scene. So Zach would be fine, too. Meredith Grey said so.

At the very moment Zach's face hit our bathroom floor, I was literally dreaming I was in surgery with Meredith Grey. Not because I have ever even vaguely aspired to be a surgeon, but because it was simply the only material my subconscious had to work with come nightfall. I'd been bingeing *Grey's Anatomy* nearly every night for the four months prior—partially because I'd watched *Killing Eve* and craved more Sandra Oh, partially because I was living at home to save money, but mostly because I was going through a breakup and wanted a new personality and elected for one based solely on the Shondaland tentpole. I'd watched the first couple of seasons in high school, but I fell off before the long-standing, seminal queer romance between Drs. Callie Torres and Arizona Robbins. I intended to just rewatch the first two seasons; how naive I was. Shonda Rhimes does not create content of which one can simply "watch a few episodes." And so, single and living with my parents, I watched fourteen seasons of *Grey's Anatomy* in four months. At the time I left Chicago for California, my brain was about 70 percent *Grey's Anatomy*.

When we use the word *escapism*, we're generally talking about a person's desire to leave reality, to withdraw from some terrible set of IRL circumstances. So, when we describe a book or movie or TV show as *escapist*, we mean it's *so* different from our real, everyday world that engaging with it lets us forget that the real world exists. Entertainment labeled *escapist* is usually absurd, or pulpy, or heightened to an unrealistic extreme. Fantasy shows are an obvious example—*Game of Thrones* brings the viewer into a whole new world of dragons and White Walkers and full-frontal male nudity.

But escapist media can also be just a slightly removed version of real life. Musical theater allows us to escape into a world where streets full of New York City strangers burst into coordinated song and dance. The *Real Housewives* franchise lets us leave our own lives to peek into the gauche, surreal environs of permadrunk, middle-aged baronesses, who lead lives utterly unlike our own. *Escapism* is a euphemism for *guilty pleasure*, used in an attempt to obscure the embarrassing fact that we, as a species, love silly and frivolous stories. It's a highbrow-sounding word that validates our cravings for the idiotic. *Escapist* is grown-up code for, "I *know* it's canonically asinine—just let me fucking watch it."

One could characterize my *Grey's Anatomy* binge as escapist, but I wouldn't. No matter how outlandish the world or story, I find the whole notion of escapism to be disingenuous. Or, at least, I think it's an unhelpful way to describe our experience of engaging with pop culture. The word *escape* implies attaining some kind of permanent state of freedom. It's a word with a wide-open future. That doesn't really fit for how we engage with entertainment. Watching a TV show is a finite experience. Even when we nurse a post-birthday hangover by watching season three of *30 Rock* in one sitting for the forty-fifth time, that binge eventually comes to an end. We come back to reality, come back to the doldrums or nightmare or whatever it is pop culture helped us avoid. We turn on the TV, and then we turn it off. We go away for a while, and then we come back.

So, perhaps, thinking of pop culture as escapism isn't the right framing at all. Maybe it's actually vacationism, or retreatism, or getting-the-fuck-away-for-a-whileism. And like most getaways, we usually bring some kind of souvenir back with us. If our vacation is, say, a bachelorette party in New Orleans, we return with a daiquiri-stained tongue and Mardi Gras beads. If it's a trip to Canada, we *at least* return with a moose keychain. If we're a white tween girl and it's a family trip to Jamaica in 2002, we return, tragically, with cornrows. But when we vacation to pop culture, we always return, toting a little emotional or intellectual memento along with us.

So, like a full idiot, when I walked into the neuro ICU the afternoon following Zach's fall, I thought, *Oh, the neuro ICU, from TV,* as if I'd seen a bottle of Proactiv on a drugstore shelf.

I can't pretend I wasn't disappointed to learn Zach's neurosurgeon wasn't Dr. McDreamy (even if he had died way back in season eleven). Dr. Patel was young and kind and communicative and flanked by a group of four eager residents. Dr. Patel told Zach and our family that he was going to insert a shunt into Zach's brain. "It's a permanent apparatus that will divert the excess spinal fluid that Zach's brain has been producing," he told us. We didn't know why Zach's brain was producing extra fluid, Dr. Patel explained, but the good thing about a shunt is that it's not dangerous once left in the brain. I definitely would've felt more secure had he been wearing a scrub cap with ferryboats on it while he told us the plan, but this guy seemed good.

"A shunt is a super common procedure," I assured my parents once the doctors left, my confidence that of an elite neurosurgery fellow. I'm not sure they were even listening to me in that moment—why would they? I had gathered this information from a *Grey's* episode where McDreamy is complaining about how bored and under-stimulated he's been lately. "I'm doing three shunts *a day,*" Dr. McDreamy whines to Meredith. His brilliance can't shine through in such a routine, safe procedure. The fact that a very fictional doctor could've performed this operation on my big brother with his eyes closed made me genuinely optimistic about Zach's health.

I'd spent plenty of time with Zach at the hospital before this particular incident, but never mid-*Grey's* binge. This hospitalization,

my brain processed my environment in terms of (and only in terms
of) the medical drama. I couldn't help it. I imagined Dr. Patel's
team of neurosurgery residents brushing off through the hallway
of the ICU together. I imagined their real talk: "I mean, it's got to
be the leukemia in his CNF, right?" that skinny resident with the
curly bun asks Dr. Patel.

"Probably," Dr. Patel replies, his voice a bit sharper. It's his real
voice, not his patient voice. "But we can't tell the family that until
we *know*. Let's get a consult with the patient's onc team. Who's the
lead on that?"

"Um . . ." The shorter guy with the broad, flat face flips through
Zach's chart as they walk.

"C'mon, Lacey. You've already reviewed his chart, you should
know this."

"It's Dr. Becker," blurts Curly Bun again. Lacey rolls his eyes.
She's always outdoing him.

"He's lucky. Becker's a real piece of work. For now, let's just
let him rest. The patient's had a major trauma. He's lucky to be
alive."

Obviously, those residents *must* have been banging each other.
If we're going by *Grey's* rules, two combinations of them have
fucked in an elevator, one had a pregnancy scare, and one found
out they were secretly the half sibling of another (but luckily,
those two wouldn't have hooked up). Do they actually have on-
call rooms in hospitals? I wonder where theirs is. Probably down
that Employees Only hallway. If I were to strut through those
doors with confidence, would I find Dr. Patel enwrapped in sustained, penetrative eye contact with Curly Bun? Or worse, would
they share such loving gazes over my brother's open skull?

Of course, I "knew" in my "brain" that *Grey's Anatomy* isn't real
life. I wasn't *completely* delusional. But once I entered the neuro
ICU, once I saw my sweet big brother's busted teeth and flocks of

surgical residents and real-life scrub caps, I became incapable of leaving Grey-Sloan Memorial Hospital.

Because no matter how "escapist" the pop culture, when we turn off the TV, flecks of it come back with us—and often remain with us. As a kid, the Animorphs book series—where a ragtag group of teens obtains the power to transform into any animal they touch and uses said power to combat an invasive alien-slug species called the Yeerks—inspired my dolphin imitation whenever I entered a swimming pool. An episode of the '90s teen mystery series *Ghostwriter* instigated my childhood constipation issues; I believed a purple, pleather-trench-coat-clad "slime monster" named Gooey Gus (his catchphrase: "Slime, anyone?") lived in my toilet, and I thus spent as little time sitting on it as possible. We grow up, and the motifs we extract from pop culture might become less literal, but they permeate nonetheless.

As those references (and this book's title) should indicate, I'm a millennial. I was born in 1989. If we bookend the Generation Y birth years from 1981 to 1996, I'm not just a millennial but a smack-dab-in-the-middle millennial. I became a ninety-words-per-minute typist by ferociously gossiping on AIM. I've worked for apps where clients rate me out of five stars. I wear glasses I ordered online and have gotten most of my dates via various cursed apps. By any boomer's standard, I am a cliché. I'm fine with that, honestly; I just needed to get that admission out of the way. If you haven't done the math yet, that means I was a teenager from 2002 to 2009. I became a full person in the aughts. And thus, 2000s teen pop culture had an acute, intimate effect on the person I am now. If our dexterous and identity-seeking teenage brains look to TV and movies for guidance, flashes of my adult self can be traced back to aughts pop culture. And my adult life is a very gay one.

Once and forever a teen of the aughts, I use this collection to explore the pop culture I devoured as a kid. I'll pick apart Harry Potter, *The O.C., Gossip Girl, Real World/Road Rules Challenge, Mean Girls,* early Taylor Swift, Disney Channel Original Movies, *Best in Show, Moulin Rouge! The Office, The L Word,* and, finally, *Glee.* Indeed, each time my brain went on vacation to Newport Beach or Scranton, Pennsylvania, or Montmartre, it returned to "real life" with insights and opinions and role models. Only some of these pieces of media have openly gay characters in them, and the queer characters of the aughts are—well, *incomplete* is a kind way to put it. Still, despite the utter dearth of fully realized gay plotlines and characters in the 2000s, I still gained a hyper-specific brand of queer identity from the pop culture of the decade.

This isn't to say good gay pop culture didn't exist in my teen years. After all, millennials grew up online. Gay content was out there, just harder to find than it is now, and I was too closeted to bring myself to do the work of scouring the internet for it. A lot of LGBTQ+ friends of mine sought out queer content and community online via message boards and the immeasurable world of fan fiction. Lots of queer women I know were fervent followers of *Queer as Folk,* deluding themselves into believing it was because they were good gay allies and not because they, too, were raging queers. While I was *just* too young for *Buffy*—it went off the air in 2003—I'd later learn that gay peers of mine cultivated a clandestine obsession with Tara and Willow, the first recurring lesbian couple on prime time. But I was neither cool nor self-aware enough to get into *Buffy* as an adolescent.

This collection examines the particular smattering of media I've chosen because a) this was the pop culture I was genuinely into then, and I can't well retroactively enlighten myself, and b) these shows/movies/books were, for the most part, very popular, and thus they had the most broad appeal and broad effects on millennials on the whole. These were the pieces of pop culture I loved, talked about, posted quotes from on my friends' walls on a nascent Facebook dot com.

Which brings me to this book's title: *The 2000s Made Me Gay.* I don't think pop culture, as ubiquitous and intoxicating as it might be, has the power to plant seeds of desire within us. Whatever part of us wants to bang in a nonhetero way is always in there, somewhere. I think I've had some latent queer beast within me since childhood, one who clung to the exhibitions of nonnormativity I saw in media—on *The Real World,* in Disney Channel Original Movies, in Olivia Wilde's sheer existence. But equally strong was—and is—compulsory straightness. These two forces duke it out within queer people until it all comes to a head, and we eventually, if we can, come out. And then, as out and proud and open and happy as we might be, the two keep duking it out internally until we die. It's great, really, existing like this.

I do think, though, that pop culture can shape our responses, internal and external, to such preexisting gayness. The ways gender and sex and relationships play out in movies and TV and books and plays can bolster either side of that queer vs. non-queer duel. Sometimes, the same piece of media can fuel both sides. For a gay man in 1998, seeing *Will & Grace* might validate and amplify his queer identity—"Wow, I, too, can be out and normal and happy!"—while simultaneously telling him that he could only be out and happy if he were wealthy and thin and white and cis and lived in New York City and spent all his time with Debra Messing. Seeing Britney Spears and Madonna kiss onstage at the 2003 MTV Video Music Awards might've jolted awake some bisexual yen in young women—and some might've embraced that lust—and others (like me) might've built a great big barricade in their brains to entrap it, ideally forever.[a]

This collection explores that push-pull. While the aughts were a period with more gender-bending and gay characters in mainstream media than ever before, such depictions were imperfect: incomplete, discreet, overwhelmingly white and cisgender. Which is to say, yes, the 2000s made me gay, but not without a whole heap of caveats and complications. Perhaps a more accurate book title would've been *The 2000s Are to Blame for the Specific Kind of Gay Person I Am Today,* but I never would've finished the book, as I'd have been utterly drained upon finishing writing its name.

That said, I didn't write this book to relitigate the relative lack of wokeness in 2000s pop culture. First of all, that's no fun. Example: I loved *Garden State* (2004) in high school. My excuses are fourfold: I was fourteen, in search of some Profound Meaning to my life and the world, liked the Shins, and had a latent crush on Natalie Portman. In 2012, a friend and I got day drunk, listened to "Your Ex-Lover Is Dead" by Stars, and agreed to an immediate *Garden State* rewatch. It was a terrible idea. *Oh God,* I realized, several rum cocktails and fifteen minutes into the rewatch, *this movie might actually be extremely bad.* Nearly two hours of faux-

---

a   When I played *The Sims* as a kid, I used a cheat code to get infinite money with which I'd throw Sim parties, build lavish home additions, and, crucially, make my Sims have sex. I'd fully ignore my Sim children, and inevitably, a Child Protective Services Sim would come to take them away. When this happened, I would pause the game, build four tiny walls around the CPS Sim to entrap them in my Sims' living room. Then, I'd un-pause the game and go about my Sims business, ignoring my captive CPS Sim. The CPS Sim would bang on the walls and scream pleas for freedom in Simlish—"Aiii, geysh geysh za rao!"—but could never get out and could never take my Sim children.

For most of the 2000s, I treated my desire to kiss girls like a Child Protective Services Sim.

deep platitudes and the standard-issue Manic Pixie Dream Girl later, I emerged horrified and enraged that Zach Braff's directorial debut had so duped me as a teen. *Garden State* is a particular example; revisiting art I loved as a kid typically fills me with warm nostalgia, a fondness despite myself. But the point still stands—ruining what we loved in adolescence is saddening and needlessly judgmental of our younger selves. It's a futile exercise meant only to flex our contemporary understanding of what's good and what's not.

But more than that, condemning pop culture we once loved installs an artificial barrier between who we are now and who we once were. Yes, of course I've grown up and gained perspective (have taken exactly one feminist philosophy class) since 2004. But in 2021, roasting, say, *Wedding Crashers* (2005) for the whole "date-rapey guys lying to women to get them in bed" thing (bad!) is just, well, obvious. Sure, *Wedding Crashers* deserved to be panned in real time for that plot, but hindsight criticism is too easy to be interesting. When we say a movie doesn't "hold up" today, what we're really saying is that, assuming we loved it at the time, *we've* changed—the audience has evolved, our shared values and understanding of what's okay and what's not has shifted. I'm more interested in examining the ways in which those pieces of pop culture have weaseled their ways into our current lives and shaped who we are now, for better or for worse.

The line between fiction and reality has always been a precarious one. With near-infinite episodes of television to binge, not to mention actors' social media presences, the distinction is harder to nail down than ever. Pop culture might be an escape from real life, but I haven't been able to escape pop culture itself. It's glommed onto my psyche, it's shaped my view of myself, my reality, my body, my sexuality, as it has for most people: when we ride the subway in quiet hope for a meet-cute, or we huff, frustrated at our hair for not flowing like Harry Styles's, or shame ourselves for not having a large group of hot friends with standing plans at the same bar every Friday night.

After Dr. Becker confirmed that Zach's cancer had spread to his nervous system, I walked in a fog around the hospital food court. It was early evening and quiet. Most of the doctors and nurses and techs had gone home for the day. I flopped down into a big chair outside the Au Bon Pain, cried big, sloppy tears, and thought, *I wish my friends were here.* I didn't mean my real-life friends, the ones who'd known me my entire life, who loved my family and brother, too. I absolutely, unironically, meant the characters on *Grey's Anatomy.*[b] I'd spent the whole summer and into the fall so alone, so isolated, consuming so much Shonda-land that these characters were, to borrow *Grey's* terminology, my *people.* All I craved in this moment was Cristina Yang to tell me exactly how she was going to beat this disease's petulant ass into the ground using some technology that doesn't actually exist in real life. Or for Miranda Bailey to shed her tough exterior and use her soft, motherly voice with me. Or even for Alex Karev to say, "It freakin' sucks, man." I wanted that skeezy, corn-fed former wrestler to wrap me in his arms.

I'd like to say that I knew, intellectually, this trauma was real life. But being in the neuro ICU felt so otherworldly that I let myself pretend, or at least hope, I was on a set. My *Grey's* delusions

---

b   Had I been living in *Grey's* as I'd fantasized, I wouldn't be in the episode. I wouldn't have made it past the first draft of edits, cut as an unnecessary character. "Why did you write in a character who's just silently sitting in the corner, looking scared and playing Candy Crush?" the showrunner would ask. "Cut that." The story would certainly have centered on Zach and his girlfriend, Molly, and the doctors, of course. I wasn't in the OR while they operated on Zach a few days later. I didn't accompany him to his follow-up chemo infusions, which successfully cleared his spine of leukemia blasts. Even those appointments wouldn't have made it into *Grey's,* considering they were nonsurgical and totally uneventful.

gave me an emotional coat of armor because in *Grey's Anatomy*, every doctor at Grey-Sloan Memorial Hospital is a straight-up genius. Sure, they're fully fictional. But at least in my mind, Zach was in the hands of award-winning surgeons. And, while I was crying in the food court, that fantasy felt good.

REAL-WORLD GAYS AND
REAL WORLD GAYS

Something you must know about me: I have big feet. Long, weird, flipper-like feet. I always have. I wore a women's size seven—as in, adult women's size seven—in second grade. From that point on, my shoe size went up about a half size every year and capped off at a size eleven running shoe in early high school. They're also very slender (a brag)—my sister calls my toes "prehistoric" and "prehensile" and "freakish" and "stop touching me with your feet." This is hyperbole. Sure, I can pick up shirts and bags and wallets with my lowest joints, but it's not like I can *write* with them. My feet are, though, avian enough that one can see the outline of a bone sticking out from each of them. These are my outermost metatarsal bones, and they protrude laterally from both feet. Let me be very clear: they are not bunions.

This information was completely unknown to my teacher, James (Montessori school), in June 1997. Each year of elementary school, the first, second, and third graders spent our final week of school at a YMCA camp in Wisconsin. Our teachers acted as camp counselors, and I was in James's cabin. One night of camp, I was on my top bunk, socks off, about to tuck into my sleeping bag, when James walked past my bed. He was exactly at eye level with my big, freaky feet, and he locked eyes with my protruding metatarsal bone. James gasped a dramatic, over-the-top gasp, lavish with worry: "*What happened to your feet?*" It was peculiar to me, a seven-year-old, to have to reassure a six-foot-two adult man that my feet didn't hurt. I wasn't bleeding, I was cozy and comfortable, besides some mosquito bites. I was happy! I was at camp!

In retrospect, this was a deliriously alarmist reaction to a first grader's too-thin appendages. But James's gasp has stuck in my head all these years not because I was self-conscious of my skeletal flipper feet. Rather, it was a landmark in my tender, queer life: I'd heard my very first gay gasp.

I didn't register James's gasp as a *gay* gasp at the time, though that's precisely what it was. I didn't even realize James was (probably) gay until many, many years after he publicly shamed my seven-year-old feet. At that point in my life, I actually didn't know any gay people. I mean, I did, sure: there was my mom's friend from choir; her hairdresser and confidant, a boomer drag queen; my two female camp counselors, who I'd hear through the grapevine years later had been a couple. These people were out to the other adults in their lives, I believe, but weren't presented explicitly as gay to me as a child. I wasn't told they were straight; rather, their sexualities simply weren't addressed. Perhaps my teachers and family thought mentioning gayness was too explicitly sexual to acknowledge to me, a prepubescent tomboy, or that explaining a person's sexual taste first meant explaining sexuality on the whole.

Lucky for me, my curiosity (and older siblings) led me to a space unruffled by sex talk: MTV's *The Real World*.

The Real World: Chicago was the eleventh season of MTV's reality show where seven strangers live together, drink, bicker, hook up, and fight over use of the communal landline phone. There's no real "point" or "plot" to *The Real World*, which, I guess, is in itself the point of the show. The Chicago season shot over the summer and into the fall of 2001 and aired the following winter—it's best remembered for covering the 9/11 attacks and aftermath.

The cast's house was the penthouse loft of brand-spankin'-new construction in Wicker Park, on Chicago's North Side. Today, the North Side enclave is home to Shinola, North Face, and Adidas brick-and-mortar stores, but back in the early aughts, it was, well, cool. "Wicker Park still has posters of Karl Marx and plenty of 23-year-olds who ride one-speed bicycles and don't have cable," the *Chicago Reader* published in a 2001 piece on MTV's presence in the area.[1] "They think corporate media is a virus." Naturally, those types had a problem with MTV's presence in the neighborhood but mostly with what that presence foretold for the area's future. Which is to say: they were pissed about gentrification. During filming, groups of protestors gathered outside the *Real World* house, chanting, "WE'RE REAL! YOU'RE NOT!" One night in July, fifteen people were arrested for blocking traffic, disorderly conduct, and impeding a police officer.

The city was abuzz with *Real World* talk, good and bad. Even as a rising sixth grader, I was well aware of it. The show was only in its eleventh season, so it was still edgy, still sexy, still ostensibly a reflection of "youth culture." Getting a *Real World* season meant Chicago, too, was sexy, edgy, and youthful. To me, a twelve-year-old writing a musical called *Funky Farm*—a *Romeo and Juliet* story between a wolf and a sheep, set to '70s disco covers[c]—I believed *The Real World* was a peek into my future. A future where I, too, would be sexually active, where I, too, would work at North Avenue Beach. And was I really that far off? I was, by all accounts, youthful (hadn't gotten my period), and I knew all the words to Weezer's

---

c   The show's opening number, "Funky Farm," was a cover of the Lipps Inc. jam, "Funkytown." Other highlights included: a fox, played by my friend Jack, dancing to "Fox Stuff" ("Hot Stuff" by Donna Summer) in a chicken coop, flanked by hen backup dancers; and me, the comic relief as a (male) pig determined to make it to Broadway. Fifteen years later, my sixth-grade teacher informed me she was almost fired for allowing *Funky Farm* to take the stage for an all-school production.

Blue Album, so I thought myself quite edgy. And, having just broken things off with my first (and only ever) boyfriend, Paul, at the end of fifth grade—well, I wasn't *sexy,* but I saw a future in which boys would be attracted to me and vice versa.

While I certainly didn't understand the gentrification debate or how bicycles could have more than one speed, I did know one thing: I needed to watch *The Real World: Chicago.* I wasn't technically allowed to watch it, though, so I did so in fits and spurts, when my parents weren't in the basement with me, or at a friend's house. In doing so, I met my first openly queer person: Aneesa Ferreira.

Aneesa was so, so fucking gay. She was unapologetic. Her main things were yelling at fuckboi dykes and walking around the house naked. In the pilot episode, her housemate Theo admits his immediate attraction to her and is fully flabbergasted when she comes out as a lesbian right off the bat. (Aneesa later came out as bisexual.)[2] In another episode, Aneesa's mom tells her to "try not to be gay" while in Chicago, and Aneesa revolts by fucking a girl in their loft's elevator. Later, Aneesa and Chris, a sweet, sensitive, artistic gay man, have a heart-to-heart about their issues coming out to their family, which we simply love to see.

Aneesa's most memorable scene on *Chicago,* though, is her breakup with the aforementioned elevator hookup after two weeks of dating. (More memorable to me, apparently, than the 9/11 episode?) Veronica, the now-ex, comes to the loft to pick up a bag she left and is accompanied by her latest fling. Aneesa wastes no time in fully flipping out. "You're a crazy bitch!" she proclaims in Soffe shorts and a spaghetti-strap tank-top. "You need to take your ass out of my house!" The ex takes the elevator back down, but Aneesa takes the stairs to the lobby, where she calls her a "cunt" and curses her out for all of North Avenue to hear. It was thrilling! I couldn't imagine calling someone a cunt, and yet, I admired Aneesa's rawness. *The Real World* at its best.

Aneesa wasn't the first openly queer person on *The Real World*. Norman Korpi was openly bisexual on the very first season in 1992. Beth, Genesis, and Ruthie were all openly into women on their seasons throughout the '90s. Pedro Zamora of *San Francisco* was HIV-positive and an AIDS educator himself, and he's largely credited for humanizing the HIV-positive community on a massive scale. Pedro even got married on *The Real World*, making MTV the first network to broadcast a gay commitment ceremony.[3] On *The Real World: New Orleans*, openly gay Danny dates a guy in the military, whose face is blurred out in every appearance thanks to Don't Ask, Don't Tell. But because Aneesa was in my city, in my shoe-size-ten-at-age-twelve stomping grounds, she stuck with me.

I wouldn't come out, even to myself, for another eight years after watching *The Real World: Chicago*. I wasn't even remotely aware that I was queer at the time I watched it, especially not after my whirlwind romance with Paul, who, let it be known, gave me three rocks for Valentine's Day. But this was my first exposure to what being openly gay looked like, and Aneesa's queerness scared the shit out of me. Not enough to keep me from watching the show, but enough for me to fixate on Aneesa, roll my eyes at her, to call her crazy. I was drawn to her but was sure to maintain an emotional distance from her, to even root against her. That's a common thing for queer kids unaware of their queerness, to yelp and run and hide at the sight of others'. Not because I was afraid of those gay people in and of themselves; rather, because the glimmer of ourselves we saw in their nonnormativity fucking terrified me. I saw bits of myself in her tomboy swagger, in her confidence, in her unapologeticness, and it all made me prickle in fear.

It's true, objectively, that Aneesa yelling at a woman on the street didn't present a particularly inviting portrait of queer adult-hood. Most of the other cast members spent the season talking shit about how often Aneesa popped off about seemingly innoc-uous things or how her ass was constantly laid bare for the whole group to see. Tonya from Walla Walla, Washington, called her "rude and crude." Aneesa was messy. In retrospect, it seems like she was really going through something while on the show, and perhaps her passionate lashing out was linked to her terrifying de-sire to come out to her dad. Aneesa wasn't me, exactly, nor was she the kind of adult I sought to become. But I got to see what happens when people stop being polite and start being loud, naked gays.

The *Chicago* season may have been my first love in the *Real World* extended universe, but in the end, it wouldn't be my great-est. I'd meet the *Funky Farm* wolf to my own *Funky Farm* sheep in 2003. It was *Real World/Road Rules Challenge: Battle of the Sexes.*

—

I'd been taught from a very young age that, as a blanket truth, *girls can do anything boys can do.* My parents' and teachers' edu-cation pounded this idea into my head, optimistic that I was born from scratch, absent any societal norms or millennia of patriar-chy. It seemed—well, it was presented to me as—such a crystal-clear idea, like midcentury housewives simply didn't *know* they were equal to men. In a similar way that saying "I don't see color!" seeks to wash away the messy nuances of race relations and rac-ism itself (not to mention, any responsibility to undo it), "girls can do anything boys can do" oversimplifies sexism and gender dynamics. Beyoncé's 2010 single "Who Run the World?" did the same thing. It's a nice idea, that behind all the bravado and power struggles and machismo, it's in fact the second sex who's pulling the strings. But it's just not true, because sexism entrenches male power in far deeper ways than a simple lack of self-confidence.

That said, adults often believe kids can only comprehend over-simplified ideas. I don't think my mom should've amended her words of empowerment to "girls can do anything boys can do, but be careful: as a woman, you'll get absolutely whomped in MTV's *Real World/Road Rules Challenge: Battle of the Sexes*."

Real World/Road Rules Challenge, now simply called *The Challenge*, is a competition reality show where teams of hot people face off to win thousands of dollars. Originally, it brought together personalities from MTV's two big reality shows: *The Real World* and *Road Rules*, which was another competition-based reality show where teams traveled around in a van for prizes. *The Challenge* first aired in 1998, as *Road Rules: All Stars*, and was later rebranded as *Real World/Road Rules Challenge*. It lasted under that name for seventeen seasons, seventeen glorious seasons, starring alumni from the two stalwart MTV reality shows going head-to-head on ropes courses for lumps of cash. By season nineteen, *Road Rules* had been canceled, so, out of sheer lack of participants, non-*RW/RR* cast members were brought in to sustain the franchise, an infusion of meathead platelets in Aeropostale. It was thus rebranded as *The Challenge* and remains so today. Yes, this relic of the '90s is still on TV, blessed be. The show's thirty-third season, *War Of The Worlds*, featured alumni from a sweeping breadth of the reality TV cinematic universe, MTV and otherwise: *Are You The One?*, *Floribama Shore*, *American Ninja Warrior*, *Love Island UK*, *Survivor Turkey*, and far too many more.

Each episode of *The Challenge* features—you guessed it—a challenge. They've gotten more physically demanding in recent years, but in the early days, the challenges were typically similar to YMCA summer camp high-ropes courses or team-building exercises at corporate retreats, except they're attempted by horny and hungover twenty-two-year-olds driven to mania in their desire for fame and fifty thousand dollars. Over the past twenty years, challenges have included: staying submerged in a cold pool full of snakes; completing a low-ropes course on top of a truck driving around a racetrack at fifty miles per hour; slamming mouthfuls of mayonnaise; riding a Razor scooter on a six-inch-wide beam a hundred feet in the air; the list goes on. It is titillating, and dehumanizing, and excellent reality TV. In the '90s and '00s, winners would earn their team prizes like a trip to Greece, Razor scooters, and a year's supply of Blockbuster rentals. In those early days, the grand prize was typically around one hundred and fifty thousand dollars (to be split between the three winners); now it's one million. In most seasons, each team votes a member off every episode, regardless of whether they won that day's challenge. Drama on *The Challenge* is bountiful, inescapable, inane. Again, like summer camp.

Each season of *The Challenge* has a theme. Sometimes that theme pertains to who they cast (season twelve, *Fresh Meat*, featured competitors who'd never been on reality TV before); sometimes it is based on the rules of elimination (at the end of each episode of *The Gauntlet I–III*, two cast members would duke it out in what can only be described as an adult jungle gym, the loser sent home in disgrace); or sometimes it is based on the location (season sixteen, *The Island*, was on—wait for it—an island). In the early days of *Real World/Road Rules Challenge*, the teams were typically split along those reality show lines, but that got old pretty quickly. One season, *Inferno II* (2005), was split into "Good Guys" and "Bad Asses," based on the personas the MTV stars had curated to that point. *The Gauntlet II* was split into "Rookies" and "Veterans." But in the two seasons I consumed so ravenously, with such intense glee, the teams were split along gender lines.

Battle of the Sexes (2003) and *Battle of the Sexes II* (2004) were the sixth and ninth seasons of *The Challenge*, respectively. They were both hosted by Olympic gold-medalist Jonny Moseley, a man with less charisma than a cardboard cutout of Jonny Moseley. After winning a gold medal in Nagano in 1998, Moseley was given the key to San Francisco and graced the cover of *Rolling Stone*. Though he failed to medal in the 2002 games, he hosted the post-Olympics episode of *Saturday Night Live* that year. For his opening monologue, Moseley skied down a ramp to the Studio 8H stage, sporting an oversize sweatshirt that conjured visions of Grimace, the McDonald's monster, covered in Cheeto dust. Moseley delivered his self-deprecating monologue in the same cartoonish, California-skater-boy, "no bad vibes" voice he'd use to say, "The inner circles can deliberate, and we'll meet back at the Chili's lounge in an hour" as the host of *Battle of the Sexes*.

Every weekend, my best friend, Jack, and I would retreat to his basement to catch a rerun of that week's latest *Battle of the Sexes* episode. Today, Jack is a cartoonishly handsome, broad-shouldered architect. In middle school, I was still taller than him, and he wore a smooth leather jacket and oval sunglasses in some adolescent *Matrix* cosplay, if Neo went to midnight *Lord of the Rings* screenings and played a lot of *Mario Party,* and I will never forget that about him.

We had been friends since first grade when he invited me to his brick two-flat home in Andersonville to play with Beanie Babies. We found we had very compatible imaginations: we'd draw worlds full of winged dogs on printer paper taped together to span his entire kitchen table. In fourth grade, we started making movies with my dad's video camera starring my stuffed animals in American Girl dolls' clothes—the villain of one was a bear in a green dress named Fiona Catherine Brains, who went by Fi C. Brains. In fifth grade, we discovered three-way phone attacks. In fifth grade, we re-created our entire class in *The Sims*: we'd make our nemeses swim, then pause the game and remove the ladders from the pool; we'd coax our crushes, Paul and Harley, into heart-shaped beds with us (again, we were eleven). Yes, girls can do anything boys can do, including puppeteer psychosexual mind games with our peers' avatars on Windows 98. Our genders never really played a role in our friendship, not in any overt way. We never had crushes (or even performed crushes) on each other. We had sleepovers pretty much every weekend until seventh grade or so. We've never kissed. And together, we became extremely invested in *Battle of the Sexes* right as we both hit puberty.

Aneesa from *Chicago* appeared on both seasons of *BOTS*. However, her antics (walking around naked) had waned in between seasons (she was always clothed now), and I lost interest in her narrative (subconsciously wanted to be watching naked Aneesa). My eye was drawn toward Ruthie, the MVP of both seasons. Ruthie, too, had calmed down, as her partying on *The Real World: Hawaii* had landed her in rehab. She came to the *Real World/Road Rules Challenge* centered and sober and competitive. She was quiet and focused and carried a lilt of dyke swagger, her hair smooth and dark and always fastened in a low ponytail—the sapphic Bat Signal.

More than Aneesa, I saw myself in Ruthie. As a member of a *travel* soccer team (yes, thank you very much), I considered myself an athlete, too. I admired her focus and tenacity, the way she tried her best to extract herself from house drama, an unspoken "I'm not like the other girls." I thought myself unlike other girls at that time, too. Though the girls lost both *Battles,* Ruthie's unique ability to hang upside-down from a trapeze longer than any of the men reaffirmed my instilled belief that girls can do whatever boys can do.

Ruthie's sexuality is rarely made explicit on those seasons of

The Challenge. She's not particularly outspoken about it, and has no on-camera canoodling to speak of. The only unambiguous discussions of her orientation are in the context of queer friendship. Specifically, the friendship between her and openly gay Genesis from *The Real World: Boston.* More than once, Ruthie vouches to the other Inner Circle members of Genesis possessing tenacity and sportsmanship, even after lackluster challenge performances— Ruthie wants Genesis to win a piece of that grand prize. Later on, the two look at the leaderboard, which Ruthie tops the entire season, and Genesis calls her the "top dog lesbian" in a delightful expression of platonic sapphic endearment. There isn't a whiff of sexual tension between the two.

The gay alliance crossed team/gender lines, as it also included Shane, who originally competed in *Road Rules: Campus Crawl.* When Genesis gets voted off, Shane gives her the Lifesaver (go with me here), which keeps her around for another episode. Ruthie appears genuinely crushed when Genesis gets voted off the first episode of *Battle of the Sexes II,* but it's undeniable that Genesis just couldn't bear-hug a dangling punching bag midair like the other women could.

The portrayals of gay and bisexual people on those mid-aughts episodes of *The Challenge* are, overall, surprisingly positive. There's little homophobic spew from straight cast members, even by today's standards. (Well, in episode one of *BOTS I,* infamous *Real World: San Francisco* cast member Puck enters the girls' villa and roars, "You guys are gonna have some straight lesbian sex in this room!" Gross, sure. But years later, we'd learn that off-camera, that's *precisely* what happened in the girls' villa during *Battle of the Sexes.*) This is surprising, not just because casual frat boy homophobia was rampant at the time but because of that particular era of MTV. This was the epoch of black light exposing ejaculate on sheets on *Room Raiders,* bikini-clad binge drinking on

MTV Spring Break, and shrieking, "NEXT!" at the first size ten to walk off the coach bus. MTV was unafraid to be cruel, so long as its audience was shocked. Its programming was the perfect blueprint for teenagers in search of fresh ways to psychologically torture their peers. But *The Challenge,* for the most part, lacked that element of cruelty.

Perhaps *The Challenge* was unique in that the cast's goal was not strictly to inspire America's moms to march into their dens and wordlessly snap off the TV. Their goal was prizes and cash. Some of the quintessential *Real World* drama did make it into *The Challenge,* like Tonya straddling Theo in the back of a minivan, mic clipped to the back of her low-rise jeans, which Theo dubbed, "like two kids at summer camp, you know, sneaking across the lake in the middle of the night to go play crazy games with each other's body parts." (Very gross.) And the challenges themselves often echoed *Spring Break,* like the one where everyone had to melt gigantic chunks of ice with their bare asses to retrieve the flip phone encased therein.

But because the show is results-oriented rather than strictly drama-oriented, players have a sense of "Look, I don't care if you're gay or straight, as long as you perform well." That's particularly true of Shane, who competed in both *BOTS* seasons. After completing one challenge—building a playhouse out of what are essentially giant Lincoln Logs—Puck asks the camera, "Who says gay guys can't build houses?" referencing his partner, Shane. Shane looks to the camera, too, and mumbles, "I don't know," palpably exhausted by Puck, as we all were.

"There's an interesting thing about being gay, and hiding your whole life from it, and then all of a sudden coming out," Eric, who's straight, muses to Shane during some downtime on *BOTS II.* "But not only coming out, but coming out to *the world.* That definitely brings out a whole lot of confidence." He's talking about Shane being out on *Road Rules* a few years prior. "There's a lot of people who you've changed their lives," says Eric. Despite Eric's nonsensical syntax, it's a sweet exchange. That episode, Shane muses on the importance of queer solidarity on *The Challenge* in his confessional. "It's nice to know that I've met someone who's gone through the same experiences I have," he says of Nick, another gay dude on his team. The episode fades to black with shirtless Shane grinding his ass into Nick's crotch in a mostly empty nightclub. It's kind of sweet.

Anyway, the women's teams got absolutely spanked in both seasons of *Battle of the Sexes*. In my thirties, rewatching those *Battle of the Sexes* seasons is demoralizing to say the least. I can't imagine my thirteen-year-old self, flying sky-high on girl-power feminism and ego-tripping hard from making the travel soccer team, felt anything but crestfallen watching adult women get their asses handed to them by men challenge after challenge then clique up and talk shit and call each other sluts. But man, I ate it up. I wanted the girls to win so much that I brought refreshed, Spice Girls–induced optimism to each episode viewing. *They've lost the past four missions,* I thought. *They can't* possibly *lose another!* But they sure did. Between the two *Battle of the Sexes* seasons, the women's team blew every challenge from packing a car with luggage really quickly, to remaining in a tank filled with crabs the longest, to a series of high-noon shootouts with laser guns. They lost and they lost and they lost. *Battle of the Sexes I* ended with the men winning eleven missions and the women, five; *Battle of the Sexes II* was 13–3, men.

The goal of any Battle of the Sexes, be it on the tennis court or on MTV, is to figure out which of two genders is better: men or women. Accepting this as a valid question means accepting gender essentialism as a valid theory, which most contemporary feminists would vehemently oppose. Gender essentialism is the overly simple idea that a person's essence, abilities, and characteristics are intrinsically linked to their assigned gender at birth. When people say Neanderthalian shit like "Men are wired to want sex and women aren't," or, "Women are better at housekeeping," that's gender essentialism. It insists gender is natural and birth-assigned and inflexible, not a construct. When people or communities or societies adopt such ideas, gender essentialism can become a self-fulfilling prophecy. It's an ideology that can lead to men feeling entitled to sex, that devalues women's labor and/or earning potential. It's an ideology that leaves no room for transgender people, as it asserts that a person's essence is always and fully tied to their genitalia. It's an easy way to explain how people are, which is appealing, because the way people actually are can be a terribly confusing thing.

Gender essentialism is the bedrock of both seasons of *Battle of the Sexes*. Lazy observations of "what boys are like" and "what girls are like" is the entire point of these two *Challenge* seasons; it creates the friction, the drama that reality TV needs. In *BOTS I,* the girls' rally cry is "Vagina! Vagina! Vagina! Vagina! Vagina!" During a challenge of "Who can sit on this block of ice the longest?" Mark tells the confessional, "Women do have a lot of toleration for pain, i.e. childbirth. But men are motivated." A couple episodes later, when Emily skips a mission that requires nudity but her boyfriend, James, competes, she forgives him to the camera, rationalizing, "Men are programmed to compete." Girls are this way, boys are that way. I think, on some level, I went to *Battle of the Sexes* for answers. I wanted to see if girls really could do anything boys could do, sure, but I really wanted to know who I was.

The voting-off process is integral to the watchability of *The Challenge,* so please bear with me: a competitor from each team is voted off every episode, regardless of the team's performance, meaning there's opportunity for backstabbing and tears in each installment. In *BOTS I*, each individual player was awarded points based on their performance in the challenge. We start with eighteen players per team; in mission one, the top male and female performers got thirty-six points, the next got thirty-four points, and so forth. The points accumulate over the season. Each week, the three team members with the most points form that team's Inner Circle and are tasked with deciding who on their team gets sent home.

In the first episode of *BOTS I*, the men decide that whoever has the lowest points each week has to go home. Clean and simple. No discussion, no hard feelings. The women, uh, don't do that. Julie from *The Real World: New Orleans* is sent home in the first episode because her former co-cast member, Melissa, alleged she "did some shady business stuff to [her] in between seasons." Okay. That set a precedent for vengeful bootings-off for the rest of the season.

From there on, the women's Inner Circle chooses who has to leave based partially on performance, but mostly on *energy*, who's not a *team player*, or whatever other euphemisms they decide to use for *I don't like or trust this girl*. Of course, this means that the girls fulfill their stereotype of being catty brats fully absent of clear-eyed competitive drive. It often manifests in mid-level girls being sent home without any real reason—or at least, no reason communicated to them—which frankly makes for great TV. When Rachel gets unceremoniously dumped by the girls' team in episode seven of *BOTS I*, she tells the camera, her voice shaking from angry tears, clad in a leopard-print crop top, low-slung jeans, and a puka shell necklace: "The Inner Circle is ugly. This game is ugly. And I don't want to be a part of it anymore. Peace!"

The two divergent voting-off systems became the central theme of *Battle of the Sexes I*. The show's essentialist declaration was this: boys are logical, and girls are emotional. Even more so than physical strength or pain tolerance or puzzle-mindedness, the voting-off systems became an implicit referendum on which sex was superior. Would the men's reliance on cold, hard numbers help them win? Is there an advantage to being emotionally attuned to the team's desires, as the women tried to be? The answer, according to MTV, was that numbers (and therefore men) are better.

The penultimate episode of *Battle of the Sexes II* is particularly brutal. Going into it, the women hadn't won a challenge in five episodes. Only four players remained on each team: Eric (a man whose personality was "I have a jump rope wrapped around my head"), Mark, Dan, and Theo for the men, and Ruthie, Coral, Arissa, and Sophia for the gals. It was by all accounts absurd that Arissa had made it this far. She was afraid of heights while competing on a show that's 90 percent high-ropes courses. I'm sure she had a lovely, well-rounded personality full of nuance and dimension off-camera, but on *Battle of the Sexes II,* her whole deal was "I'm Arissa, and I'm afraid of heights." It seems like she was generally well liked enough to not get voted off, though she should've been scrapped around episode nine. But somehow, Arissa made it to the final four. Because Arissa was so useless, the guys wanted to ensure she'd make it to the final challenge, where a hundred and eighty thousand dollars was on the line. They did so by ensuring she'd be safe from elimination that round. The mechanisms of how they did this are complicated to explain and, frankly, unimportant, so I'll just tell you the result: the men's team threw the match, which meant Arissa couldn't be eliminated, which meant the women's weakest player was on their final squad. The final prize cash was in the bag for the man-children. Strategically Napoleonic, admittedly.

Considering it was only their third victory of the entire season, the four gals were beyond elated to win the challenge. They had zero clue the match had been thrown. And only afterward does the audience learn what had happened, in a devastating split-screen. On the right, the girls hug and shriek and celebrate their underdog victory, a small proof that "girls can do anything boys can do." On the left, the guys cackle and revel in their deviousness. It's hard to watch. It's every insecure teenage girl's fear: that no matter your success, there's always a pack of boys howling at you, like hyenas wearing head-to-toe Quicksilver, who think you suck. Who manipulate your victories, who mock your pride and self-worth, who always, always, define the terms in which you feel good about yourself.

So why was I so particularly drawn, out of all *Challenge* seasons, to the two *Battles of the Sexes* if it merely crushed my childhood dogma that girls are just as good as boys? Perhaps on a subconscious level, I watched *Battle of the Sexes* for the gay content, but it's not like these seasons of *The Challenge* are particularly gayer than any other. Truthfully, I came to *Battle of the Sexes* yearning for guidance on my own gender identity.

Adolescence is a time of exposure to adult existence, when the world reveals itself as a much more complex beast than we knew it as children. One might even call it a time when things stop being polite and start getting real. *Battle of the Sexes* came into my life in middle school, a time of seismic shift for many, myself included. My body was changing, and with that, social dynamics morphed, too. I wasn't invited to sleepovers with the boys anymore. While Jack and I remained friends, I found a new group of girls to clump up with. Boys and girls had begun dating each other—not like Paul and my polite, rock-exchanging romance in fifth grade, but actually *making out*. While being a sporty little tomboy might've been innocuous, even *cool* pre-seventh grade, the new flutter of sex hormones made my boyishness a turnoff to boys, and therefore a social impediment. As someone who'd existed in between the girls and boys in middle school—I cast myself as neither a wolf nor a sheep in *Funky Farm* but as the *comic relief pig*—this burgeoning dichotomy left me scrambling for an appropriate way to be.

Even though the men obliterated the women in both seasons of *Battle of the Sexes*, I think I found comfort in the idea that "girls are this way" and "boys are that way." Some kids recognize their own atypical gender performance as a reason to revolt against rigid structures. I, on the other hand, was freaked out by the space I occupied, freaked out by my own similarities to queers like Aneesa, and sought guidance on how to be a girl. Perhaps this is because I was both a know-it-all and also really, *really* wanted to be well liked. But I saw in my clothes and hobbies and attitude that I was different from my straight girl friends, and I sought a remedy for my burgeoning queerness. It's not that I admired the backstabbing, the afraid-of-heights-ness, the nonsensical voting system of the girls' team on *Battle of the Sexes*. I knew I didn't want to emulate these women. (Especially not Arissa who, it bears repeating, should not have made it to the finals of *BOTS II*.) But in a time when I was confused about how to be a girl, I was comforted by the notion that there *could* be a right answer, even if *Battle of the Sexes* wasn't it. I hoped that life could be simple, black and white, boy vs. girl. MTV laid out a lazy worldview that I, with an underdeveloped brain and a host of social anxieties, ate right up.

It wasn't terribly surprising to either of us when Jack and I came out to each other sophomore year of college. We'd spent high school trading nasty barbs about each other's gayness—he went on my Facebook behind my back and joined every group he could find with the word *vagina* in it, and I retaliated by writing something to the effect of "everyone knows you're gay" on his wall. Internalized self-loathing, it turns out, can harm more people than just yourself. But finally, one of the frozen, last nights of 2009, I told Jack I'd been seeing a girl at school. We zipped up

Lake Shore Drive in my green Eurovan as he asked me those big, establishing questions: *Who else have you told? So are you still into guys? Was there ever anything going on with you and Claire in high school?* Driving, it turns out, is an excellent activity to do while revealing the kinds of people about whom you daydream, as my eyes were responsibly glued to the road. I felt understood and not judged.

But if I had to do it again, I'd do it Rachel from *Road Rules* style: "Compulsory heterosexuality is ugly. The patriarchy is ugly. And I don't want to be a part of it anymore. Peace!"

HARRY POTTER AND THE HALF-ASSED GAY CHARACTER

At a Q&A at Carnegie Hall, J. K. Rowling casually mentioned that fictional wizard genius Albus Dumbledore is gay.[1] It was October 2007. The seventh and final book, *Harry Potter and the Deathly Hallows*, had been out for three months; the series was complete. A fan had asked the author if, for all his espousing of the all-conquering power of love, the Hogwarts headmaster had ever found love himself.

"My truthful answer to you..." Rowling replied, "I always thought of Dumbledore as gay." The gaynouncement was met with huge applause. Rowling further explained that she imagined Dumbedore's brief-yet-explosive friendship with the all-powerful Gellert Grindelwald as young men, explored in detail in *Harry Potter and the Deathly Hallows*, as a romantic one. She never wrote anything in the book that explicitly confirmed Albus and Gellert were a couple, but, sure, perhaps *gay dude* is written somewhere on a self-imposed character worksheet she filled out in an Edinburgh café in 1997.

Predictably, the news outraged conservative groups. But even among liberals, a fierce debate was sparked: Can an author decide something about a character that isn't explicitly written in the text? It's hard to imagine this cultural debate would've been a Thing had Rowling dubbed Dumbledore, say, a straight widower with a dead wife who was never mentioned in the book, but no matter. The subtext became, *Is Dumbledore* really *gay?* And, on top of that, why does it matter if a fictional wizard is gay?

"Ms. Rowling quite consciously makes Dumbledore a flower, more human wizard than [J. R. R. Tolkien's wizards], but now goes too far," Edward Rothstein wrote for the *New York Times* Arts section, in an opinion piece that bends over backward to argue why Dumbledore isn't "really" gay.[2] (Remember: we're talking about a *fictional wizard* here.) Over at *EW,* writer Mark Harris championed the headmaster's proclaimed identity an LGBT triumph.[3] He praised the move, saying, "Rowling's announcement about Dumbledore isn't a plot twist. It's a challenge to look at the world—even a world of wizards and magic—as it really is."

"To me, it wasn't a big deal," noted cisgender heterosexual J. K. Rowling told actor Daniel Radcliffe in a 2012 conversation.[4] "This is a very old man who has a very terrible job to do. And his gayness is not really relevant."

As for me, I cared deeply about the Harry Potter series at the time. In classes, I regularly fell into a daydream where I was Harry's wittier and less moody twin sister, Grace Potter. (Imagine my horror when the indie frontwoman of that name came to my attention in the late aughts! As if a private piece of my inner desires were extracted from my brain and put on display. Humiliating.) As Grace Potter, I lived the exact same circumstances as Harry: dead parents, all-powerful noseless snake-man attempting to murder me every June (conveniently canceling final exams), Weasleys for friends. It wasn't a very creative fantasy. At age sixteen, you may think I was too old for such daydreams and, reader? You might be correct.

I credit this emotional attachment to my matching Harry's age at all seven books' releases. Since I was born in the late '80s and J. K. Rowling wrote each book between 1997 and 2007, the Boy Who Lived and I were in the same life phase at each book's release. As Harry experienced first crushes (book four), torrential hormone-induced mood swings (book five), and, eventually, the initial freedoms and consequences of adulthood (book seven), so did I in real life. This was true for anyone who graduated high school in the late aughts; we spent our entire middle and high school experiences in the thick of unrepentant Potter mania. I'll thus always feel a deep allegiance to this series (not to Rowling, mind you), as if part of me grew up in the tapestried walls of Hogwarts, a sentiment I share with millions of fellow Gen Y-ers.

My friend Erin is one of those smack-dab millennials. On the day the sixth book was released in 2005, Erin's older brother flipped through to the end of it and casually told his baby sister that Albus Dumbledore dies at the end. Totally indifferent to the series, he blew its biggest twist, just to be an emotional terrorist. In a moment of delusional teenage fury, Erin sought vengeance. If she couldn't have the surprise of Dumbledore's untimely death, that crushing, childhood-ending moment of literature—*no one should have it.*

So she did what any pubescent demon blinded by spoiler-induced rage would do in 2005: she logged on to AOL Instant Messenger. She clicked to edit her away message. Erin's would typically read *away* with her cell phone number, or maybe a semicryptic Broken Social Scene lyric or quote from *Eternal Sunshine of the Spotless Mind*. But not on that day. She typed a new one: *DUMBLEDORE DIES.*

Unsurprisingly, when Erin returned to her computer an hour later, she was flooded with furious messages from friends and acquaintances and total randos alike: "R U KIDDING ME?!" and "WHAT THE FUCK" and "hahahahhh ur fucking w/ ppl rite???" She successfully spread the disappointment her brother had gifted her. She took the message down after an hour or so.

A *lot* of people told Erin she'd ruined the book for them, which she isn't proud of. To me, Erin's impulse to spoil a Harry Potter installment via AIM away message is as perfectly 2005 as Kanye West in a polo shirt.

All of this is to say: my friends and I really, really cared about Harry Potter. And about the fate of Albus Dumbledore.

And yet, I didn't have any visceral reaction to J.K.'s gaynouncement. I was a closeted seventeen-year-old and a Potter nerd, so I stuck to the text, and nothing in the text explicitly confirmed Dumbledore's sexual identity in any which direction. For context, I was mid-relationship with my (female) best friend, yet in total denial of my queer feelings. The self-loathing structures of Closet Brain cast jet-black shadows over many of my memories of late high school; perhaps that's why I can't recall my exact take on the news at the time. All I know is that, in the scheme of things, I cared *much* more about Snape killing Dumbledore than Dumbledore's alleged gayness.

It's true that every good writer concocts some backstories that, while they inform a character's disposition and choices, are irrelevant to the story at hand and thus don't explicitly make it to the page. In that same conversation between Rowling and Radcliffe, the author described a whole backstory for transfiguration Professor Minerva McGonagall she'd had locked and loaded but never found a reasonable place to explore in the books. To Rowling, Dumbledore's queerness, too, was a backstory that didn't warrant explicit exploration. Personally, I think that in describing two critical/powerful characters' intense friendship over one intellectually invigorating summer—*and* making said relationship integral to the central character's fate and the plot of the final book—the fact that they were also in love and Frenched on the reg is extremely relevant information. I have a hard time envisioning Rowling omitting a relationship's romantic aspect were Dumbledore straight and Grindelwald a woman. But, for whatever reason, Rowling opted for coyness. On Dumbledore and Grindelwald's boyhood tryst, she says, "I liked leaving that open so that perhaps a more worldly reader could see that that may have been in that relationship," Rowling told Radcliffe. "And perhaps a nine-year-old would think he made a great friend and he trusted him. So I was okay with that." Have your cake and eat it, too, Joanne.

Rowling's irritating wink-nudge approach to Dumbledore's queerness makes me wonder if she felt the character would have to change were she to have made his sexuality explicit in the books. Imagine J.K. had written in, say, a tender, teenage kiss between Gellert and Albus to confirm their romance, as she did with Harry and Cho, and Harry and Ginny, and Ron and Hermione, and—you get it. It's not like droves of fans would protest that Dumbledore *hadn't seemed gay* in the other books. He's an occult-obsessed dude who wears beaded robes, lives alone in a tower with a theatrical and (literally) flamboyant bird, hoards receipts of memories, and whisks off to "meetings" late, late at night. Nothing about Dumbledore reads as blazingly straight, to say the least. "Oh yeah? If he's gay, why is his beard so ungroomed?" fans would surely not be asking. "Where's his Madame Maxine–inspired drag persona? And *how* do you expect us to believe this is a gay man, if we *not once* see him doing poppers over *seven books*?"

Fourteen years later, Dumbledore's sexuality has yet to be depicted on page, stage, or screen. The *Fantastic Beasts and Where to Find Them* film series premiered in 2016, and documents the American Wizarding World about seventy years prior to the *Harry Potter* series. Much of it centers on a young Albus Dumbledore, including his friendship with Grindelwald. So far, two films (of five, total) in that series have been released, and neither has explicitly confirmed Dumby's sexual leanings. That's not to say it won't happen in the coming films. In fact, given how (relatively) gay-friendly the entertainment climate has become and how Rowling has triple- and quadruple-downed on her "Dumbledore's gay!" announcement since 2007, I'd be surprised if the films don't depict Albus and Gellert's romance on-screen. After all, in an extended feature on the *Fantastic Beasts: The Crimes of Grindelwald* Blu-ray/DVD released in 2019, Rowling did confirm there was a "sexual dimension" to the wizards' relationship.[5] But still, all we've got is Jo's word. Also, as a Potter purist, I think of the *Fantastic Beasts* series as, like, a fun but unnecessary bonus franchise, but perhaps that's just me.

Rowling's extratextual expansion of the Wizarding World hasn't stopped with Dumbledore. Like anyone with a Twitter account, the woman can say whatever she wants to strangers online. And apparently, what Rowling wants to say are Harry Potter–related tidbits a decade after publishing the final book of the series. Things we've learned about the Potter world from Rowling tweets include: Hogwarts tuition is free.[6] Dumbledore saw his family in the Mirror of Erised. Harry's son was sorted into Gryffindor, Remus's into Hufflepuff. The confirmation that Hogwarts is a safe place for LGBT students (. . . k!).[7] The clarification that Anthony Goldstein of Ravenclaw was Jewish.[8] These are details that expand the Potter universe, sure, but don't really matter and aren't relevant to the story; critics interpret them as retconning contemporary standards of white feminism into the series. Twitter makes it incredibly easy for Rowling to fire off a quick reply to a fan's unnecessary question, and, wow, doing so just might be her greatest passion. Considering she created a multibillion-pound franchise and her career would carry on just fine sans social media presence, J. K. Rowling tweets *a lot*. Over the course of the 2010s, the author's seemingly off-the-cuff coloring in of Potterverse became so common that it's an inside joke on the internet. The "Performatively Woke J. K. Rowling" meme posits the writer as providing increasingly sexual and unnecessary details that absolutely no one has ever asked for.

According to this meme, J. K. Rowling has written in her mind a whole depraved subworld of the Wizarding World, where all the characters fuck a ton and most of them are queer in some respect, with bestiality and inanimate objects so far totally inbounds. Twitter users have joked about J. K. Rowling retconning everything from the Sorting Hat's disinterest in sex (though, it *can* fuck), to Buckbeak the Hippogriff's casual BDSM curiosity, to a great number of details about Dobby the house elf's genitalia.[9,10] Those of us who inhaled Rowling's novels as closeted teenagers are now full-blown, openly queer adults who grew up to be a bunch of monsters fully comfortable posting gross jokes on Twitter and who are quite comfortable rolling our eyes at empty, if potentially well-intentioned, gestures of allyship.

Rowling's apparent addiction to posting has gotten the author into trouble with fans. In the late 2010s, J. K. Rowling got canceled about once per year. In 2016, Rowling was accused of appropriating Navajo tradition in a history of American magic on her website, Pottermore.[11] The following year, amid the rise of the #MeToo movement, Rowling defended the casting of Johnny Depp in the *Fantastic Beasts* franchise, despite public evidence of him abusing his then-wife, Amber Heard.[12] Fans saw this as traitorous, given her vocal defense of women online—not to mention, given the values she instilled in the Potter books themselves.[13] Then in 2018, Rowling doubled down on the *Fantastic Beasts* casting choice of Korean actress Claudia Kim as Nagini, Voldemort's snake and Horcrux, which critics argued played into the "dragon lady" stereotype that plagues East Asian women.[14] And by the end of the decade, J.K. really outdid herself, tweeting a defense of a transphobic woman who'd lost her job for making transphobic comments at work and online.[15] Her goodwill with the LGBTQ+ community all but vanished, as fans interpreted Rowling's comments to mean the author is a trans-exclusionary radical feminist, or TERF.[16] At this unfortunate TERF turn,[d] my sister yowled, "Joanne, why can't you just let us enjoy the wizard teens in peace?" It is remarkable how simple it is to not tweet, and yet.

In parallel to this trickle of additional Potterverse info, the generation that grew up alongside Harry Potter has grown up to be the gayest generation to date[17] (only to then be handily out-gayed by Gen Z).[18] Those who read the Potter books as kids are now adults in a much more queer-friendly world than the one in which we grew up. The State of Gay in America has changed dramatically from October 2007 to now. Only 37 percent of Americans supported gay marriage then, against 61 percent in 2019.[19] We have openly gay senators and rock stars and supermodels and even non-Broadway actors! It's way less okay for straight dudes to call some innocuous shit their buddy does "so gay" now than it was when the Harry Potter books came out. In the broadest sense, American culture has become substantially more gay-friendly since Dumbledore was outed. There remains tons of work to be done. But if you're an affluent, well-connected, cis, white gay dude, things are pretty good. And what wizard fits that description perfectly, hm?

So there's this great chasm between the progress our cul-

---

d   But wait, there's more. In June 2020, Rowling published an essay on her personal website elaborating on her views on "sex and gender issues." In it, Rowling doubles down on her belief in the importance of birth-assigned gender. After describing her experience with mental health and body issues—and, later, of surviving sexual assault and domestic violence—she writes, "[. . .] if I'd been born 30 years later, I too might have tried to transition. The allure of escaping womanhood would have been huge." To trans activists (and to me), this seemed to suggest that trans men are people who bailed on womanhood because it was too hard. *Accio* empathy.

ture has made since 2007 and the way J. K. Rowling handled Dumbledore's queerness at the time. In today's context, claiming a character's queerness without demonstrating it feels pointless and ridiculous. Considering how gay young adult TV and movies and books are now, it feels disingenuous to color a character's sexuality without actually exploring it in the canon. That's the generous read. A more cynical take is that Rowling used "Dumbledore's gay!" to seem "woke," to cash in on the rising *coolness* of being gay. With only extratextual implications, "Dumbledore's gay!" feels hollow, meaningless—a cheap way to score points with a super gay-friendly generation. Sure, some writers in 2007 dubbed the wizard's casual outing an LGBT victory. But we've grown more cynical. Or perhaps we were always cynical—now we just have our high school diplomas and Twitter accounts of our own. Now we're controlling the cultural conversations.

But back to that question the *New York Times* asked in 2007, when J.K. dropped the bomb that she wrote Albus Dumbledore as a gay man. If an author embellishes upon characters but those details don't appear in the text itself, do those extra-narrative details "count"? In other words, when J. K. Rowling taps *send* on a tweet about how there once were no bathrooms in Hogwarts (she did this, once), does that detail ascend to the Harry Potter canon? Is Dumbledore's sexuality officially part of the Wizarding universe? I neither have nor care to find an answer to this question. I can see the argument for both sides and can also see myself being bored to tears as each side makes its case to me. What I do believe, though, is that queerness exists within the world of Harry Potter, but on a very precarious, *does-it-or-doesn't-it-count?* basis.

It exists with Dumbledore, sure, but even more so in the indisputably noncanonical world of Harry Potter fan fiction.

Online, fans pen their own stories about canonical couples—
Harry and Ginny, James and Lily, Ron and Hermione—which,
in terms of sheer absurdity, pale in comparison to noncanon
ships.[e] Fans have dreamt up millions of words of Harry Potter
erotica, including one where Draco Malfoy runs an in-school
business selling Polyjuice Potion for the explicit purpose of allowing others to turn into and have sex as him (Draco); Madame
Pince and Professor Slughorn banging in the Restricted Section
of the library; and Professor Snape and Hermione engaging in
worship fetish in the bejeweled prefect's bathroom. Thank you,
Al Gore, for your internet.

Slash fic, the subgenre of fan fiction that reimagines characters
in queer relationships, runs rampant in the online Potter world.
I've encountered a steamy Ginny/Cho hookup in the Quidditch
showers; a one-night tryst between Harry and Neville in Berlin after the Battle of Hogwarts; and a particularly beguiling one where
a twentysomething Dumbledore goes to an underground sex club/
dungeon in Knockturn Alley, where he meets Gellert Grindelwald,
who repeatedly punishes Dumbledore's ass with a paddle with the
Deathly Hallows symbol carved into it. But the biggest slash ships
online are Drarry (Draco and Harry) and WolfStar (Sirius Black
and Remus Lupin). Revisiting the books as a gay adult, yeah, these
two pairings do reflect adolescent queerness in the canon itself.
Draco and Harry's mutual hatred is a full-blown obsession, an infatuation that leads Harry to save Draco's life in book seven. As for
Sirius and Remus, the two lithe boys spent their Hogwarts glory

---

e   Short for *relationship*. When fans ship two characters (or celebrities), they're
     rooting for them to get and/or stay together. They often insist they've picked
     up on a spark that's gone unfulfilled. Stucky shippers want Captain America
     and his friend Bucky Barnes to get together in the Marvel Universe; Larry
     shippers insisted that Harry Styles and Louis Tomlinson of One Direction
     were secretly a couple. Personally, I live the quiet, satisfying life of shipping
     Jina (Ina and Jeffrey Garten).

days transforming into canines and running off into the night together—it's easy, at least for a gay fan, to imagine where that might go.

The point is, if Rowling can bulk up the Potter stories post-publication, so can random fans online. Sure, Rowling's tweets carry more weight than Archive of Our Own posts from 2007 do. But given the sheer magnitude of Potter universe expansion in the form of slash fic, I'm equally convinced of Sirius and Remus's boyhood romance and Dumbledore's non-straightness. Which is to say, I'm moderately convinced.

⌒

I grew up over the sprawl of the Potter series, forging my own opinions and values and sense of identity. I was asking really big questions, normal for someone of that age: What does being a good friend really mean? Do I believe in God? What do I want my future to look like? One evening when I was eleven or twelve, I walked down to the kitchen where my mom was watching TV. (She was a producer for Chicago's public television station and got a small TV for the kitchen so she could watch the news while cooking dinner.) I told her, in a sturdy voice I'd practiced in my mirror upstairs, "Mom, there are some things that I disagree with about the Catholic Church." I was petrified to tell her this—and that I didn't think I wanted to be confirmed in eighth grade. I unfolded a small piece of paper, on it a bullet-point list of the church's most obvious offenses to a burgeoning liberal tween: women can't be priests, they don't accept gay people, etc. My mom politely listened and said she agreed but that to her, the church's good outweighed the bad. That satisfied me, I guess, because I chose Saint Cecilia as my confirmation name a couple years later.

While I went along with Catholicism, I found a more profound and palatable sense of right vs. wrong in Harry Potter than the Bible. Each Potter book followed more or less the same structure: We follow Harry et al. through the school year as they repeatedly stick their noses in places they shouldn't, and in doing so slowly unravel a Voldemort-related mystery. Then, at the end of the school year, Harry finds himself face-to-face with some version of the Dark Lord, wriggles his way out, and finds himself back in the hospital wing or the headmaster's office or, in the last book, limbo. Here, we read a very satisfying chapter where Dumbledore answers Harry's outstanding questions about what the fuck just happened and why this pale, noseless man is hell-bent on murdering a tween boy. Reading the series as a kid, I knew, however messy things got, we'd always find Harry back in Dumbledore's office, questions being answered. Even in the final book, after Dumbledore's been dead for a year, we're treated to a penultimate chapter where a half-dead Harry gets to ask the headmaster all the burning questions that have been eating at him, and us, the whole book: *Why didn't you tell me I was a Horcrux? What was up with your friendship with Grindelwald? How did your sister really die?* In the end, Dumbledore is revealed to be flawed and pained like any other human, which only makes him feel more godlike to me.

The headmaster drops quotable quotes in nearly every chapter of the series, but J.K. crammed a particularly high quantity of wisdom bombs into these wrap-up chapters. He ties up loose ends for the reader—yes, a piece of Tom Riddle's soul was trapped in the diary, and yeah, the deputy headmistress gave a thirteen-year-old a tool to warp time so she could take more classes. But he also churned out quippy life lessons, which boiled down to a) do the right thing, even (especially) when it's hard to do, and b) love, be it familial, romantic, or friendly, is a stronger force than any charm a wizard could summon. Type *Dumbledore* into Etsy to reveal hundreds of pages of framed quotes from the wizard in bright colors and gaudy fonts. To many, Dumbledore is the literary equivalent to a weighted blanket.

These end-of-book explanations made the Hogwarts headmaster the ultimate representation of clear reason and morality to tween and teen me. And in adolescence, clear reason is very comforting. Dumbledore wasn't literally *God* to me, no. But he represented some kind of greater plan, a universal goodness, the notion that someone, somewhere had all the answers at the end of the day. I reveled in the idea that I could go through some confusing and frightening hell—be it dueling a giant snake in a subterranean cave or a nasty fight with a friend—and emerge to find an older person telling me exactly what just happened and why everything would be okay. I craved a role model or a mentor. I wanted my own Dumbledore. And though I was closeted, I believe on some level, I craved guidance from an older, queer person, something I completely lacked.

It makes me a little sad to imagine how lovely it would've been had Dumbledore been openly gay through the whole series. At the point I was reading them, I'd never seen any gay character who'd been a story's moral and intellectual center—I'd pretty much only seen gay people on reality TV. What if my Ultimate Source of Order and Reason had been an old, heartbroken, gay spinster? And to have been betrayed, tragically, by someone he loved at a young age—how humanizing. I would've killed for an all-knowing being who spent his entire life sulking over his high school ex-boyfriend. *Killed.* To be able to say, "I am both right and gay at all times" is the absolute dream. And Dumbledore didn't belong just to me—what if the person an entire generation of kids looked to for reason and comfort and existential guidance had been queer? I wish I could say I would've seen my own queerness sooner or had the courage to come out sooner, but that's impossible to really know. But I can say with confidence, it's very nice to think about Dumbledore, the Wise Gay.

But that's not what happened. Whether or not you accept Rowling's post-publication additions to the Wizarding World as canon, the phrase "Dumbledore's gay" remains shrouded in skepticism and eye rolls. He's a queer hero with a big asterisk. By electing to omit Dumbledore's sexuality from the text and retcon diversity in post-publication, Rowling ensured her intentions would be scrutinized, and her godlike character would never be quite the gay icon he could've been. If Rowling did indeed write Dumbledore as gay, it's hard to imagine she never computed a cost-benefit analysis when deciding whether to include that detail in the books (and movie adaptations). Perhaps if Rowling had a little more Hufflepuff in her, we would've gotten Dumbledore, the Wise Gay in earnest. Instead, Dumbledore's sexuality is just a letdown to gay fans.

Throughout the 2010s, the internet produced about fifty billion think pieces containing the words *representation matters*. It became a sort of rallying cry for millennial bloggers and was overutilized to the point of diluting the message. Yes, underrepresented groups saw themselves on-screen more in the 2010s than in previous decades: *Crazy Rich Asians* and *Black Panther* broke ground with (nearly) all-Asian-American and all-Black casts, shows including *Pose* and *Euphoria* put transgender characters front and center, and even Disney's uber-popular *Doc McStuffins* featured an interracial lesbian couple (voiced by Portia de Rossi and Wanda Sykes, no less) in one episode. Progress!

But audiences' pressure to add such characters to shows and films also led to really poorly constructed characters, whose race and/or sexuality and/or disability either didn't come up or felt so clearly written by a white/straight/able-bodied person that their place on-screen felt like a letdown. Max on *Happy Endings*, a sloppy, bro-tastic dude who just happens to love dick, felt like he was conceived by well-intentioned straight creators, as if to say, "straight people and gay people are the same!" And while I adore that character, in doing this, the show failed to give Max any real, lived-in gay identity. When MTV's *Faking It* had one of its leads, Amy, a lesbian, sleep with a cisgender, straight guy, critics argued the show was more interested in advancing plot than honoring queer women's experiences.[20] When Hulu reimagined *High Fidelity* for 2019, record-store owner Rob became a Black queer woman (Zoë Kravitz). But the character doesn't feel *meaningfully* queer— she seems to approach relationships with men and women identically, seeing no difference between them, which felt like a straight person's *technically-respectful-but-ultimately-lacking-any-nuance-whatsoever* understanding of bisexuality. While I think Dumbledore was well crafted on the whole, his lack of queer life/identity in the text makes him, while not necessarily "not really gay," at least a worthy addition to a long list of poorly crafted gay characters with unfulfilled potential.

Because queer TV and film characters are (even still) relatively rare, when they do appear, the stakes are higher and the potential for misrepresentation is bigger. Even if written by well-intentioned straight people, mishandled non-straight characters send inaccurate or misguided messages about LGBTQ+ people to straight audiences. Representation doesn't matter for the sake of visibility in itself but for the sake of communicating the lived realities of queer people.

The reveal of Dumbledore's gayness was utterly bungled, and because of that, it feels less legitimate than had he been out in the text. Yes, some of us had the Potter slash fic ships if we sought them out, but it does mean something for queerness to be canonical. When gay characters and gay narratives are done right, it feels like the authors have our backs, and thus gives the illusion that powerful institutions like publishing and Hollywood do, too. It's easy to imagine how such a botched job could lightly traumatize millennial gays into appreciating the importance of well-done queer characters. Perhaps it's made us skittish around gay characters, more suspicious of them and their creators' intentions, more trigger-happy with our bullshit radar guns. For millennials, ham-fisting diversity into stories simply doesn't work: it comes off as fraudulent, and members of the group represented can smell it from a mile away. We can tell when diverse characters only exist in an attempt to score "wokeness points"—or, at least, we're highly suspicious of that happening. Our generation's demand for fully realized LGBTQ+ characters stems from witnessing so many letdowns.

The Harry Potter series is rife with life lessons invaluable to young people: that familial love burns eternal, that the truth is always worth telling, that death is an inescapable part of life. Harry showed us how to turn to love and friendship in the face of grief and heartache, how to discern confidence and real courage, how to find our own, new families. Thanks to J. K. Rowling's post–*Deathly Hallows* media existence, I'd like to add another quip to the pile of Potter wisdom: Don't ever trust half-baked gay characters.

THE GOSPEL ACCORDING TO
MEAN GIRLS

Going into freshman year, I half expected high school to be like *Mean Girls*," I told a church full of my classmates and their families. It got a laugh. Tina Fey's high school comedy had come out four years earlier, at the end of eighth grade. And even then, in May of my senior year of high school, the movie had years to go before it became a classic, and before "*Mean Girls* day" jokes each October 3 would strip the film of any cool factor. It was a *just* niche enough pop culture reference. I nailed it.

I was giving a speech at our Baccalaureate Mass, a senior class service on the eve of our high school graduation. This exact moment was the peak of my personal Catholic faith; it would all cascade downhill from here. I'd just completed four years at a Jesuit high school. The head of the Department of Formation and Ministry—we called it FAM (and, I regret to report, we called its regular participants the FAM fam)—asked me to give a speech reflecting on my time in high school in the context of my faith. I talked about "getting to know my true self and getting to know God," and being "fortunate enough to be called to lead Kairos," and "praying and reflecting on my service work."

Our school's church was so ugly, we called it Catholic Disneyland: life-size statues of the Saints peered down at parishioners, their robes painted vibrant blues and pastel pinks, their complexions distinctly European. Behind the altar, big, bright, exposed light bulbs dotted the apse as if it were a vanity, making the parishioners Judy Garland prepping for our close-up and Jesus our sleazeball manager, alternately feeding us speed and sleeping pills. Pontificating from the pulpit, I was the very closeted poster girl for Jesuit education.

—

I saw *Mean Girls* in a packed movie theater. My friend Nora and I went to the Biograph on Lincoln Avenue, back when the Biograph still screened movies. We walked back to my house, cackling and quoting the Plastics, and then we immediately watched Lindsay Lohan host *Saturday Night Live*. That episode—May 1, 2004—was best known for the inaugural "Debbie Downer" sketch, though I best recall the one where Lohan plays Hermione Granger with gigantic boobs. (Hm.) As Nora and I shrieked with laughter in my basement, I knew I'd fallen in love with *Mean Girls* and perhaps with Lohan, too.

I liked the cadence of the jokes in *Mean Girls*: the surprising lyricism of the phrase "heavy flow and a wide-set vagina"; the way, as Karen Smith yearns to mack on her cousin, "Seth Mosakowski" rolls off her tongue; the uniquely high school catchiness of the words "the projection room above the auditorium." It has a unique tempo, marked by a tender heart interwoven with gentle digs at the genre. ("You know, it's not really required of you to make a speech," Tim Meadows's Principal Duvall interjects during Cady's sentimental spring fling address.) When I watch *Mean Girls* now, it's like revisiting an old album I've worn to death, scratches be damned. I get chills with the honeyed way Regina asks the newest Plastic, "Cady, will you please tell Aaron his hair looks sexy pushed back?" and in her equally evil but cool, "Because that vest was disgusting!" The humor sounds like music to me.

Mean Girls made me feel seen and my insecurities understood. In the content, yes, but mostly in Fey's writing, which treated teenagers how they really are: smarter than they look. *Mean Girls* doesn't talk down to kids, neither in how it treats teen girl drama (as genuinely hurtful and lasting) nor its jokes. It hit me right at the perfect age, fourteen: I'd had enough health class to know chlamydia doesn't start with a K yet lacked the life experience to have any idea what "butter your muffin" means. I was familiar with the cringey trope of cool moms, sure, but I had to laugh along with "What are marijuana pills?" to not look like an absolute dweeb. The jokes felt a *step* out of my age bracket, and I loved that challenge—nothing makes a joke funnier than *getting it* despite it being intended for someone smarter than you, nor more satisfying than that smugness. It was the humor, more than the story itself, that made *Mean Girls* feel so personal to me.

After that first viewing with Nora, I wanted *Mean Girls* injected into my veins and got as close as I could without getting blood poisoning. Two weeks after seeing it, my eighth-grade class went on a trip to New York. We saw the Lower East Side Tenement Museum and the Statue of Liberty and *Hairspray* with Michael McKean as Edna. But what sticks out most in my mind were the two hours our teachers just let us cut loose (?) in Chinatown (??) to buy a bunch of bootleg crap (???). I bought a DVD recording of *Mean Girls* someone had taken from the back of a movie theater with a handheld camcorder. It wobbled and flickered, the sound grainy and distant like it was playing from the end of a very long hallway. (I also bought a similar DVD of *Troy*, which is the first and last time I'll be mentioning *Troy* in this book, despite its flagrant homoeroticism.) I watched that bootleg recording on my pink desktop iMac nearly every day of that summer; by the time freshman year began, I knew it word for word. Not because I actually thought it was an accurate depiction of high school—I lied in that baccalaureate speech to get the laugh, sorry—but because I felt the jokes respected me. Before I knew what a *personal brand* was (I still don't, really), *Mean Girls* was my personal brand. The jokes were smart and funny, and my loving them meant that I was smart and funny, too. It became part of my identity.

Despite an obscene number of *Mean Girls* viewings, only as an adult did I register the movie's most brutal insult is a homophobic one: "Janis Ian—Dyke." It's written in the Burn Book and photocopied for the whole school to see. The big offensive thing here, in the world of *Mean Girls,* isn't that the Plastics use a gay slur. The mean thing the Plastics do is call Janis a lesbian. It's more than that, though. In eighth grade, Regina started a rumor that Janis was gay, which ostracized Janis at school and prompted the end of their friendship. "I couldn't invite her to a pool party! There were going to be girls there in their *bathing suits,*" Regina says, explaining the roots of their years-old feud. "I mean, right? She was a *lesbian.*" It's posited as a reasonable prompt for Janis's unbridled hatred of Regina and is even perceived as degrading to "too gay to function" Damien. When Cady takes a page out of Regina's book and accuses Janis of being in love with her, he slams on the brakes and urgently defends his friend—"Oh no, she did not!"—knowing Cady had just cut Janis where it hurt most. In *Mean Girls,* calling someone a lesbian is treated as an insult unto itself; it's the worst version of "grotsky little byotch." It's simply an insult, a *bad* insult, an insult cruel enough to tear up a friendship, to incite a year-long revenge plot and a burning urge to fully destroy the girl who made that claim.

No one likes to be misrepresented, sure. But the fact that being called a lesbian is an insult is, well, pretty insulting to lesbians. One could argue the movie isn't trying to be homophobic, that Regina's the homophobic one, that the writing mimics the casual homophobia teens used in the mid aughts. And, yes, it would be natural for self-conscious teen girls to revolt at being called a lesbian—I know I did. And all that might be true. But the writing certainly doesn't stick up for queer women, either. Despite Janis wearing a purple tux to Spring Fling, Fey is sure to disprove Regina's allegation in the final scene, as Janis makes out with Kevin G. in pure, blissed-out heterosexuality.

After upward of seventy-five viewings of *Mean Girls* 2004, I internalized the idea that, like Regina argued, lesbians shouldn't be allowed to go to pool parties with straight girls. I worshipped the movie—and Fey, too. And so, a subtle but disappointed narrative nestled into a corner of my brain for years after 2004: it's cool for guys to be gay. It's cool for girls to be friends with gay guys. But it's an insult to be called a lesbian. Or, as Liz Lemon puts it in a *30 Rock* episode, "My boyfriend and I aren't married, but we might have a baby together anyway. And I hope it's gay! Male gay. Because with the ladies, it's too much hiking." To be fair, that's not untrue.

My high school experience wasn't like Cady Heron's for a whole host of reasons, ranging from "I wasn't a homeschooled jungle freak" to "no boys wanted to have sex with me." But, especially, there was the whole Catholic thing. To answer your first questions, no, my school wasn't single-sex, and no, we didn't wear uniforms. We instead stuck to a dress code that insisted we look like the assholes in every '80s movie: collared shirts, no jeans, knee-length skirts. (My friend Anne so relentlessly abused the mid-aughts pleated miniskirt trend that I believe she single-handedly inspired the school's skirt minimum length to be extended from mid-thigh to knee. Brava to Anne.) Defying the dress code would earn one a Jesuit school detention called a JUG, which stands for Justice Under God, something so on the nose, it's not even worth unpacking. But the most Catholic thing about Catholic school—including crucifixes in every classroom and all-school masses and praying as a team before cross-country races—were our required religion classes. In 2007, while Lindsay Lohan began her famous will-they-won't-they dance with rehab, I was taking my junior year Catholic ethics class with my religion teacher, Mr. Baird.

Mr. Baird was a Texan Marine turned high school religion teacher, a broad-shouldered action figure of a man. He looked like a redheaded Jesse Plemons—so much that, a decade after I left high school, my father would watch *The Post* and remark on the talent of "that guy who looks like Mr. Baird." In class he was abundant with energy, nimble even, which I guessed was a holdover from his morning commute up Lake Shore Drive on a recumbent bike. He was a passionate educator, who firmly believed in hard-assedness as a means of teaching hard lessons. Mr. Baird appeared to delight in rules and was ruthless in giving JUGs; I had to wear socks with my (heinous) Birkenstock clogs every damn day of junior year. Despite the demons the veteran undoubtedly wrestled on those low-to-the-ground bike rides, he was warm, and funny, and alluring, and spoke with such passion on just about every subject that his words always wiggled into my brain and nestled into its folds. If you asked me at my Baccalaureate Mass, I'd tell you I'd learned more from his class than any other in high school.

Mr. Baird's Catholic ethics class was my first introduction to philosophy. Catholic dogma is more based on philosophy than it is on the Bible—a call to return to the text itself was the whole point of the Protestant Reformation, after all. And Mr. Baird seemed to relish Catholic thinkers' place in the larger tradition of Western philosophy. And in order to understand contemporary Catholic teaching, Mr. Baird insisted, we needed to read Catholic philosophers like St. Augustine, Thomas Aquinas, and C. S. Lewis. And understanding *those* thinkers required conversational fluidity in Plato, Aristotle, and Socrates, and even Kant, Freud, and Marx. We had pop quizzes on our dense reading assignments several days a week. His class was hard, and he expected us to rise to the text. Like Tina Fey, he treated our minds as adult ones, and I liked that.

We spent the first semester pretty much exclusively reading and discussing Plato and St. Augustine of Hippo, whose philosophies, Mr. Baird was delighted to present, were parallel. St. Augustine's whole thing was that Original Sin has made us all terrible messes, and we should do all we can do to free ourselves of our bodies' desires and be closer to God.[1] Fair enough. We read excerpts of St. Augustine's *Confessions* (400 A.D.) just two years after Usher's album of the same title was released. In what's basically a memoir, Augustine writes as a fortysomething about his teens, twenties, and thirties, the sins that paved his way to eventual Christian conversion. It's heralded as both the earliest autobiography and a cornerstone Catholic text and is essentially a magnum opus on how desperately the fifth-century North African thinker wanted to bone.

Before getting to sex, Auggie kicks things off with a story of teenage folly. As a sixteen-year-old, he and his buddies stole a bunch of pears from a nearby orchard, despite having plenty of pears of their own. They ate a couple then gave the rest of the pears to some pigs, apparently delighting in the sheer fun of stealing shit when you're a bored teenager. Augustine uses this as proof of Original Sin. Okay.

Post–pear incident, St. Augustine's main thing is: he's horny. He spends most of his twenties banging an unnamed woman (exclusively, he does note), and though they're not married, they have a son together. When he's twenty-nine, his mom, St. Monica, sets

Augustine up with another woman to wed. He breaks up with his baby momma and then finds *another* woman with whom to cheat on his new wife. Come on.

Looking back as a Christian forty-year-old, Augustine describes this as the worst time of his life. He writes, "I had been extremely miserable in adolescence, miserable from its very onset." He's really, really hard on himself for having been a twentysomething with a sex drive. Augustine isn't really concerned about the women he's cheating on; rather, he ruminates strictly on his personal moral failings and how giving in to his urge to sin only widened his well of unhappiness. Sex, he says, drew him further from God. In that time, youthful and captive to the wants of his schlong, he prays, "Grant me chastity and self-control, but please not yet." Which is extremely funny, as it essentially translates to, "I'll stop masturbating to my memory of a crumbling bust of Venus . . . uh, *tomorrow*, I swear."

Eventually, St. Ambrose helps him convert to Christianity. The rest of *Confessions* consists of prayers, spiritual meditations on human nature, and general disdain for being a human being trapped in a human body with human needs. At the time, it was written as a how-to guide for early Christian converts, a sort of *Early Christianity for Dummies*. Mr. Baird felt about St. Augustine the way St. Augustine felt about cheating on his wife: simply addicted. My teacher nearly drooled in hysteria the day he finally replaced the descriptors in Plato's allegory of the cave ("cave," "shadows," "sun") with language from Augustine's Theory of Knowledge ("Original Sin," "temptation," "God") on the chalkboard at the front of our classroom. I had a galaxy-brain moment then, too.

As my introduction to Western philosophy, Mr. Baird's class was also my introduction to the malleability of philosophy to support otherwise arbitrary opinions. Based on what he discussed in class, his own Catholic ethics, suspiciously, matched Bush-era

Republican talking points at the time (abortion bad, immigration bad, death penalty good, war good). My family was and remains Chicago Catholic: blue-voting descendants of Irish immigrants, loyally fueling the city's iron-fisted Democratic Machine, for better or for worse. *Liberal Catholic* may sound like an oxymoron, given the whole "abortion is evil" and "we loathe women" things, but given the sheer global expanse of Catholics, Pope-followers run the political spectrum, from liberation theologian Oscar Romero on the left to Pope Benedict XVI on the right. Mr. Baird was a different kind of Catholic than I'd known to that point. He did something even wilder than joining the armed services in wartime: he *chose to be a Catholic*. Mr. Baird converted from Anglicanism, which is basically just Catholicism, except women can be priests and people can divorce, after teaching Catholic ethics for years. Apparently he didn't like ladies turning bread into Jesus, or the ending of marriages. He became all the proof I needed that converts are always the most intense religious types.

—

St. Augustine might say that Lindsay Lohan's twenties, like his, were defined by her succumbing to earthly and bodily desires and subsequent descent into heathenism.

Lohan's public fall from grace began just after that first *SNL* gig that Nora and I watched in my basement. Double-starring in the 1998 *Parent Trap* reboot had placed Lohan firmly in the seat of Disney stardom. In the early 2000s, she continued that trend, with starring roles in *Get a Clue* (2002), *Freaky Friday* (2003), and *Confessions of a Teenage Drama Queen* (2004) before stepping onto the PG-13 scene with *Mean Girls*. Fey's movie, while ostensibly for teenagers, was Lindsay's chance to show the world she was funny, dammit—like, *adult* funny—and could carry films outside the Mouse's purview. Around the time *Mean Girls* was released, her parents' messiness started to make regular tabloid headlines. Her father, Michael, had spent time in prison in the '90s for criminal contempt, then spent additional prison terms for violating his probation.[2] In 2004, he went to prison for a DUI, and later was arrested again for walking out of a hotel without paying his thirty-eight-hundred-dollar bill.[3] Soon after, Lindsay's mom, Dina, filed for divorce.[4]

Things got real messy for Lindsay after her parents' split. Her partying ratcheted up post–*Mean Girls*, until, throughout my entire high school experience, her name became inextricably linked to the disastrous young Hollywood party culture of the 2000s. *Lindsay Lohan* was synonymous with *shitshow*. It just kept going and going. The actor partied her way through the filming of *Herbie: Fully Loaded* in late 2004, and around then she started appearing in tabloids with Hollywood party girl du jour Paris Hilton.[5] In December of that year, *People* wrote Lindsay was "looking notably thinner."[6] In May 2005, a year after her first hosting gig, she returned to *SNL* blond, rail-thin, and with a heap of messy tabloid photos under her belt. Backstage, Tina Fey and Lorne Michaels "held an intervention of sorts," imploring Lohan to take care of herself so she didn't literally die. Per Fey's telling in *Vanity Fair*, Amy Poehler told Lohan, "You're too skinny . . . I'm not going to ask you why, but you're too skinny and I don't like it."[7]

The *SNL* family's tough love approach didn't exactly get the job done. Lohan went to rehab in early 2007, but in May she crashed her Mercedes SL-65 on Sunset Boulevard around five thirty a.m. after a night of club hopping.[8] She was busted for a DUI and cocaine possession. Just two months later, she was taken into custody for driving with a suspended license, coke possession (again), and a DUI (again). She pleaded guilty in August, and got a whopping one day in jail, community service and a treatment plan. She famously spent eighty-four minutes in jail, released early due to "overcrowding."[9] Lohan would spend the next few years in and out of rebab, clubs, cop cars, and the occasional film set. Despite her personal tumult, studios and directors remained eager to draw out the pitch-perfect performances she'd proven capable of in *Mean Girls, Freaky Friday,* and *A Prairie Home Companion* (2006).[f]

Lindsay Lohan and Cady Heron were synonymous in my mind. That meant just as *Mean Girls* felt personal to me, so did Lindsay Lohan's public unraveling. And, I mean, I'd *trusted* Lohan, after all. She'd carried the first piece of cinema I felt *got me,* and therefore, she *got me*—right? So what did it say about me, that this A-lister of my own generation, whom I'd been rooting for since *The Parent Trap,* had become a tragic punch line? I felt bad for her, probably, but mostly I felt bad for me. Perhaps I judged her cruelly, as teenagers often do. I disregarded the overwhelming stress she was under personally and professionally and instead thought of

---

f   For contrast, my own teenage partying went like this: after her parents would casually say they were going out for a bite around the corner for like, an hour, Anne (the one whose skirts forever changed our school's dress code) would invite about twenty people over. I'd imagined high school parties to be like those in *Mean Girls* or *10 Things I Hate About You*: hundreds of kids crawling all over the house, keg stands, Julia Stiles dancing to Biggie on the dining room table. Turns out, the more people, the more likely you are to get caught drinking. So our parties weren't parties, they were "having people overs." At Anne's "having people overs," we'd stand around her kitchen, drinking raspberry Smirnoff out of water bottles, downing Mike's Hard Lemonade, and throwing the bottles out in her neighbors' trash across the alley. We'd listen to "Yeah!" from Usher's *Confessions* and the Ying Yang Twins and soul-chopping Kanye, songs that reveled in the kind of freedom found after several bottles of champagne in strobe-lit clubs, the places where Lindsay Lohan hung out. Our gaggle of semi-athletic, Abercrombie collar–popping future frat stars would spend the following two hours playing quarters and half-heartedly soliciting hand jobs from my friends (let me be very clear: no boy ever wanted a hand job from me). Most nights, I stuck to my hard-and-fast rule of not drinking after nine p.m. in order to sober up enough to talk to my parents at my eleven p.m. curfew.

her only as a peer who'd gone off the deep end. It's not that Lohan had been a hero of mine, per se. Rather, I struggled to tease apart Cady Heron and the woman the paparazzi kept snapping crumpled up in a pile on Sunset Boulevard, like a half-burned, abandoned campfire with a wig thrown on top. Like the imagery of said campfire, the whole thing was sad and a bit confusing.

—

Our final project for Mr. Baird's Catholic ethics class was a group project, the most cursed of projects. Each group was given a hot-button "ethical dilemma" of 2007, which—gird your loins—were: abortion, gay marriage, immigration, euthanasia, the war in Iraq. (This was when I learned the ongoing moral panic had not, in fact, been about "youth in Asia.") Each group had to present on what each writer we'd read would say on the issue, make a determination of what side of the issue they'd take today, and give an overall PRO or AGAINST on each issue. Then, Mr. Baird would dress each group down in class, poke holes in our arguments, and bend philosophy in the direction of the conservative Texan worldview he espoused in class without once using the word *conservative*, like magic. My group did the death penalty. We went NAY based on "the sanctity of human life," the same tenet Catholics use to reject abortion; per Mr. Baird, we were wrong, but abortion is still a terrible sin. Hm.

Naturally, I remember no presentations other than mine and the gay marriage group. They, too, were a group composed of liberal Chicago Catholics, and had gone PRO on gay marriage. We may not have been open-minded enough to actively embrace and support queerness, but dammit, we liked the *idea* of sounding open-minded! Of course, Mr. Baird appeared thrilled to announce, they, too, were wrong.

"Homosexuality is like alcoholism," Mr. Baird told us.

He explained. A person is genetically predisposed toward substance abuse, but like Augustine with constant masturbation, he can resist the impulse to drink. (Augustine's mother, St. Monica, is the patron saint of alcoholics.) Similarly, one might feel the urge to smooch people of the same gender—apparently conceding that homosexuality isn't a choice, so there's that, I guess—but we should shove it away, resist it, in order to inch nearer to existential truth and happiness. Never mind that alcoholism, when unmanaged, can be a life-ruining disease.

It turns out that argument is a common one among conservative Christians. Mr. Baird might've been the first person I'd heard make it, but he wasn't the most famous one. His fellow Texan, Rick Perry, said the same thing during a 2014 speech in San Francisco.[10] And, upon hearing the news that my friend, Jack, had come out in college, a conservative classmate of mine asked another friend: "He's not going to *act on it*, is he?"

In that moment in class, I knew Mr. Baird was wrong. I didn't process his comments as harmful to me, personally; I hadn't yet allowed myself to grapple with my sexuality. I was just entering the phase of my closetedness where I simply fancied myself a really great gay ally. Maybe a part of me knew I'd fall for my friend, Claire, in just a few short months. But no, I was fired up about gay shit because I *fucking loved justice,* not because of my own Augustine-esque illicit fantasies. But Mr. Baird was a very good teacher—he was funny and charming and passionate—and that idea, that being queer was something worth resisting, stuck to me. I think that's why, years later, the false simile has stuck with me. It's easy to brush off homophobia when it spews from the mouth of an obviously sinister wacko. It's much more confusing from someone you trust, someone you admire. It affirmed my instincts to repress my sexuality, at least for a few more years. I wasn't as hype on Mr. Baird's Catholic ethics class as I had been on *Mean Girls*, but just as "Janis Ian—Dyke" seeped into my brain by embedding itself in a piece of art I loved, "Homosexuality is like alcoholism" crept its way in under the guise of Catholic logic from a trusted teacher.

—

Given the alleged link between substance abuse and homosexuality, I can only imagine Mr. Baird would've had a judgmental *field day* with Lindsay Lohan had he ever glanced at the cover of *Us Weekly*. Because in 2008, Sam Ronson happened.

Lindsay Lohan dated the openly gay DJ (and sister of producer Mark Ronson) from 2008 to 2009, on and off. They'd run in the same cocaine-fueled Hollywood party circles for a couple years but were spotted, as Principal Duvall of *Mean Girls* would say, "canoodling" in public over summer 2008. Lohan confirmed their romantic relationship later that year. It appeared to come out of nowhere. Lohan hadn't publicly dated women before, though she's alluded to sleeping with some. And Sam Ronson was, well, a total dyke. She had short, boyish hair and definitely clenched her jaw in photos to carve definition into her high cheekbones. She wore fedoras and slouchy jeans and jean vests over oversize tees, a skinny skater boy aesthetic that echoed her fictional peer, Shane McCutcheon. And there she was, mean-mugging in the club with Hollywood's hottest twenty-two-year-old on her arm.

A famous person dating someone of the same gender so casually (and so publicly) was a rarity at that point, especially without any sort of declaration of sexuality. This was years before supermodel Cara Delevingne and actor Michelle Rodriguez went to the Knicks game together, handsy and wasted; Kristen Stewart wouldn't tell the world, "I'm like, so gay, dude," for another eight years. In interviews at the time, Lohan comes off admirably confident about dating a woman and with sexual fluidity at large: "I appreciate people, and it doesn't matter who they are," Lohan told *Harper's Bazaar* in a 2008 cover story.[11] "I feel blessed to be able to feel comfortable enough that I can say that." She told her profiler, Marshall Heyman, that she "maybe" identified as bisexual (though, definitely not as a lesbian), and that she simply didn't know whether she'd end up with a man or a woman.

While some outlets applauded Lohan's casual queerness—like the *LA Times*, which wrote, "It's bigger than both of them"[12]—gossip blogger Perez Hilton labeled the couple "saMAN and LezLo," a wild reminder of how comparatively low the standards were for internet humor in the aughts.[13] Today, I'd agree with the *LA Times*; in 2008, my peers and I tended to use Perez's language. Sure, many of us had more or less liberal families, but gay rights hadn't yet landed on the mainstream liberal agenda quite yet. And in school, our teachers presented us with allegedly rational perspectives on why being queer was a moral failing. The guys called each other *faggot* and *fucking gay* on a near-constant basis. I might've believed, intellectually, that being gay was fine. But homophobia seeped into my bones and stuck there, invisible and gross, for years. I still find gobs of it in my marrow to this day.

Lindsay Lohan was trapped in a constant downward spiral of her own creation. That was the narrative that surrounded her throughout the late aughts, anyway, and it's the one I bought into, however much it bummed me out. St. Augustine would have called her the poster child for giving in to temptation—she partied, she was in a queer relationship, she was lust-driven, and if there were a pear orchard in West Hollywood in 2008, Lindsay

Lohan would've stolen all of the pears. And because Lohan was this Tasmanian Devil–esque cyclone of cocaine and auto-tuned songs and tube-top-miniskirt dresses, I felt like everything she did was symptomatic of a steady, public unhinging.

So, on a subconscious level, I came to understand Lohan's bisexuality as another byproduct of her partying, her parents' drama, her general derailment. Even more broadly, the conversation about Lohan made me think that a person exhibiting queerness, or sexual fluidity, or non-straightness at large, meant something was wrong with them. And because my parents weren't divorced and no one would even offer me cocaine for another ten years, that couldn't be me.

Revolutionary as they might or might not have been, Sam and Lindsay were abject chaos. After a heavily paparazzi'd on-again, off-again thing, they finally broke up for real. Then, Lindsay publicly backtracked on all that gayness. In 2010, she told *The Sun,* "If I wasn't with Samantha, I would probably be with a boy next. She's the only woman I've been attracted to."[14] Then, in 2013, she told Piers Morgan, "I know I'm straight. I have made out with girls before, and I had a relationship with a girl. But I think I needed to experience that, and I think I was looking for something different."[15] She told Wendy Williams the same thing five years later and explained her sapphic dabbling a decade prior as, "I was living in L.A."[16] Which, sure. All that is to say, Lindsay Lohan might've banged down the door for Hollywood's messy lesbian couplings of the 2010s, but her shame-adjacent feelings toward queer identity muddle her place in LGBTQ+ history.

Internalized homophobia is a sneaky thing. For most queers, its most common form is not intentionally closeting oneself, nor is it telling Wendy Williams that we're actually straight. It's much more subtle than that. It crops up at inconvenient times, making our insides feel icy and our heads briefly disassociated from our bodies.

I feel pangs of it when I opt to wear a dress to a family wedding instead of a suit, or when I kiss a girl on a busy street, or when I insist that I don't want to chop my hair off because "I don't have the face for it." It sits inside me. It's that gross part of me that feels validated by straight girls crushing on me, valuing their straightness over others' queerness. In my first decade of being openly gay, I've learned how to spot it, name it, and question it. That usually shuts it up. But I don't think I'll ever shake internalized homophobia, though, not entirely.

Gay self-loathing may never really end, but it does start somewhere. I'd be dishonest if I blamed my Catholic upbringing for the brunt of it. (But wait, is that just Catholic Stockholm Syndrome? There's no winning.) Sure, a Napoleonic ex-Marine shrieked ancient texts condemning lust at me for a swath of my pubescence. But I also had my very favorite, soul-affirming movie tell me that if I were gay, none of my female friends would want to be around me while in bathing suits and that their discomfort was reasonable and valid. And those conclusions surely informed my latent understanding that queerness and public meltdowns go hand in hand. It's easy to blame organized religion for all our fucked-up sex hang-ups—and that's usually warranted, at least in part. But I think singling out my Catholic ethics class, or those all-school masses, or my CCD classes as the places where I inherited negative ideas about queerness lets the secular world of the 2000s off way too easy.

At the Baccalaureate Mass, the night before my high school graduation, my internalized homophobia was so deep, I hadn't yet excavated it. In that moment, from that pulpit, I was proud of the grown-ass eighteen-year-old I'd become. I felt truly called to live a faith-based life, and on some level, truly felt homosexuality was an ailment, that succumbing to it would be a loss. The fact that I'd been making out with my (girl) friend for months was stuffed

CHERRY CHAPSTICK

When this comes on at parties, you *know* what girls are gonna do!" Sean shouted to his buddies over the music at a sweaty, vodka-heavy party in the coach house above Mike's garage. He wasn't a close friend of mine but was one of the "good guys"; Lord knows what the not-so-good guys were saying about this song. It was the summer between senior year of high school and freshman year of college. That particular time of life when, had we been in a movie, we all would've been scrambling to lose our virginities to one another on terrifying dares. Like, whoever hasn't fucked by Labor Day has to drive their dad's Toyota into the lake. Something normal.

Instead, my friends and I spent the summer enjoying that final sliver of time together before we were scattered from Boston to New Orleans to Seattle for college. We drove aimlessly around to *Late Registration* and *Hot Fuss,* snuck Smirnoff Ices down to beach bonfires in Michigan, became intimately familiar with the late-night taco options on Lincoln Avenue. When I wasn't at work bussing tables on a dinner cruise ship on Lake Michigan—one with a dance floor where the "Cupid Shuffle" played every single night at nine fifteen—I was laughing my ass off with my roving crew of sexless pals. That summer, I encountered the genitalia of absolutely zero people other than myself. Which was fine! The five of us were a subunit within a larger mob of recent grads, including

Sean and Mike, who spent that summer reveling in one another's company. There's no ego boost like being a senior, and these three months felt like a bonus burst of seniordom. That eager energy bubbled away at coach house parties.

The song that Sean was getting publicly horned up about was Katy Perry's "I Kissed a Girl." And the thing girls were to do when they heard this song was, of course, to make out—with lots of tongue!—with lots of boys watching. Maybe even hooting, who knows. Sean didn't have to spell that out for his buddies to get the point. Jimmy, my tall crush, clasped his hand in Sean's and smacked him on the back with his other: the straight male equivalent of raw, emotional honesty. For the record, no girls at the coach house made out to "I Kissed a Girl" that night. I can't speak to how that went for Sean up in Madison that fall.

As the sweaty Midwest summer reached its peak in temperature and restlessness, the bop encroached upon me from all angles. "I Kissed a Girl" was released in late April 2008, about a month before my high school graduation and two months before the release of Perry's second studio album, *One of the Boys*. Co-written with Max Martin and produced by Dr. Luke, the single was destined to be a pop smash, and so it was. "I Kissed a Girl" dominated airwaves that summer and helmed the Billboard Hot 100 charts for seven weeks straight.[1] It was the song of the summer, in that final trickle of years before streaming algorithms existed and "the song of the summer" could still be a thing. "I Kissed a Girl" was *everywhere*. At least, it was everywhere for partially employed teenagers who had nothing better to do than zip up and down Lake Shore Drive and listen to 103.5 KISS FM all night.

The song—in case you're blessed enough to have never heard it, or I guess if you're currently a tween?—details a girl-on-girl make-out session framed as an "experimental game." Here's the first verse, translated for your ease:

This was never the way I planned
Not my intention

Rough translation: "I haven't been *thinking* about making out with girls, I promise."

I got so brave, drink in hand
Lost my discretion

"I'm drunk, babe!"

It's not what I'm used to
Just wanna try you on

"I don't plan to make this a lifestyle, don't worry."

I'm curious for you
Caught my attention

"Not only am I drunk, but I am in fact ready to get it on!"

You get it. "I Kissed a Girl" is a bop about getting drunk and making out with a girl, couched in metaphorical asterisks that assure the listener Perry isn't *really* gay.

The song's lyrics were surely engineered to spark controversy, or at least conversation, which it did. It outraged Christian groups for obvious reasons. But even within the queer community, there seemed to be little consensus whether the song was harmful or innocuous or even helpful. Was it homophobic of Perry to sing about making out with some random girl—then turning around and clarifying that she, the real-life Katy Perry, was actually straight? Or is that assessment biphobic, or at the very least admonishing queer experimentation? The editor of the UK's decades-old sapphic magazine *DIVA* drew a very simple conclusion: Katy Perry is an idiot. She told *The Guardian*, "I don't think she's being homophobic. I think she might be a bit dumb...a bit un-self-aware."[2] This seems like an overly simplistic (and kind of sexist) response from a purported authority on queer women's issues. Perhaps the relief of seeing a queer female narrative, however questionable, dominate pop culture overshadowed the song's potential damage to the LGBTQ+ community.[g]

The American blogosphere loathed "I Kissed a Girl." *Vulture* ran a listicle titled, "Six Reasons Katy Perry's 'I Kissed a Girl' Isn't the Song of the Summer," calling it a "lumbering ode to part-time bisexuality" that you can't dance to, whose lyrics are a "cheap grab for attention."[3] *TIME* hated it, too. They wrote, "Perry turns brushing lips with the same sex into a cheesy, aggressive form of exhibitionism—like Wrestlemania without the cuddling."[4] In a post headlined, "Why I Hate Katy Perry," a *SPIN* blogger asked, "Why are people buying her album and not Zooey Deschanel's?" which was, apparently, reasonable to be asking in the Year of Our Lord 2008.[5] The sheer shamelessness of the pop song seemed to outrage more cultural writers than the purported homophobia did. Which might've been its whole point. "Oh, I'm completely shameless!" a twenty-three-year-old Perry confirmed to *The Guardian* in an interview that summer.[6]

Truly *everyone* had a take on the song. To my roving crowd of sweaty high school seniors, the song was scandalous. To our parents, it was the pinnacle of the oversexed, attention-obsessed generation they'd birthed us into. To boys like Sean,

---

g   Also on *One of the Boys* was a song called "Ur So Gay." In it, Perry taunts an ex-boyfriend who is "acting gay" by doing gay (?) things like "wearing an H&M scarf" and reading (notoriously macho literary icon) Ernest Hemingway. That one, unlike "I Kissed a Girl," was universally panned by gay groups as blatantly shitty and homophobic, even in 2008. Which, yes, correct.

it was an indication of how girls *could* act, or *would* act when they're drunk, or perhaps even *should*. To some girls, it was an instruction manual for getting guys' attention. To my core unit, the song was catchy and frivolous. (We preferred *The O.C.* soundtrack, because we were cultured and "got it.") And, to closted me, "I Kissed a Girl" was a rude bird cawing directly in my face, a bird that somehow knew the way my stomach jolted every time I caught a whiff of a friend's hair as she put up her ponytail.

It felt like "I Kissed a Girl" had been dropped into my life for a *reason*, because when you're eighteen, you're the heroine in your own screenplay. Coming of age is in and of itself an inciting incident. The tone of my charming indie flick, I envisioned at the time, would be some godforsaken combination of *Garden State* and *Juno*. Quirky, punchy, sickeningly optimistic, and low-key laced with conservative values. And in screenplays, there are no random occurrences, there are only plot points—or at the very least, meticulous world-building. In any case, my late teens were in part defined by a self-centered conviction, or hope, that everything happens for a reason. And so, I was certain that Katy Perry's "I Kissed a Girl" had been inserted into my life for one purpose: to mock me.

There are two major reasons I felt this way. The first was that the singer of this ode to tonguing unidentified chicks had the exact same name as my seventy-eight-year-old grandmother.

Well, with a slightly different spelling. The only Katie Perry I'd known up until this point was a four-foot-eleven, cranky Irish lady who lived for parish gossip, cheating at Scrabble games against her grandchildren (by flipping over tiles to create blanks), and her daily Manhattan(s). The content of "I Kissed a Girl" was scandalous enough, but the fact that its singer's name matched my grandma's? Chef's kiss. Hearing a woman with your grandmother's name purr,

"*It felt so wrong/It felt so right/Don't mean I'm in love tonight*" all over the radio is, for the record, a total mindfuck. And pretty funny to a pack of eighteen-year-olds. Especially eighteen-year-olds with zero LGBTQ+ sex ed or visible lesbian role models, fictional or in real life.[h]

But my grandma wasn't the only reason I felt "I Kissed a Girl" had arrived strictly to ruin my life. By the time the song came out, I'd already kissed a girl and I'd already liked it. We'll call it: the Claire Thing.

I'd just emerged from my first gay relationship—using *relationship* in its most liberal sense possible. Claire and I became friends our sophomore year of high school but became *best* friends, an important distinguisher at the time, our junior year. From the end of junior year to senior spring, we had an intense friendship laced with romance. We'd spend all our time together. We ran on the cross-country team together, carpooled, spent weekend nights together. I convinced my parents to take her with us on a ski trip. We organized a service trip to Appalachia over Christmas break— any excuse to spend more time together, even if it meant a nine-hour van ride to Kentucky in the dead of winter.

Peers and teachers alike knew we were obsessed with each other. "Two peas in a pod!" our coaches called us. But codependent friendships like that are common between teenage girls. So common that I convinced myself that Claire and I were those kinds of teenage girl [space emphasized] friends: naturally in-

---

h   My Katie Perry passed away in 2015. After her funeral and the reception at an old North Shore country club, my extended Perry family gathered at Uncle Tim's house in Wilmette to continue drinking. (Irish funerals.) After several Manhattans, one cousin suggested it'd be funny if we watched the "California Girls" video, as sort of a tribute to the "Original Katie Perry." We snapped it off after one chorus and a dozen glimpses of whipped cream on titties, nary a glimpse of Snoop Dogg. It was one of the worst Perry family ideas to date.

timate, yet totally platonic. I ignored the lurch in my stomach that sprang up whenever she held my hand. Which, by the way, we did on the bus to every cross-country meet our senior year. Claire had read somewhere that holding hands relieves stress, and since we were both absolute basket cases before our weekly three-mile races, it was settled: we'd hold hands on our way to meets, if only to increase our chances of running a PR. That said, holding hands in pursuit of athletic success is arguably gayer than holding hands in pursuit of a girl.

Our friendly obsession with each other was so intense that it sometimes got physical, though, honestly, not *that* physical. We stayed cuddled up in the air-conditioning of my parents' base-ment for most of summer 2007, pretending to watch *Gossip Girl*. When we said, "I love you," we both knew it was to be received like one straight girl saying it to another. Never mind that we were kissing when we said it.

Crucially, we never, ever, ever talked about what would happen physically between us. We shared a wordless understanding that this was simply what we did when we were alone together. That seems absolutely absurd now. But, at the time, we pretty much left our brains on the shoe mat when we got home, then promptly curled up together. Claire's family was very conservative. Her dad was a big-time Republican; her grandpa had a building named after him at a fancy Catholic college; her extended fam-ily all wore color-coordinated Lacoste polos in their annual group portrait. My family unit was (and remains) a matriarchy, helmed by my journalist mother, who instilled in me a deep mistrust of trickle-down economics by the time I'd finished nursing.

Since we were at Catholic school, both of us were fairly reli-gious at the time. Once, I told Claire that I liked my family's parish because it was relatively socially liberal, as far as Catholic parishes go. I mentioned to Claire that the church hosted weekly meetings for LGBT Catholics. (I didn't go. I only knew that because they'd announce that week's meeting times at the end of the eleven fifteen mass. *How nice for the gays,* I would think, distant, as if I hadn't spent the entire Liturgy of the Eucharist thinking about Scarlett Johansson's lips in *Ghost World*.) I liked that, I told Claire, fancying myself a supportive ally and absolutely nothing more.

As I spoke, she froze. Silence welled up between us. "What?" I asked, genuinely confused.

She burst out laughing. "*Oh!* I thought you were about to tell me that *you're gay!*"

"No!" We both cackled at the misunderstanding. Imagine! Me, gay! As if I hadn't had my hand on her leg under the blanket as we'd watched an ABC Family teen drama the night before. Our physicality existed in another sphere of the universe than our conversations did. Like if we verbally acknowledged that we didn't cling to any other friend—emotionally or physically—like we did to each other, it'd become real. We instead laughed aloud at the sheer prospect of one of us being gay.

I later learned that my closest friends suspected *something* had been happening between us. Mostly based on the fact that it was, uh, really obvious: how I *insisted* Claire sit in the front seat of my Eurovan on the drive to school, how I lunged for my Motorola cell phone when Jack started to read my texts, how we cuddled the entire long, January van ride to Kentucky for our service trip. My and Claire's relationship wasn't unlike that of Queen Anne and Lady Marlborough in *The Favourite*: totally fucking gay to onlookers, but of an era lacking the vocabulary for or understanding of what homosexuality was.

"Okay, *hot*." That's the knee-jerk reaction I get from people of all genders and sexual preferences when I reveal I had a down-low lesbian affair at Catholic school. Admittedly, it does sound like prototypical pornography. But the truth is, from my experience, clandestine gay love affairs get really old, really fast. It's far darker than it is fun. The psychological undoing of not being able to openly crush on your crush far outweighs the fun of a secret romp. The acute, silent pain of knowing you can't take her to a dance, let alone tell your parents, or that even telling your other friends will prompt scandal and gossip. That it would just be a whole *thing* if you tried to. If you didn't have low-key gay make-out sessions in high school, please, you have nothing to be jealous of. I would absolutely have sacrificed a secret fling for a school environment that let me be myself.

Whatever was between us had gasped for air in the no man's land between the platonic and romantic, and ultimately it sputtered out with college on the horizon. When the Claire Thing ended, it ended quietly, a fade-out. Because we never talked about us, we never verbally broke up. It just happened, we just drifted. By that summer after graduation, it was fully over. I wasn't hung up on her, because I'd managed to create a great gorge between what my body wanted and the thoughts I allowed to actually pass through my brain. I hoped that the Claire Thing was a misstep to move on from, merely teen horniness born from our mutual lack of boyfriends, and, fingers crossed, that we'd go to college and be straight and coupled up with guys. (Deep denial disguised as rationalization.) Despite said necking, I still thought myself straight. I was so disconnected from my body and my own wants that I couldn't even come out to myself. I knew in my gut that I wasn't entirely straight, but I couldn't even think the words "I'm gay," or "I'm bisexual," or "I'm attracted to girls," or even the obvious truth, "I'm attracted to this one girl, at least, and by the way, kissing you is super fun and I'd like to continue doing it if that works for your schedule?" Not even to myself, in my head.

As the Claire Thing petered out, "I Kissed a Girl" ramped up into teen ubiquity: at those sweaty summer parties, all over the

radio and iTunes charts, on "for the drive to college!" mix CDs.
And that meant the topic of lesbianism, in general, was everywhere. I had to dodge it at every turn.

My public reactions to the bop were measured, if I dared ex-
press them at all. A strong response to hearing "I Kissed a Girl"
would be, I feared, a tell that I'd spent the past year kissing a girl
and liking it. If I pumped it up in the car? Gay. Snapped it off? Sensitive, gay. Told Sean et al. off for being gross about it? Gayest option of all! Only a dyke would get sensitive about guys being horny
for dykes, right? Kanye West, the patron saint of aughts Chicago,
would famously "do anything for a blond dyke"—so it was socially
acceptable for the boys to thirst accordingly. Being a gay teenager
when "I Kissed a Girl" came on felt less like being locked away in
the closet and more like standing naked onstage in front of the
whole school as they leered at your every move.

"I Kissed a Girl" had such a deep impact on my psyche because
it was the first time I can remember the topic of lesbianism being
discussed so openly among my peers. It's ridiculous to imagine
this just ten years later, but the song was one of the few examples of lesbian desire I'd encountered in mainstream pop culture.
Whether I was subconsciously searching for queer guidance or
not, Katy Perry was teaching me about what being gay looked
like. And because I had no other pop culture figures to look to, I
listened to her.

The more I heard this woman with my grandma's name sing
about making out with girls, the more I was "forced" to think about
making out with girls. It wasn't just that I was afraid I'd be "found
out" as gay—I was genuinely afraid of *being* gay. It seemed like the
worst, most humiliating, ostracizing life event possible. I was afraid
to even let myself think about how I would come out or what that
would look like. Wouldn't all my friends think I'd been lying to them

all this time? Didn't gay people know they were gay from birth? I didn't know what I wanted, ergo I couldn't be queer.

Plus, lesbians weren't like, *real*, right? If I'd learned anything from *The O.C.*, bisexual dabblings were a phase of female adolescence to be moved on from and laughed at in retrospect. Also, weren't lesbians just women men didn't want to fuck? I hadn't fucked any guys—mostly because absolutely zero dudes wanted to fuck me—but wouldn't my coming out a lesbian just highlight that very real truth? Plus, how could I *know* I was gay if I was so inexperienced with boys? *Maybe if I just sit tight, the whole thing'll blow over.* Maybe I'd meet a guy in Boston who would sweep me off my feet. Maybe I'm bisexual? But is bisexuality real?

I was, to be kind to myself, a mess. I both was and lived in constant fear of being Tammy Metzler in *Election* (1999): "It's not like I'm a lesbian or anything," she says in a voice-over, "I'm attracted to the person. It's just that all the people I'm attracted to happen to be girls."

Going into college, I felt—on a subconscious level—like I could take one of two paths: I could confront the fact that I was for sure into girls, or I could continue to push it away in the hope that it stayed away. And then, Katy Perry sauntered into the picture with her cherry ChapStick and her Jock Jams drumbeats and convinced me there was a third option: the "I Kissed a Girl" narrative. And in my screenplay, no major plot point goes unexplored.

The "I Kissed a Girl" narrative means doing, basically, what Katy Perry does in "I Kissed a Girl." It's coming out as queer only after kissing a girl by happenstance, preferably publicly, double preferably with a boyfriend present to affirm you're not lezzing out, because lezzing out means boys don't like you because you're ugly. The narrative allows the apparent luxury of a vast emotional chasm between the participant and the girl she's kissing. It is a meet-cute with one's own sexuality. It is waltzing, girlish and glib and feminine out of the closet. And most important, it is extremely hot to straight men.

That narrative was tempting to me. "In or out" was too conclusive! Too much pressure! My own experience having same-sex feelings had been overall painful, unfulfilled, and embarrassing. I couldn't even tell the girl I was kissing, "Hi, I like kissing you." I felt I had to lie to all my friends about the extent of our closeness. I hated the part of me that curled up close to her at sleepovers. I didn't want that anymore. That couldn't be *my* story. I wanted something easier. I wanted the Katy Perry path. I wanted my sexuality to be something I merely encountered, instead of what it was: a series of lingering hugs with friends strung together in my head to culminate in one, pseudo-erotic experience. Stumbling is easy; stumbling is a plot point, something that happens to you because someone else wrote the story. Flat-out unrealized wanting is scarier and realer. And at any age, it's so much more embarrassing.

So, freshman year, I tried to take the Katy Perry path: I assumed I could passively wait for some hot girl to kiss me at a party and take it from there. "I'd never thought about being with a girl before," I'd tell my cool new college friends. "But—I don't know, she's so into me." My friends would assure me that this imaginary suitor was, although female, hot nonetheless. In this fantasy, I was extremely sought after, not a creepy lesbian fantasizing about straight girls. I'd be, best of all, the object of desire, not the *haver* of desire. Far less embarrassing. I wouldn't have to tell my cool new friends about Claire—I'd never mention that whole mess—or let on to the fact that I had ever wanted anything or anyone ever before stepping foot on campus in August 2008.

Shockingly, the "I Kissed a Girl" narrative didn't work out for me. Instead of illuminating an unembarrassing, suave way to come out, it duped me into thinking there was a path available that excluded honest self-confrontation. Perhaps some people have meet-cutes with their own sexuality, but I didn't. Instead, my gayness was the annoying coworker I'd been hoping would shut up throughout adolescence but had to learn to love because they wouldn't fuck off. All "I Kissed a Girl" did was give me an excuse to stave off the genuine conversation I needed to have with myself. I eventually did that early sophomore year and almost immediately started telling friends, one by one, that I was into girls in some capacity, maybe bisexual, maybe gay.

In hindsight, I was totally incorrect in thinking the only options at this time were "in or out of the closet." I didn't *know* if I was gay or bi or pan or queer or what. I shouldn't have had to declare anything conclusively. I was eighteen! Experimentation is good and fun and healthy and something everyone should do at some point. Why not take the time and space and energy to figure out what you really want and need sexually? And it's not just me saying this—studies show more Americans than ever are experimenting sexually.[7] And honestly, there are so many people who didn't think they were gay, then got drunk and made out with someone at a party Katy Perry–style and realized something new about themselves that made their life better. Katy Perry might've even been one of them! But still, I don't think that's exactly the framework "I Kissed a Girl" lays out. Experimentation for the sole purpose of satisfying the porn-driven fantasies of straight men is, dare I say, less good. When your sexuality becomes packaged as something that should exist to satisfy everyone but you—well, that rarely offers any real clarity.

To her credit, Perry has partially reckoned with "I Kissed a Girl." She's confessed she regrets recording such clichés, and she's publicly alluded to non-straightness and/or queer sexual experiences—though doesn't necessarily identify as bisexual. "If

I had to write that song again, I probably would make an edit on it," Perry told *Glamour* in 2018. "Lyrically, it has a couple of stereotypes in it. Your mind changes so much in ten years, and you grow so much. What's true for you can evolve."[8] That's nice to know, I guess, but it doesn't change the fact that at the particular crux of my life in which "I Kissed a Girl" entered, it warped my brain on a very intimate level.

It's fun to wonder what it would be like if some big cultural phenomenon happened in a different era, but it's rare that we get to actually see it happen. We got that payoff with "I Kissed a Girl." A decade after Katy Perry's cherry ChapStick took her to the international stage, Rita Ora tried to re-create Perry's let's-get-drunk-and-kiss-girls model of success. The singer/actor/erstwhile *America's Next Top Model* host/Adidas collaborator unveiled her single "Girls," ft. Cardi B., Bebe Rexha, and Charli XCX, in June 2018. The chorus plays thusly:

Sometimes I just wanna kiss girls, girls, girls
Red wine, I just wanna kiss girls, girls, girls

It's pretty complex content, I know. It was a weird, out-of-era déjà vu, like "I Kissed A Girl" had dropped back in ten years later, just to check in and see how we're doing and if this whole "drunkenly making out with girls" thing is cool yet/again. Ora even admitted the lyrics were inspired by Perry's 2008 girl-smooching anthem. How could they not be?

"Girls" debuted to near-immediate backlash from queer fans and artists alike. Which is to say, Twitter got mad. Millennial lesbian pop artist Hayley Kiyoko, known to her fans as Lesbian Jesus, called the single "downright tone-deaf, which does more harm than good for the LGBTQ+ community."[9] It was as if a generation of queers who'd come of age to "I Kissed a Girl" finally got the chance to nip that song in the bud, and it was taken out on Ora, Cardi, Rexha, and XCX. Ora publicly apologized. She also stated she's dated both men and women, possibly to give herself more cred, possibly to recenter the hit as a genuine coming-out anthem. That narrative didn't save the single.

My take on "Girls" is still blurry. I think, today, there's more space for people who don't identify strongly with any sexual identity group—gay, straight, bisexual, or otherwise. Today, there are *so* many more queer narratives in TV shows, movies, books, and pop music that one of them being "I like to get drunk and make out with girls sometimes!!!" doesn't bother me too much. It's true for a lot of people! That's fine. I think "I Kissed a Girl" fucked with my head so much because it was the *only* mainstream pop lesbian narrative I could look to during a particularly sad and confusing sliver of my life. The whole thing makes me feel for those gay writers in 2008, trying to figure out what the hell to do with Katy Perry.

The 2018 gay pop music landscape would be utterly recognizable to someone in 2008. Artists including Kiyoko, King Princess, Khelani, Troye Sivan, Kim Petras, Big Freedia, Arca, and Perfume Genius sing about queerness not to exploit the LGBTQ+ community but to explore their actual lived experiences. Honestly, I'm jealous of kids who have these artists' music at their fingertips. LGBTQ+ teenagers still have all kinds of difficult and often confusing emotional unpacking to do, though the "I Kissed a Girl" problem seems to have been a strictly millennial one. Katy Perry isn't single-handedly responsible for warping my view of my own sexuality. But it's tough not to imagine what my biopic would've been like with a different soundtrack.

BE THE PR TEAM YOU WISH TO SEE IN THE WORLD

There are moments when I feel so gay that I've been stripped of any nuance, my defining cracks smoothed such that I am a plastic Easter egg indistinguishable from any other pastel orb in the garden. I had one of those moments in late 2019, when I saw my most played song of the year on Spotify: "Pussy Is God" by King Princess. I wasn't shocked—I'd spend hours of the spring and summer wandering Echo Park with the cocky twenty-year-old crooning in my earbuds, tapping repeat twice to loop one song only. Still, I became overcome with a strange sense of solidarity. Without trying to perform my queerness for anyone, I accidentally listened to "Pussy Is God" literally hundreds of times in one calendar year. I promptly screenshotted my Spotify Wrapped 2019 digital card, and sent it to my entire phone book.

"Pussy Is God" was released by nineteen-year-old Mikaela Straus, aka King Princess, in 2018. The title is almost a joke in how horny it is, suggesting a sexual depravity that really isn't found in the song. *Pussy* might be a hypersexual word, but the song isn't, really. It's a tender bop that describes finding clarity in love. It's sweet. *"Your pussy is God and you know I / Think you're so cute when you get high,"* King Princess sings in the second verse. Yeah, it's a song about literally worshiping pussy, but she's *so damn cute* about it. I wanted to inject King Princess's confidence directly into my veins. An overconfident nineteen-year-old so settled in her queerness that she dares worship at the high altar of pussy, for the world to see? I needed that.

The release of "Pussy Is God" capped an eventful 2018 for King Princess. Earlier that year, the teenager shot to stardom almost instantly. She'd already signed to Mark Ronson's label, Zelig Records, and they released her first single "1950" with pretty much no promotion. Harry Styles tweeted lyrics from the song—*I love it when we play 1950*"—and boom, King Princess was a Thing. And it's easy to see why: King Princess oozes cool, Gen Z queerness. She grew up in twenty-first-century Williamsburg and spent her childhood toying around in her dad's recording studio before getting Harry Styles's coveted stamp of approval.[1] And of course, she is brazenly gay.

King Princess was unabashedly queer from the get-go. Her stage name is an in-your-face mosaic of gender identities. The song "1950" is a tribute to Patricia Highsmith's classic lesbian novel *The Price of Salt,* which was adapted into the Oscar-nominated 2015 film *Carol.* She released her ode to pussy within the first six months of her music career. King Princess has always been far more interested in *being* gay than in *becoming* gay, even as a teenager.

"I guess I really came out in middle school," she told the website *them.* in 2019.[2] "I had my first queer kiss in eighth grade. It was over the summer, and this girl I was friends with asked me directly if I wanted to kiss her at a party. Immediately after we kissed I was like, 'Fuck. That was good. I'm gay.'" What? How! She presents such confidence and nonchalance in her sexuality that it makes me feel like she never grappled with it at all. I'm sure Mikaela Straus did. But the character *King Princess* never really came out; King Princess was always out. In King Princess's world, the closet does not exist. The closet never existed.

—

"Coming out of the closet" is the kind of phrase my English teachers would have begged me to avoid: a mixed metaphor. According to *Gay New York: Gender, Urban Culture, and the Making of the Gay Male World* by George Chauncey, the phrase "coming out" was first used in pre–WWII Manhattan.[3] "Coming out" was shorthand for "coming out *to homosexual society*" as a debutante. It wasn't a reference to *leaving* a place of repression or darkness, not an escape from emotional and sexual cloistering, but rather, coming out and *into* gay society. I love that analogy, likening newly out gays to be-gowned teen girls. It frames the whole process of expressing one's true self as a celebration rather than an unshackling or a freedom from darkness. That being gay is an elevation of one's social stance and an official declaration of one's freshness and potential. As if to say, "Oh, you're still straight? Grow up."

It's less clear where the closet part came from, but it certainly gives the phrase a real bummer context. Chauncey guesses that addition was borrowed from the idiom "skeletons in one's closet"—that is, to be hiding secrets, darkness, scandal. *The closet* implies a literal, physical boundary dividing one's life before publicly declaring queerness, and after. It's a threshold impossible to recross, two distinct places to live: in the darkness, or in the light of one's self-truth. It doesn't promise stepping into the light will be easy, but it does imply a fundamentally altered human experience.

Such a dichotomy was only written down within the past one hundred and sixty years. The German philosopher Karl Heinrich Ulrichs, often regarded as the first queer theorist, fancied the disclosure of one's sexuality was a means of self-emancipation. Throughout the 1860s, Ulrichs wrote a series of pamphlets on queer identity, including one called *Researches on the Riddle of Man-Manly Love,* a phrase I'd love to have tattooed on my neck. In 1862, he sent a letter to eight of his relatives saying he was an

Urning—or, as it was translated to in English, a *Uranian*. Ulrichs coined that word, using it to refer to a third, homosexual gender, conflating sexual preference and gender identity. He'd continue writing about gay identity under a pseudonym (Numa Numantius? For whatever reason?) until 1868, when Ulrichs started using his real name, effectively outing himself to the public.[4] That's considered by many the first public coming out in modern history. To Ulrichs, coming out and making *Urnings* visible was critical to changing public opinion on homosexuality—an early #RepresentationMatters guy. How I'd love to time travel and tell Ulrichs about Ryan Murphy. "Indeed, I am proud that I found the courage to deal the initial blow to the hydra of public contempt," Ulrichs wrote of his coming out, which is objectively metal as fuck.[5]

The first high-profile American wouldn't come out publicly for nearly eighty years after Ulrichs. It was the poet Robert Duncan, who wrote an essay for *politics* magazine in 1944 titled "The Homosexual in Society." Self-identifying as gay, Duncan defined homosexuals as a marginalized group—not just some smattering of pervs—and called for gays to be treated as equals by society at large.[6] Following Duncan's lead, members of the Mattachine Society, a necessarily secret, pre-Stonewall gay men's organization, would come out, too. Also, Robert Duncan dated Robert De Niro Sr., father of the actor, which is neither here nor there in the crusade for gay rights, just juicy.[7]

If coming out to the public is, as Karl Heinrichs Ulrichs characterized it, a means of chipping away at homophobia and normalizing queerness, no person in modern American history proves so quite like Ellen DeGeneres. The sitcom star infamously declared her sexual identity on the cover of *TIME* in April 1997, her image accompanied by three unforgettable words: "Yep, I'm Gay." A couple weeks later, Diane Sawyer interviewed her on *20/20* (imagine, for a moment, Barbara Walters uttering the words "her first sexual encounter with another woman" to intro the segment).[8] A few days later, Ellen did the whole thing again on *The Oprah Winfrey Show.* In both interviews, she gets a chance to fully explain herself: how she'd struggled for years with being gay but now loved herself and felt sharing her true self with the world was more important than any career backlash, and how she'd been with men, but it never felt *right.* She did the work of explaining to Oprah, and thus to straight people at large, the experience of feeling like she wasn't living in her own skin. She clarified that she loves men, just not sexually, so as to bat off the "scary, man-hating lesbian" stereotype, and that she was still the same lovable, girl-next-door Ellen DeGeneres she always had been.

Despite her careful wording and general pleas for equality and love across the board, Ellen's step out of the closet sparked controversy. Diane Sawyer told Ellen that in a poll they'd conducted, 41 percent of parents wouldn't let their kids watch *Ellen* for apparent fear that learning about gay people would make their kids gay. A terrifying and unblinking white woman in the *Oprah* audience opined that homosexuality was being shoved down her family's throat on TV: "Right now we've got the lesbian wedding on *Friends,* there was the lesbian relationship on *Relativity,* I just found out there was a lesbian relationship on *NYPD Blue,* and now there's *you,*" she tells Ellen to her face.[i] "I just feel like we're being stuffed like this right now, down our throats! It's like, why!?"[9]

Real-life Ellen's coming out coincided with her character on her hit ABC sitcom, *Ellen,* doing the same. It had been rumored for months that Ellen Morgan would come out, and she eventually did, on an episode titled "The Puppy Episode." The script

---

i   Disclosure: I tried my best to obtain this random woman's exhaustive catalog of lesbian TV plotlines for research for this book, to no avail.

had been kept on an ultrasecret lockdown and was reportedly printed on maroon paper so it'd be impossible to photocopy and just *barely* possible for the actors to read. A-listers including Laura Dern, Demi Moore, and Billy Bob Thornton appeared in the episode. A bomb threat was made to the studio when they were taping it. Around forty-two million people watched the episode when it aired.[10] After, Ellen gave hour-long interviews with two of the biggest women on television to elaborate on who and how she loved.

All of this is to say: Ellen DeGeneres's coming out was a whole fucking *Thing*. Necessarily so. She had little choice but to march directly out of the closet and onto magazine covers, into Harpo Studios, unapologetically and unwaveringly so as to make gayness as *relatable* (a word so integral to Ellen's public gay identity that she'd use it as the title of her 2018 stand-up special) to Middle America as possible.[j]

Then there's a strange, long gap in between Ellen's coming out in 1997 and the deluge of queer celebrities of the 2010s, for a pretty simple reason: declaring her queerness damaged Ellen's career, badly. Despite the sky-high ratings of "The Puppy Episode," *Ellen* was canceled the following year. Ellen couldn't get work for years after that; her career was all but over. Laura Dern, who's straight, has said even she couldn't get work and needed a security detail after appearing as Ellen's love interest in the episode.[11] That said, when celebrities did come out during the 2000s, it, like Ellen's, was always *a Thing*, said quite literally into a microphone

---

j   Ellen remained America's dyke sweetheart until 2020, when a big asterisk appeared on *The Ellen DeGeneres Show*'s "be kind" mantra. Reports emerged alleging rampant workplace abuse and sexual assault on the part of the show's executive producers. Meanwhile, on Twitter, a tweet soliciting "the most insane stories you've heard about Ellen being mean" garnered over twenty-six hundred replies.

for an audience. Rosie O'Donnell screamed, "I'm a dyke!" onstage at a fundraiser for ovarian cancer in 2002.[12] *A Thing.* Wanda Sykes came out onstage at an anti-Prop 8 rally in 2008.[13] *A Thing.*

Famous men, too, only trickled out of the closet in the aughts. Neil Patrick Harris came out in a stale, PR-y sounding statement ("I am a very content gay man") to *People* in 2006, though gay rumors had swirled around him for years.[14] *Star Trek*'s George Takei came out in erstwhile LGBT print magazine *Frontiers* in 2005.[15] Lance Bass came out in a *People* cover story that same year (headline: "I'M GAY").[16] They all made these official, proud, unflinching declarations, typically paired with extensive interviews wherein they argued gay people are just the same as straight people, calling for equality and understanding, just as Ellen had. Their coming out was also *a Thing*, upon an unsure American public's unspoken request. Ellen says she didn't want to or plan to expose her private life during her comedy career, not to mention give in-depth interviews about it on TV, but felt a higher obligation to do so and thus help normalize queer people in American culture. To do just as Karl Heinrich Ulrichs said coming out would.

Over two decades on, it's now clear Ellen did just that. She is widely credited as a trailblazer for gay entertainers. President Obama even gave the comedian the Presidential Medal of Freedom in 2016, reflecting on the impressive shift in American views on homosexuality in the years since "Yep, I'm Gay" hit newsstands. It's easy to forget, Obama mused during the ceremony, "just how important it was, not just to the LGBT community, but for all of us, to see someone so full of kindness and light, someone we liked so much, someone who could be our neighbor or our colleague or our sister . . . Push our country in the direction of justice."[17]

While White House recognition is certainly powerful, even more so is the direct effect Ellen's actions had on the subsequent generation of gay entertainers. At the 2020 Golden Globes, *Satur-*

day Night Live's Kate McKinnon presented Ellen with the Carol Burnett Award, a lifetime achievement accolade for excellence in television. McKinnon recalls contemplating her own queerness around age thirteen and what seeing Ellen come out meant to her, directly:

> ... Attitudes changed, but only because brave people like Ellen jumped into the fire to make them change. And if I hadn't seen her on TV, I would've thought, "Oh, I could never be on TV, they don't let LGBTQ people on TV." And more than that, I would've gone on thinking I was an alien, and that I maybe didn't even have a right to be here. So thank you, Ellen, for giving me a shot at a good life.[18]

McKinnon is likely on the younger end of those directly inspired by Ellen's coming out. Six years McKinnon's junior, I didn't see Ellen as any grand symbol or beacon of light. I don't remember her coming out—I was in first grade at the time—and I don't remember my parents having her sitcom on in the house. Honestly, I didn't know who Ellen DeGeneres was until seeing *Finding Nemo,* which did more for me in terms of forgetful fish representation than lesbian visibility. And beyond *Nemo,* I've never felt all that connected to her girl-next-door comedy.

But my own coming out process, even being the non-famous plebe I am, was undoubtedly shaped by Ellen's, and Rosie's, and Lance Bass's, and George Takei's, and so on. After all, no gay kids came out in my high school, so I only had these models of queerness in pop culture. And they showed me that coming out had to be Official: premeditated, unwavering, taking confident control of my own narrative. It required gracious explanation and a willingness to answer questions. I needed staunch certainty and sense of self—never mind that Ellen was nearly forty, having lived double the life I had, when she calmly debated that unhinged lesbian plot-line documentarian on *Oprah*.

Such fanfare reinforces the dichotomy the closet presents. In giving so much attention to the coming out process itself, we re-state the notion that life is different *inside* and *out of* the closet, and even that gay people are somehow fundamentally different humans inside and outside of it.

That might be partially true. In a twenty-year retrospective on "The Puppy Episode," *Ellen* costar Joely Fisher recalled the literal, physical difference in Ellen DeGeneres after the whole coming-out frenzy: "I saw someone literally get lighter in her feel and in her vibe," she told *Vanity Fair*. "She was like a caged bird . . . I saw a shift in her gait; I saw a shift in the way she carried herself."[19] A 2013 University of Montreal study found tangible health benefits of coming out, including lower stress levels and a smaller chance of depression among those who had come out to their family and friends than those who hadn't.[20] Many queer people, myself in-cluded, felt a sort of weight lifted after disclosing their sexuality to their friends and family.

Being closeted is a multifaceted and tailored experience with dozens of layers, but there are three big ones. The first is just in-side the door. There, you can see the light pour in by the thresh-old's crack and hear the murmurs of those on the other side; you can visualize, sometimes more clearly than others, what life could look like for you on the other side of it. In the shallow closet, you know you're gay but haven't found the right circumstances, or perhaps courage, to alert your social orbit. You self-identify as queer privately, in your head, when talking to yourself. Maybe you watch gay porn, or sneak episodes of *The L Word* and *Queer as Folk*, or journal about how Kate Bosworth made you feel in *Blue Crush*, contemplating when and how you'll bust open that door. Maybe it means waiting for college, or severing some toxic ties, or telling your spouse. In the shallow closet, you may have a beard to safeguard your secret to the public, or maybe not. What defines this stage is the awareness of the nature of your lust. It's where you watch *Brokeback Mountain* hoping to astral project into Heath Ledger's cowboy boots. It's also the place where having visible LGBTQ+ role models matters most acutely—where seeing Ellen and Portia on the red carpet might give hope that there's a good life waiting for you beyond that door. (That particular infatuation will fade rapidly once you're out.)

In the next layer in, you're sitting on boots, at the bottom of your coats. You know you have same-sex attraction, but you've rationalized it in some way: it's a hiccup, maybe, or a fleeting feeling that can be undone. Perhaps you're attracted to many genders and tell yourself that, because you *can* have other-gender relationships, you're probably just straight. "It's impossible for any human to *not* be turned on by *Brokeback Mountain*," you rationalize to no one in particular. Maybe you log on to Grindr—or, in the aughts, gay dot com—for anonymous hookups but tell yourself it's an easy-to-access release rather than any reflection on your core self. Or, if you're like I was at this phase, you say you're only hooking up with a girl because you don't have a boyfriend and you're simply seventeen and need a warm body. The thought of self-identifying as queer—even telling others, maybe—has crossed your mind in quick flits. It's waved away, the idea more of a gnat than anything that could take flight with dignity.

Then there's the final layer of the closet, way back there, in that narrow, suffocating space between the winter coats and the back wall. The garments have fully blocked any light from permeating back to you. This is the place where you're so closeted, you don't even know you *might* be gay. You've fully convinced yourself you only love *Brokeback* for Michelle Williams's emotional journey. Maybe, maybe, you've felt it on a cellular level—one mitochondria getting a liiiittle too cozy with another—but the thought of actively self-identifying as queer hasn't even crossed into your mind. Perhaps you haven't met any gay people, a common reality for '00s high schoolers. Perhaps you haven't even "met" any gay characters on TV; you have no reason to tune in to *Will & Grace,* right? Perhaps homosexuality as sin has been beaten so thoroughly into you, it's fully dislocated your brain from your somatic wants. Or maybe it's just plain-old, secular homophobia doing it to you. You're not navigating the world with a secret, because you have to be aware of sensitive information in order to hold a secret. This might free you to learn all the lyrics to "Take Me or Leave Me" and think you're just a really great ally. There is a core of you, an essence, that's been so tamped down that you don't even know you're not totally you. You might be smart, but there's a certain self-awareness you lack. Those in Plato's allegorical cave, which Mr. Baird so diligently hammered into my teenage brain, are so deep in there that they think their own shadows dancing on the wall are reality. They don't even know they're in a cave, that there's a whole outside world awaiting them. The deep closet isn't so different. And, given those similarities, it's not terribly surprising that Plato suggested in the *Symposium* that the Greek army should be comprised entirely of gay lovers.

These layers pay no heed whatsoever to who you're dating or how others perceive you—others suspecting you're gay doesn't necessarily make you *more* closeted, it just makes it harder to understand why you're not out. The closet is about self-awareness and self-identification. Ellen existed in the first level of the closet for a long time before "Yep, I'm Gay," because there were virtually no famous gay people to help her open the door. I fluttered between the deep and midrange closets throughout high school, even as I fell for my best friend. By the time I got to the shallow closet—when I finally admitted to myself that I'm into girls—I could only stand to exist there for about a week before charging to my college library, locking my friend Allister in a private study room, and telling him. Given the wealth of openly queer cultural figures and characters now, I suspect there are fewer people toiling in deep closet obliviousness than there were in the 2000s.

But it's more than that. If Ellen DeGeneres modeled a way of coming out for people my age, celebrities like Kristen Stewart, Amandla Stenberg, and King Princess are doing the same for the next generation. And these figures' public journey indicates—at least for sexuality—that the whole three-tiered notion of the closet isn't really a thing. That is, the way celebrities came out as queer over the 2010s eroded the whole idea of the closet altogether. That whole rant I just went on about the three layers of the closet? It's already so, so dated.

~

After I came out to Allister, I pumped the brakes on self-disclosure for a few weeks. It had felt good to get the news off my chest to exactly one (1) person, but I also wanted to come out strategically, as coolly as possible. I'd decided that the best and easiest way for me to announce my queerness to my peers and my parents was to get a girlfriend. "I just fell for this *person*," I'd say, as surprised as my friends, "I really wasn't expecting to!" No need to disclose the hours I'd spent fantasizing about mysterious girls with bangs who lived across campus, filling in the blanks of her personality. God, how much easier it would be, I felt, if coming out were something that just *happened to me*. For queerness to seek me out, and not the other way around. To be a passive observer in my personal journey than to participate in my own life. Being sought after by a girl would make me seem *wanted* and *cool* and *sexy*; coming out sans girlfriend, on the other hand, would make me a lonely, creepy dyke. Sure, I'd failed to stumble into my sexuality

Katy Perry–style. But I could still present to the world like that's exactly what happened.

There was one hiccup in my newfangled search for a girlfriend: I knew hardly any gay girls. Until I came out during my sophomore fall, my social life revolved around my largely heterosexual cross-country team, a gaggle of goofy-humored straight girls in Patagonia half-zip sweaters and waifish guys in short shorts, all of whom, regardless of gender, seemed to consume about a jar of peanut butter per day. I loved my team, despite the fact (or maybe because) it was a straight-up cult. The flocks of shirtless twigs in short shorts flittering across Somerville were total mysteries to everyone else on campus. My runner friends were all straight and simply wouldn't stop hooking up with one another, and then one another's friends, and roommates, and teammates. It was messy and fun to gossip about. Being queer, I got to comment (thoroughly) on the messy team incest without dipping a toe in, but I also knew that only socializing with trackies wasn't a sustainable plan if I wanted any kind of romance. So I grew my circle of non-runner friends over my sophomore year, largely fueled by a primal need for gay friends, and also sex.

Still, I was in a Catch-22. I wanted to come out by having a girlfriend, but I couldn't get a girlfriend if I wasn't on any gay girls' radars. I couldn't get on any gay girls' radars unless they heard through the grapevine that I was queer. The grapevine wouldn't know I was queer unless I *told* the grapevine I was (at this point, identifying as) bi and told *enough* of the grapevine that I was (at this point, identifying as) bi. This put enormous pressure on Allister, the only person who knew I was gay for the month of October 2009, to find me a girlfriend. But, knowing everyone on campus, Allister floated another recently out queer girl I didn't know until then: Zan.

Zan had a bro-ey, stoner affect and hung out with hipsters. I think she was premed—some science something?—and I had a vague sense that she was good at school. She had long, wavy, chestnut hair and a kind of skater swagger I now recognize as deeply dykey. She had a warm ease to her and was incredibly easy to like. After Allister casually introduced us one day at the student-run coffee shop, we'd always stop and chat whenever we saw each other at the library or the campus center. These chats were awkward and lasted far too long, considering we had nothing in common other than our friendship with Allister, who was friends with everyone, and the fact that he'd told each of us separately that the other one was recently, formally, into chicks. I'm also confident I made far too much eye contact with her.

I wanted to kiss her desperately, though, because I wanted to kiss any girl desperately, and I wanted to be able to tell my friends I was kissing a girl. We had about as much chemistry as I had with most straight men, which is to say, none at all. Throughout college, I'd see Zan smoking cigarettes on the back porches at parties and would join her, the chat worth compromising my pink runner lungs. Our conversations were only slightly easier under the influence. Once, I mentioned I'd worked at a marine biology summer camp months earlier. Stoned, she was absolutely mind-blown by my exhaustive knowledge of humpback whale feeding behaviors, and her enthusiasm only let me ramble more. That was, by far, our steamiest conversation. Despite her knowing well I was queer (I made that *clear*), it never worked out between us.

Over the course of the 2010s, it appears that a lot of famous women had the same strategy as I did: come out with a girlfriend and little explanation of the true *stuff of you* is really necessary. (Never forget, Lindsay Lohan pioneered the technique in her Sam Ronson era.) In 2014, supermodel Cara Delevingne—now one of the most visible queer women on the planet—shared her fluidity with the world in equally messy terms. She and Michelle Rodri-guez, at that point openly bisexual and a star of the *Fast and the Furious* franchise, were snapped blatantly tanked at a Knicks game, making out and puffing e-cigs from their courtside seats. *Us Weekly* called their behavior "bizarre" three times in one article.[21] St. Vincent's nonheterosexuality was only made public when she was caught close, repeatedly, with Delevingne in 2015 and 2016. Actress Kristen Stewart appeared in the tabloids holding hands with her once-assistant Alicia Cargile over 2014 and 2015, and then with French musician Soko, and then St. Vincent, and then with Stella Maxwell—Jesus, Kristen—all before publicly declaring she's "like, so gay, dude" on *Saturday Night Live* in early 2017.[22] They all came out with girlfriends, as I'd so badly wanted to.

Not immediately but eventually, all these women were asked about their sexualities in magazine interviews, where they de-scribed their identities on their own terms. "The whole issue of sexuality is so grey," Stewart told *The Guardian* in 2017.[23] "I'm just trying to acknowledge the fluidity, that greyness, which has al-ways existed." Delevingne, too, prefers "fluid" as a descriptor. Janelle Monáe came out as a "free-ass motherfucker" (by which she meant, she eventually clarified, pansexual) to *Rolling Stone* in 2018.[24] Tessa Thompson is bisexual, as she told *Porter* that same year.[25] Unlike the days of "Yep, I'm Gay," these disclosures were rarely the headlines, but rather interesting tidbits in larger pro-files. They could talk about their sexuality in more nuanced ways than audiences would've been ready for in 1997, and weren't ready for throughout much of the aughts.

My university unfortunately didn't have its own tabloids, but we did have CollegeACB. Well, first there was JuicyCampus. Juicy-Campus was essentially Reddit, but for gossiping about peers. Each major college had its own subpage on JuicyCampus, which housed hundreds of comment threads ranging from advice for incoming freshmen to ranking fraternities to a thorough catalog of which girls shaved (or didn't) their pubic hair. There was virtually no regulation or oversight, and the forum became a cesspool of slander under the guise of free speech. It got fucking mean. One of my friends was called a "cumdumpster" on JuicyCampus when she was nineteen, which we (she included) could not stop laughing about at the time, but now it makes me queasy. JuicyCampus was shut down in February 2009, not because of the national controversy it sparked but because it failed to turn a profit. CollegeACB—Anonymous Confession Board—swiftly filled the vacuum left in JuicyCampus's shutdown. ACB satiated many college students' craving for a place to say horny and/or terrible shit about the five thousand people they shared a square mile with. It was ostensibly "nicer" than JuicyCampus because users could report offensive posts, but its functionality was virtually identical. As my college's student magazine wrote in 2010, "Destroying Reputations: as easy as ACB."[26]

I read CollegeACB all the time, because I'm trash and love to gossip. And over the course of my sophomore year, I doggedly monitored an ACB thread called "hottest lesbians on campus." It was about sixty posts long and growing. I was not on it. I told all my friends I was an as-yet undetermined degree of gay during that fall and had accepted—hoped for, even—that the rumor mill would do its thing. Zan wasn't working out, but I was still holding on for coming out to my high school friends and my family with a girlfriend, mostly to avoid admitting that I'd ever considered my sexual preferences before a woman propositioned me. *Surely, the only reason I'm single is because* The Gay Community *doesn't know I'm an option yet,* I reasoned. *Surely, once word of my gayness reaches the secret lesbian campus tribunal, I will be drowning in women.* I thought the news would spread like wildfire. It didn't. Throughout the spring of 2010, the "hottest lesbians on campus" thread grew, and I remained (egregiously) unnamed. Absolutely no one gave a shit that I'd come out. I would not be preyed upon by any of the hot girls on the ACB thread, like the one femme from the rugby team or hyperconfident skater dyke who fucked straight sorority girls. Offline, I'd been casually seeing someone, but it was clear neither of us wanted anything serious from each other. It became clear that I would not have a girlfriend to present to my Catholic parents when I came out to them come May, making it unprovable that I'd ever thought about sex in any capacity before college. The embarrassing thing about coming out to my parents single was not that I was single, but that I felt I was telling them, "Here's how I would *like* to have sex, if I had anyone to have sex with on a regular basis."

When I came back for junior year, I was hell-bent on getting a girlfriend. That meant I needed to get on some radars. As I lacked a PR team to manage my baby-gay years, I needed to be on the "hottest lesbians on campus" CollegeACB thread.

I recruited my friend Devin, who, like me, kept up with ACB (though had also never posted), and who, unlike me, was too nice to tell me my plan made me look weird and desperate. He OK'd it. So I logged on to an anonymous ACB account in the sober light of day, in my bedroom (how humiliating would it be to be caught posting *anything* on the site in public!). I typed in casual lowercase, as if simply dashed away: "grace perry is so cute." Simple! True! To the point! It was the 2010 liberal arts college equivalent of calling the paps on yourself. Now it was just time for me to watch the random friend requests roll in! Which, of course, they didn't.

The functionality of college gossip threads and tabloids are really more similar than not. Maybe whatever impulse that drove me to post about myself on ACB is the same that drove Michelle Rodriguez to get liquored up and handsy at Madison Square Garden. Or what drove Kristen Stewart to traipse around LA with so. many. women. Or what drove Tessa Thompson to dress up as a literal vagina for her then-girlfriend, Janelle Monáe's, music video for her song "Pynk." Not visibility for the sake of finding someone to date—lord knows Kristen Stewart didn't need the help—but a craving to be *seen*. To be known to acquaintances and peers and people you don't know. To not have to explain yourself. Did the rest of the student body follow "hottest lesbians on campus" as aggressively as I did? Certainly not. But I still felt adding my name to an official lesbian roll call substantiated my existence in the world.

I came out at a time when coming out as gay wasn't always worthy of a magazine cover, but it wasn't quite the casual tidbit of information it is today. I was pulled between the two eras and felt like, because I'd seen Lance Bass and Neil Patrick Harris and Rosie come out with such fanfare, I owed my community a similar explanation. But I also resented that expectation. I was exhausted by the prospect of having to come out to everyone over and over and over again and just wanted the information to be in other peoples' brains. I wanted to do the Kristen Stewart thing, to just start dating women and maybe explain later if I felt like it. I wanted other people to gossip about me, and when they wouldn't, I gossiped about myself.

I started writing this essay to argue that coming out is passé, that celebrities don't really come out as gay anymore and thus Gen Z doesn't, either. But that's not really it. Of course people come out as queer—they make the world know they're gay—but on their own terms, by living their lives openly. Celebrities talk about their queerness on their Instagram pages, in their music, and when they do discuss their sexuality in interviews, they can do so without fear of as great a backlash. Straight culture at large, having seen so many people come out by now, demands less of an explanation from celebrities who come out as queer. And in real life, it happens younger now, with far less fanfare than when Ellen did and with more nuance. That said, while a sapphic coming out became casual in the 2010s, coming out as transgender and nonbinary still isn't. Instead of Ellen on the cover of *TIME,* it was Caitlyn Jenner on the cover of *Vanity Fair* in 2015. In 2019, Sam Smith's Instagram post announcing their nonbinary identity caused a kerfuffle—think pieces and misgendering galore!—that no pop star's sexuality reveal has matched in years.[27] Elliot Page came out as trans in a self-written, Official-feeling statement, which he posted to social media; simultaneously, GLAAD released a tip sheet to help media cover Elliot's story using respectful and accurate language. While celebrities coming out as transgender is still *a Thing,* coming out as not-straight now happens in public appearances and off-the-cuff social media posts or is casually dropped in interviews rather than hour-long sit-downs with Oprah. It's not the process of coming out as queer that's become archaic but the closet itself.

By embracing less rigid terms of identification, like *fluid,* those like Janelle Monáe and Cara Delevingne encompass the part of their lives where they were exclusively dating men in their sexual tapestry. In doing so, they break down the *in vs. out, dead vs. alive, asleep vs. awake* false binary that the stark visual of a closet door has created. What once could've been deemed their time in the closet is reframed as a part of who they are. They weren't living in sad obscurity and repression. They were just figuring it out, living their lives, and still are. If the dramatic nature of Ellen's coming out reinforced a dichotomy of being In The Closet vs. Out Of The Closet, the relatively casual way in which most public figures do so now blurs the lines. It means we're inching closer to a reality where the metaphor of the closet is deemed obsolete.

So much of this is the shifting tides of public opinion, that audiences can now handle a more nuanced conversation about sexuality. (Or, also likely, just aren't shocked by it in the way they were in 1997.) Because of this, we get artists like pop singer Hayley Kiyoko, who came out to her parents in sixth grade (!), being gay from the start of their careers.[28] Like King Princess, the public persona of Hayley Kiyoko was never in the closet. It's hard to imagine an artist who's nicknamed Lesbian Jesus and sings lyrics like "I only want a girl who ain't afraid to love me" was ever in the closet. Of course, she was in her own way. But increasingly, queer art is not about the process of coming out of the closet but simply existing as such.

Within months of my self-posting, CollegeACB was shut down. I'm not sure why. But I have to assume that my unabashed thirst prompted a full and irrevocable website meltdown. Or maybe the site administrators were so thoroughly bummed out to see I'd attempted to hype myself up to my college's lesbian community, they figured the world would be a better place without the forum. I have no idea if anyone ever read that post or if any queer girls actually checked that website except for me, a horned-up gossip monger. I didn't get any Facebook friend requests from random queers, nor did the art history girl with bangs I pined for stop me in the campus coffee shop and say, "I saw your name in all lowercase on a gossip forum, wanna make out?" And yet, I felt somehow more out, more officially gay, felt less of a need to explain myself.

I did fall in love with someone that year, though. Not because she read my name on an anonymous posting board, but because I was in Paris and had seen *Moulin Rouge!* far too many times to let such an opportunity go to waste.

BLAIR WALDORF HAS NOTES ON MY SEX LIFE

Pacey hands Joey the condom from his wallet. They've been arguing about sex all weekend. They're on their senior ski trip, where their peers are getting wasted and fucking and hot tubbing and potentially skiing? And until now, Joey hasn't been ready to do the deed. "You wanna throw it away?" asks Pacey Witter (Joshua Jackson). He respects that Joey (Katie Holmes) doesn't want to rush things. To his surprise, his girlfriend tells him in a half whisper: "I want to throw the wrapper away."

Oh, dear. It's happening. The teens are at it.

They're in their sexy, cozy cabin with a proud fire blazing away behind them. Joey lists all of Pacey's recent expressions of love: how he carried her bag off the bus, how he brings her napkins with her movie popcorn, how he taught her how to drive. Then she begins to unbutton his shirt. If you listen closely, you can hear millions of teen girls shrieking in unison from their basement couches. "You kissed me first, sweetheart," she says. "The second time, you counted to ten just in case I wanted to stop you." She removes Pacey's button-up to reveal a white tank top. "We were on a boat for three months, and you understood, without a word, why I wasn't ready." She peels the tank top off to reveal a body that's filled out a bit since season one. It's getting deeply horny, though they're just barely, timidly touching one another. In the words of *30 Rock*'s Devon Banks, "No touching just makes it hotter."

"Pace, I'm gonna count to ten." In the background, a song called "I Will Love You" croons, rich vocals over piano, promising, unambiguously, *"I will love you, love you, love you."* Pacey and Joey touch palms like there's a panel of glass between them. "And then I'm going to start kissing you. If you don't want me to, then you're just gonna have to stop me." Ten seconds do not pass, and she does not actually count to ten. "Ten, my love," Joey whispers to her patient and emotionally competent boyfriend. They begin kissing, and the screen fades to black.

Joey loses her virginity in episode fourteen of season four, "A Winter's Tale," which aired in February 2001. I was in fifth grade at the time, too young to be watching *Dawson's Creek.* My sister, Rachel, six years my senior, was the prime age for the teen drama. My mom didn't approve of the show—*Sex! Drinking! Weirdly adult dialogue delivered by baby-faced teens!*—so Rachel would sneak episodes in on Wednesday nights, when our mom was at choir rehearsal. I got into *Dawson's Creek* my senior year of high school, four years after the series finale. My friend Margaret and I visited my second cousin Martha at her college, and we spent 90 percent of the weekend bingeing season one on DVD. It was my first binge-watching experience, a monumental first for any millennial. Margaret and I returned to Central Time obsessed with Joey and Pacey and Dawson and Jen. We'd swoon and giggle through YouTube compilation after YouTube compilation, "ironically" enjoying it.

My senior year of high school, I easily watched the "Ten, My Love" scene on YouTube over two hundred times. My late-teen self was genuinely smitten by the "throwback" show (watching this scene from 2001 felt like unearthing an ancient Mesopotamian text). And I was smitten with Pacey Witter, especially.

"Ten, My Love" exemplified, to me, The Be All, End All of Losing Your Virginity. It seems the *Dawson's Creek* writers thought so, too. The show may be named for Dawson Leery (James Van Der Beek), but by seasons three and four, Joey and Pacey had ascended to its central couple. By the time they finally *do it,* Pacey and Joey have been a couple for nine months. They've shared all their dreams and fears, they've spent a summer on a sailboat together, they've declared their infinite love for one another. To Pacey—this show is so goddamn earnest—sex is the pinnacle of love. "For me, it's not about wanting to have sex," Pacey says to some hot girl whose name doesn't matter earlier on in that ski trip episode. "It's about wanting to share the most intimate thing you can possibly share with someone."

At the time of my "Ten, My Love" obsession, I was in the throes of the Claire Thing, and yet, still in the Middle-to-Deep Closet. Though I was experiencing my first romantic (albeit very confusing and not that physical) relationship, when I watched Joey and Pacey have sex for the first time, I wasn't imagining myself in that situation with Claire or even with Joey Potter. I imagined (hoped, assumed, contorted my brain through sheer internalized homophobic willpower) that when I did have sex for the first time, it would be with a boy, with a chatty-yet-affable sweetheart like Pacey Witter, if not with Joshua Jackson himself, if not Joshua Jackson in character as Pacey Witter. In the Middle/Deep Closet, I entirely disassociated from the way Claire made my stomach leap, refused to acknowledge or name the feelings I was experiencing for a girl. Instead, I willed my brain into attempting astral projection into Pacey Witter's arms. Because of my fear of being gay, yes, but also because TV told me this was the indisputable Right Way to lose my virginity.

By senior year, I'd fully accepted my fate of graduating high school without having sex with a boy and felt more or less fine about it. I believed that my high school boylessness all but guaranteed a whirlwind, enduring romance with a Pacey Witter type the second I stepped foot on a college campus. And that, when we did have sex, we would be a) desperately in love, b) on and/or near a mountain, and c) irrevocably heterosexual.

I can't quite claim *Dawson's Creek* as a show of my microgeneration, but I'm happy to claim *The O.C.* Two months after *Dawson's* went off the air, *The O.C.* established clearly The Wrong Way to have sex for the first time. When the series opens, Marissa Cooper (Mischa Barton), almost alien-like in her willowy, teen beauty, has been dating Luke Ward (Chris Carmack) since fifth grade. (My own fifth-grade boyfriend, Paul, went on to date my aforementioned second cousin Martha. *Sigh.*) Luke is immediately established as the Water Polo Asshole. In the pilot episode, he delivers one of the first iconic lines from the series, just after punching Ryan Atwood (Ben McKenzie) in the face: "Welcome to the O.C., bitch!" In sum, he's a dick. It's immediately established that Ryan and Marissa are meant to be together, and Luke is just the shitty dude in the way.

Anyway, the teen sex. In season one, episode six, "The Girlfriend," everyone's at the Cohens' house for Caleb Nichol's (Alan Dale) birthday party. Marissa walks in on Ryan hooking up with Seth's grandpa's twenty-four-year-old girlfriend (God, I love this show) in the pool house. She's been falling for Ryan, so this is a terrible scene for her to encounter. Marissa storms out, grabs Luke, and they hightail it for Luke's empty house. In a jealous rage at a seventy-year-old's birthday fete, Marissa makes a rash choice: it's fuck o'clock.

Marissa and Luke's sex scene is gross and sad and an overall bummer. It's ninety seconds of sweaty, skin-to-skin close-ups that feel a half step away from soft-core porn. "I love you so much," Luke says. Marissa says nothing back. The two barely communicate the whole scene. Luke, for his part, tries to open a dialogue: "Do you … are you …" Marissa says, "I'm good," in the opaquest exchange of verbal consent in history. Marissa Cooper appears even more cold and distant and emotionally ambiguous than usual. But we, the viewers, can tell she's thinking about Ryan.

It's a far cry from Joey Potter's laundry list of things she loves about her boyfriend, but at least, like Pacey, Luke has a condom. They have sex offscreen, and later Luke unceremoniously drops Marissa off at her beachfront McMansion. Ryan, our hero, sees her return. The depressed prom queen turns to the boy she's supposed to be with and delivers in delicious *O.C.* overdramatization: "You're too late." *Chills.* An episode later, Marissa encounters Luke cheating on her in Tijuana, inspiring her to hoover a bunch of pills and pass out in an alley, to then be rescued by, of course, Ryan Atwood.

O.C. creator Josh Schwartz's second YA smash, *Gossip Girl* (2007), embraces the Right vs. Wrong Way to Lose Your Virginity dichotomy also—but the show toys with it a bit. *Gossip Girl*, in its ongoing pursuit of freaking parents out, makes the wrong way seem less sad and more, well, hot. Blair Waldorf (Leighton Meester) is determined her perfect life will go according to her perfect plan. Her boyfriend, Nate Archibald (Chace Crawford) is integral to that plan: she'll go to Yale, marry into one of Manhattan's most rich and powerful families (Nate's a Vanderbilt, dammit!), rule the world. Of course, part of this plan is losing her virginity to Nate.

In early season one, Nate and Blair are on-and-off. They get into a blowout the same episode Nate's dad gets arrested for cocaine, embezzlement, and defrauding investors—a total Jimmy Cooper move. Furious, Blair skips off to see Chuck Bass (Ed Westwick), Nate's skeezy best friend, at the burlesque club he's just bought. (Sure.) A few scenes later, she fucks Chuck Bass in his limo. It's one of *Gossip Girl*'s early legendary moments: the moment they kiss, Sum 41's "With Me" ramps up into full scream. The screen flitters into a sepia/old-timey film filter. It's shocking! Scandalous! And textbook Wrong Way to Lose Your V-Card: Blair cheated on her hot boyfriend (who cheated on her first, but)! With the scummiest dude on the Upper East Side! But where Marissa Cooper's Wrong Way just pangs depressingly, Blair and Chuck's scene is, well, sexy. So sexy that they eventually become the most loved couple on the show and end up together. No wonder parents protested this show so fervently.

On the other hand, Dan Humphrey (Penn Badgley) loses his virginity to his dream girl, Serena van der Woodsen (Blake Lively), whom he adores and who adores him back, in a magical, wintry sex cathedral/DIY art installation on Christmas Eve. They might as well have THE RIGHT WAY! flashing in neon above their bed.

—

You'll be floored to learn that "Ten, My Love" didn't happen for me.

There was no whirlwind romance freshman year of college. There was no romance whatsoever. There was only learning a new campus, stressing out about papers on the Protestant Reformation, and trying to discern *actual* friends from people I just hung out with to feel less lonely. Which is to say, I was busy—a good enough excuse for why I hadn't yet found my Pacey.

I came out as "at least bicurious" early sophomore year, before I'd actually slept with a girl. Or a guy, for that matter. New sexual experience didn't lead to my coming out; no, I'd just finally started acknowledging the way my body felt around certain people and how I'd felt with Claire. But coming out while a virgin felt more like a declaration of intent than one of identity. I felt like I was unraveling a scroll and shouting from my diaphragm, "Once I can convince someone cute to have sex with me—assuming that happens at some point, though I have exactly zero romantic prospects right now—I'm open to, but not exclusively set on, that person being a girl!" Embarrassing. In any case, I felt I needed get it over with, and stat, if for no other reason than to earn my title as a Certified Gay.

But there was another part of it. Something I'd heard a lot when people came out was a question dripping in incredulity: *How do you know you're gay if you've never hooked up with a [guy/girl] before?* I don't recall anyone ever saying this to me, explicitly, but I knew it was a retort that was out there. I'd probably even said it at some point. But it's this idea that sexuality is a trial-and-error kind of endeavor. Culturally, we often talk about gay sex in adolescence as *experimentation*. It's mostly used as a euphemism for a period of gay sex surrounded by periods of straight sex. Sometimes it's the other way around; I've known lesbians who, in post-breakup hazes, have slept with guys without identifying as bisexual. But the idea of experimentation implies a trial period. It also implies, in my opinion, the implementation of the scientific method.

Ask a question: Am I queer?
Do background research: Collect number of times my stomach has lurched when catching a whiff of a girl's hair; consider middle school wardrobe composed entirely of Old Navy boys' athleisure; rewatch YouTube compilations of the Marissa/Alex plotline from *The O.C.*, note what happens to mind and body.
Construct a hypothesis: I'm . . . very queer.
Test with an experiment: Find a girl to make out with, if not fall in love with, on a semiregular basis. Repeat as necessary.
Procedure working? Yep.
Analyze data and draw conclusions: My hypothesis was correct: I'm queer.
Communicate results: See this entire book.

I knew that this question—*how can you know you're gay if you haven't had gay sex?*—was a) rude and b) misleading. And I knew that no one ever asked straight people how they *know* they're straight. But still, because I'm mean to myself, I asked that question all the time. I knew I thought about girls, I knew I'd kissed one (1), but I didn't know I could *know* I was gay until sex was involved. It was the crucial element of the whole experiment, and I couldn't be certain until I went through with it.

As I began to accept my queerness, I realized that I wouldn't be having a "Ten, My Love" first time. Not simply because it wouldn't be with Pacey—I was still sorting through my feelings for boys, so a Pacey type was still on the table for me. But by the time I came out, my views on virginity loss had evolved. Well, *evolved* implies I'd reached some higher level of thinking. Let me be clear: I'd just become more desperate. First, I wanted to be a Certified Gay, and second, I was approaching twenty, an embarrassing age, I felt, to have little to no sexual experience. I simply didn't have the *time* to fall in love with someone, sail around the world with them for a summer, learn every nook and cranny of their tender little soul, book a ski lodge, ski all day, build a roaring fire, write and recite an exhaustive list each time I tumbled more and more deeply in love with them, and *then* have sex. Who has the time for that? Teenagers on The WB do, and that's it. Coming out forced me to hit the gas on losing my v-card, which, in turn, forced me to ditch my "Ten, My Love" aspirations. It was time to pivot and to move swiftly, if I wanted to be a Certified Gay.

I don't remember how or when, exactly, Kate and I exchanged numbers that fall. But we started texting.

—

So far, according to 2000s pop culture, the unspoken requirement for a healthy, happy, satisfying first time has been unfettered heterosexuality. So what does the Right Way look like for gay people? Pretty much identical to "Ten, My Love," according to *Glee* (2009).

By the season three episode "The First Time," Kurt (Chris Colfer) and Blaine (Darren Criss) have been together for about six months. Blaine is starring as Tony to Rachel Berry's (Lea Michele) distinctly not Puerto Rican or Latinx Maria in the school production of *West Side Story*. The two feel like artistic frauds upon realizing they're telling a story about sex and love and coming-of-age, when neither has had sex despite their serious boyfriends. On opening night, Rachel encourages Blaine backstage: "Tony and Maria were soulmates. Okay? Against all odds, they found each other. I know what that's like. You do, too. So we just have to play to that." A fireworks display reading THESE TEENS ARE IN LOVE AND ARE THEREFORE READY TO HAVE SEX would've been more subtle. The episode ends with the two couples doing it for the first time in a split screen, (more specifically: lying in bed, facing each other, mostly clothed, in dim lighting) as Rachel and Blaine's duet, "One Hand, One Heart" plays. It is excruciating, but technically speaking, "nice."

For both couples, this is textbook the Right Way to Lose Your Virginity. Pushed a hair further, "The First Time" could've been a satire of the *Dawson's Creek* model. Instead, Ryan Murphy very intentionally made a statement that hadn't been made on network teen TV before: gay sex isn't really all that different from straight sex. It was revolutionary at the time, fitting queer teens into the same mold that had been created for straight teens. Similarly, on *Pretty Little Liars* (2010), lesbian swimmer teen being stalked presumably by her first crush's murderer, Emily Fields (Shay Mitchell), turns her girlfriend's room into a magical aquatic light palace, and it's implied the two have sex for the first time that night. It's quite similar to Dan and Serena's winter wonderland sex palace on *Gossip Girl*, and it is indisputably the Right Way. By fitting Kurt and Blaine into the same template as Joey and Pacey, *Glee* undid the implication that the Right Way was reserved for straight people. Or, more powerfully, that straightness was a prerequisite for achieving Right Way status.

But straightness in itself hadn't been the issue with the Right Way. The problem with that model is that it led me to believe, for a long time, that love is integral to sex. More specifically, that real, pure, cosmic love is the only avenue by which one is capable of trusting a sexual partner. It's obviously not abstinence-only sex education, but it *is* love-only sex education.

It's not that the Right Way isn't right. Yes, ideally, everybody's first time is with someone they trust, someone who makes them feel good about themselves. Also in that ideal world, every teenager falls in love, and that love is fully reciprocated. And in that world, every great first romance entails sailing the Atlantic for three months, cuddled in their lover's arms, like Joey and Pacey. Then, they spend months in fervent and mature deliberation and ultimately decide they feel ready to have sex. "I'm glad I had sex," Joey assures her boyfriend the next morning, after he expresses anxiety about his underperformance in the sheets. "I'm really glad that I had sex with you." It'd be great if no one regretted their first time—even better if we were all actually *glad* it happened. TV writers tend to care deeply about their characters. Why wouldn't they want to make their first time as magical as possible?

By making love the only prerequisite for sex, the Right Way implies that sexual trust was impossible to forge with people we anything less than love. And, on the flip side, it fails to acknowledge that romantic love doesn't guarantee your partner will be safe or communicative or able to meet your needs. The advice "be in love first" doesn't actually give teen viewers any tools we actually needed to have safe, good, empowering sex. Showing a condom on-screen is great, but what about the rest of it? How do you actually *know* you're ready? How do you say what you want? What if you change your mind? What if you don't have an orgasm? What if you have an orgasm too soon? What if you want to have sex, but you're not in love? How do you remain not pregnant? How do you *know* you trust someone? Love alone can't provide the answers.

And so, having abandoned my goal to lose my virginity the Right Way, I forged guidelessly ahead into the world of adult relations.

⁓

Naked Quad Run always fell on the final night of fall semester classes. It was mid-December in New England, so we could always count on snow and freezing temperatures. The frigid weather was the undergraduate population's excuse for getting so thoroughly drunk each NQR—to stay warm for our ass-naked sprint around the residential quad. Drinking heavily was also our means of engaging in a tacit contract with one another: you'll drink enough so you don't remember the way my tummy jiggles, and I'll get so tanked, I'll be free of the imagery of your cold, shriveled self. Not participating in said contract were the locals who'd come watch, whose presence, we suspected, prompted the unofficial event's official cancelation by the new university president my senior year. But as a sophomore, NQR was still on and had been a weird, socially obligatory and beloved school tradition for decades. Okay.

The night revolved around the nude jaunt, but that was really only a few minutes. Most of the night was the pregame and postgame partying. My track friends and I spent it scream-singing to "Bad Romance" while taking Fireball shots in an uphill, four-person suite. Kate and I had been texting lately. We'd been texting earlier that day about each other's NQR plans. Drunk at nine p.m., I texted her the Platonic ideal of lazy game: "How's your NQR treating you?" She replied. It was on.

My pursuit of Kate, a lovely person with whom I had very little chemistry—though, a fraction more than with Zan—was more of a pursuit of having said I'd had sex than anything else. I was twenty and felt totally ashamed of my lack of sexual experience. I needed to rip the Band-Aid, and there was Kate. We had mutual friends and—both history majors—mutual classes. Kate was on the rugby team, which wasn't really so much an athletic team as it was a queer drinking and mud-wrestling club that occasionally featured sprint drills. (My dad, an erstwhile rugger-turned-rugby coach, suggested I try out the sport in college. I scoffed and told him rugby was for lesbians. And the thing is, I wasn't *wrong*.) In any case, this meant she had lots of queer friends, which intimidated me. That, on top of her having had girlfriends and coming out in high school (I couldn't even imagine), made me feel completely clueless in her presence. As we awkwardly chitchatted and texted throughout November and December, I felt her palpable indifference to me. I knew she read me as an inexperienced baby gay, and I knew I wasn't at the top of the list of girls she was pursuing. I knew she still pined for her ex, who was also on the rugby team. But there she was, texting me back on the biggest party night of the semester, so I supposed I'd risen in her ranks. Or perhaps her ex just wasn't texting her back that night.

I don't recall how or at what point on that NQR night I ended up in her suite, but there I was, late. It was post-run, the dregs of the party everywhere: empty Natty Lite cans and vodka bottles were scattered about, two wobbly legged girls played another round of beer pong, while others, drunk and exhausted, lounged and chatted half-naked. "Bad Romance" was on there, too. I waltzed in, also drunk, and spoke to no one. I felt like I had a neon sign blinking above my head: HELLO, I'M HERE TO HOOK UP. I waved to Kate, and we immediately went into her room. Not because we were so engrossed in passion that we couldn't keep our paws off each other but because I was simultaneously so terrified by this roomful of queer girls and anxious about what I knew was about to happen. And, well, I was full of Fireball.

There were no long-winded declarations of love, no gentle whispers of "Are you *sure* you're ready to do this?," no awkwardly fumbling for a condom (well, obviously), but I was nervous. I wanted the whole thing to be over with, not because of her but because I was more interested in saying that I'd had sex than actually having sex with this person. It certainly wasn't the Right Way, nor did it particularly feel like the Wrong Way. It was simply A Way to Lose My Virginity.

I eventually said bye and unceremoniously scampered off. I went to grab my keys from West, the dorm where I'd been earlier that night, but no one answered. (I'd later learn about eight of them had passed out, draped over couches and in shared twin beds and one, on a staircase, and that one middle distance runner's ankle had been severely injured in the process.) Locked out and freezing, I called my new friend Devin, who kindly let my drunk, post-gay-sex self share his bed with him. I fell asleep knowing my first time hadn't been the Right Way, and yet, relieved. Happy, even. I couldn't wait to watch my primary care physician tick the Sexually Active box at my next visit. I'd revised my expectations beforehand, and the whole event had been just what I'd hoped for: fine.

⎯

For straight people, the whole concept of a first time is generally pinned to their teen years and early adulthood. It's a thing that happens, and then it's over. It gets rarer and rarer to encounter a virgin your age as time passes. But what about for queer people? What does it really mean to lose your virginity? If you have straight sex as a closeted teenager and then have gay sex a few years later, do you lose it twice? Are virginity and gay-ginity two different things? Does the first one not count if you didn't actually like it?

For queer people—especially women—that little phrase "Have you done anything before?" crops up well into adulthood. Lesbians and bisexual women, on average, come out later than their male counterparts.[1] In any case, many of us do the First Time routine as adults, and we get pretty good at it. Not just because we've had time to conquer the logistics of orgasm, but we've learned the importance of creating a comfortable environment, of communicating, of checking in, of respecting each other's limits and wants. Apart from having sex with women, writing the last sentence is the gayest thing I've ever done.

Because the experience stretches into adulthood, the reality of queer virginity loss is often more complex than Blaine and Kurt's first time on *Glee*. After my first time with Kate in college, I became the Kate to other people in return, people who felt as equally not in love with me as I had with my first partner. It happened more frequently in college and my early twenties. I was the first girl my first girlfriend had ever kissed, and when I lived in Brooklyn post-college, I dated a couple girls who'd only been with guys before. It really didn't bother me or make me feel self-conscious. At that age especially, it made sense: we were all still figuring ourselves out, deciding who we were and what we wanted in every facet.

By the time I was twenty-nine, I thought I'd grown out of this era. I apparently hadn't. One night, I met a girl at a bar while in line for the bathroom, inarguably the gayest way to meet someone. I was drunk (I asked her zodiac sign about six times; it was Aries). We went home together. I asked her if she'd slept with women before—she said she had. I woke up at six a.m., bleary-eyed and still drunk, to see her leaving my room. I told her she could stay, that I didn't mind. But she left. The following week, we texted, but she blew me off for two dates, which, frankly, was fine. About a month later, I learned we had mutual friends, and through those friends I learned I'd been the first girl she'd slept with. I'd been her Kate—that cool night in LA was her Naked Quad Run, as unemotionally charged as my first time had been.

Typically, being someone's gay first is a loaded ego stroke. Whenever I've kissed a heretofore straight girl, the most arrogant part of my brain gets cranked to eleven. I believe, for a blip, that I'm so hot that I *turned someone gay*. It's the prestige of nabbing a "straight" girl. It's like I, single-handedly, can recruit a whole fresh army of dykes. It's gross and obviously incorrect and is my internalized homophobia valuing straightness over queerness. Just like Kate didn't *turn me gay,* I'm not so irresistible that I've cast a spell on some poor, defenseless het. She was queer long before I waltzed into her life and asked her if she had the Co-Star astrology app.

So, after discovering I'd been the Aries' first, my friends cracked up and mockingly congratulated me. But instead of feeling self-congratulatory, I was pummeled with anxiety. It's one thing to know you're someone's first in the moment; learning it after the fact retroactively sours the whole thing. What I'd interpreted as a one-night stand with a cute girl from a bar had been A Moment in her life. I'd grown out of the age where such a thing was routine. *Did I do something she wasn't ready for? Am I a predator? Am I now burned into her brain? Is that why she fled my room so early, why she canceled on me twice?* I racked my brain to piece together the sloppy events of that night. My Catholic brain cropped up, out of goddamn nowhere, and suddenly hated me for having casual, drunk sex.

She did say she'd been with a girl before, and I get why—she didn't want to make it *a thing.* She wanted to rip off the Band-Aid, the same way I'd wanted to with Kate. Maybe she thought she'd seem uncool or inexperienced. Maybe she thought I'd pump the brakes. Maybe I would have. I can't say for sure what I would've done had she been more open with me. But I do think I would've treated the experience differently, perhaps with a bit more caution, a little slower, a little more consciously. That's probably exactly what she didn't want. The Aries was far from the first person to pull the "say you've done this before" move, gay or straight. But ultimately, she lied to me in order to ensure I'd have sex with her. And because womanhood is traversing a swamp of incomprehensible and unwarranted shame, I felt exactly that. For once, being someone's First didn't at all stroke my ego.

As adults, we know well that great sex can happen with people we don't know very well. Perhaps it's the cachet of a catch, the novelty of a new body, the sensuality that so often pairs with mystery. But, whatever the reason, it's very possible to have great sex with some bozo with a C-minus personality. The more sex one has, the more familiar one becomes with the important components of good sex: verbal consent, enthusiasm, attuned-ness to body language, knowing one's wants and limits while adhering to those of one's partner. And, well, chemistry, that unidentifiable *thing* that leaps from the most surprising people, where even your neurons seem to want to touch theirs. These ingredients are all attainable whether or not two people are in love. Yes, love adds a whole different, incredibly fulfilling dimension to sex—come on, I'm a gay woman. If I could huff "I Love You" sex out of a paper bag, I would. But love is not integral to good sex.

The Right Way I needed as a young queer person wasn't a gay carbon copy of the Joey/Pacey model, like the narrative *Glee* offered. Instead, I needed a model that showed kids (of all sexualities) how to have safe, satisfying sex even absent romantic love. One that taught me how to meet a partner wherever they're at. I needed a model that taught me not to fear or scoff at others' virginity (as I feared Kate would mine, and as the Aries likely feared I would hers), where I wouldn't have felt like my queer identity was contingent on my sexual experience with women. A model that showed how to cultivate trust, even absent a blazing fire in a ski lodge, even absent desire to spend daylight hours with them. Instead, I grew up with extremely specific expectations for virginity loss that instilled in me a lot of anxiety and shame leading up to my first time. An experience that, in hindsight, was quite insignificant in itself, an experience that I'm only writing about because our cultural obsession with virginity has dubbed it a Significant Moment.

Sorry to disappoint, but after that drunk December night, Kate's and my relationship did not blossom into some grand, romantic love story. We continued to see each other casually the following spring. I suspected that her list of prospects had run dry because it was months after our first encounter that she showed active interest in me again. It was a casual fling for which neither of us felt anything strong, and yet, it made me feel so good about myself. I felt like I'd finally proven myself as a sexual being, with someone who made me laugh and showed consistent interest in me and my body—and not just when we were drunk. She made me feel comfortable and confident. I knew I wasn't in love with her, and yet, feeling like a normal college kid having a normal college fling, I felt this must be the right way to do things. It was not the stuff of great rom-coms, which was fine, because my life wasn't and isn't a rom-com.

I went to work at a camp for the summer, and when we came back for junior fall, we both knew the whole thing was over. Senior fall, we took a Russian history lecture together three times a week at eight a.m. She'd usually miss at least one class a week because she'd been up all night with some sophomore she was seeing and would ask for my notes. This irritated me greatly, but by then I'd grown so fond of her friendship, I couldn't help but fork over my notes on Vladimir the Great's Christianization of then-pagan Rus.

Kate and I showed up to our five-year college reunion in very gay-looking matching outfits: black jeans, loafers, patterned button-ups. We laughed hard at this, then spent the entire evening together. We gossiped about girls who'd come out post-college, I met her new girlfriend, and we got late-night takeout. Over a buffalo chicken calzone, she admitted something sweet. Kate still lived in the area, so, like my dad did for my high school, helped coach the rugby team. She said she'd told her players that her five-year reunion was coming up, and they shuddered. "It must be *so weird* seeing like, random people you'd hook up with in college when you're that far out of it," she told me they said to her. "Actually," she'd apparently said, "some random girl I was hooking up with my sophomore year is exactly the person I'm most excited to see." I might've done the whole thing the Right Way after all.

BANTER BOYS
CHRISTIAN, SETH, JIM, AND ME

A quick brag: eighth grade was the most heterosexual year of my life. I peaked or bottomed out early, depending on how you look at it. My first kiss was on a moving Blue Line train, the dots of tunnel lights flitting by, somewhere between Division/Milwaukee and Clark/Lake. Adam and I made out in the tucked-away seating where I now realize people without homes sleep, eat, and urinate. I was popular, not by virtue of being hot and/or cool, but by being one of the less weird kids at a weird school. I knew my school was uncool when I went to soccer practice. My club team had about two girls from each other grade school on the North Side, and nearly every other girl on the field (except for the goalies, who are always gay) wore makeup and straightened their hair, two things that both baffled and scared the shit out of me. Despite my feminine failings, though, I did just fine in the make-out department with my guy friends, thank you very much.

But no matter—I was fourteen and loved kissing, and I exercised my right to do so regularly and, miraculously, with little to no shame. The kissing happened on dares and not, in basements and parks and alleys, and once on the Blue Line. And all the mouths were attached to platonic friends, nothing more. It's the most I've ever been appealing to boys who like girls, and it never went far beyond making out. I think, in part, I loved the movie *Moulin Rouge!* (2001) because the romantic leads were just constantly macking—

and never going further—as if they were, like me, still so thrilled by the sheer excitement of simply kissing.

Eighth grade was the first year I felt I had a bone fide clique of girl friends. It was me, Nora, Nora, Samantha, and Sima. Some combination of the five of us would have a sleepover nearly every weekend. Most times, we'd watch *Moulin Rouge!* then dress up and perform the songs for each other. We were particularly obsessed with "Elephant Love Medley," the mashup of '80s love songs that begins with Satine (Nicole Kidman) feigning resistance to the charms of Christian (Ewan McGregor) and ends with the two wrapped in each other's arms, confessing their mutual love to "I Will Always Love You." We knew every line, every beat, every sigh, and every harmony. We found particular hilarity in the two seconds when Christian hops onto a dangerous ledge and Satine nags him, "Get down from there!" and swooned aggressively at the song's end, when Satine whispers into Christian's parted lips, "You're going to be bad for business. I can tell." I can't help but suspect my erstwhile heterosexual allure was fueled by weekend viewings of *Moulin Rouge!* watching Satine and Christian tumble into unshakable straight love over and over again. Or maybe I just got any/all straightness out of my system in a single school year.

To be completely fair, *Moulin Rouge!* is teen girl catnip. It's set in Paris. It's a musical composed entirely of pop love songs. It alludes to adult themes (sex!!!) but never shows you more than heavy, sloppy make-outs, which is all I could really fathom for myself at the time. Baz Luhrmann's aesthetic is glittery and dazzling, with can-can dancers whirling skirts more layered than puff pastry and six-foot-four drag queens partying in sparkling bodysuits, the whole thing, to me at least, irresistible.

But more tempting to tweens than any of that, *Moulin Rouge!* tells a straightforward, formulaic love story: there's a boy and a girl who want to be together, and a bad guy is keeping them apart.

In the early aughts, I was young enough that I still saw obstacles to love—be they dukes, distance, or dads—as genuine deterrents, and if two people wanted to be together despite the hurdles, destiny would make it so. Now it's obvious to me that obstacles themselves are often the instigators of romance, that they fan the flames. In any case, *Moulin Rouge!* centers on the idea that love is an entity that exists in its own right, that it controls us, and we are merely victims of its whims. And to an adolescent trying to figure out the world, such clear, unambiguous terms are quite appealing. At least, they certainly were to me in middle school.

One of the Noras struck gold when she briefly dated Max, a boy who had seen *Moulin Rouge!* Whether he watched it on his own or because he knew all the girls liked it remains unclear to this day. I do recall, though, that Nora and Max would type the lyrics to *Moulin Rouge!* songs to each other on AOL Instant Messenger. The five of us shrieked when we realized that Max had miswritten the line "Want to vanish inside your kiss" in "Come What May," the musical's one original melody, as "Want to finish, insert your kiss." Still, I was jealous that Nora got to play digital *Moulin Rouge!* cosplay with a boy, despite his failure to google song lyrics.

I was jealous that Nora got to be Satine, but in a way, I did, too. In the spring, for a school project, our friend Samantha re-created the red dress that Satine wears during "Elephant Love Medley," a long silk gown with a plunging neckline suitable only for a person with ample chest to fill it. By virtue of having the most developed breasts of the five of us, Samantha tailored the dress to my measurements: I got to be the model. I traipsed around Nora R.'s Ukrainian Village house in full Luhrmann universe costume, belting "I Will Always Love You" as Samantha photographed me. I felt like a star; I felt feminine. I never found my Christian, despite all the smooching, but I got to be in the story we loved so much.

There are so many ways to be attracted to someone. Sexual attraction is the most obvious form—a lingering curiosity about their lips, the magnetic pull from your navel to theirs, a buzz urging you to hold their hips. But people get stuck in my head for so many reasons other than wanting to sleep with them. Most often, I'm attracted to people as friends. Maybe they make a reference to a serial killer I, too, am obsessed with (John Wayne Gacy), or maybe they flare their nostrils in impatience as a straight dude at a party talks about Quentin Tarantino films. I can tell that they *get* me, and I want them to like me. But that kinship, that draw, that seeing oneself in another is a form of attraction.

Or maybe it's just something in the way they dress: a geometric ring I'd wear, or their ability to wear the shit out of a wool sweater in a truly envious manner. I'm pulled to people as friends, as creative partners, as role models all the time. And while I'd prefer the majority of the people I choose to have in my life remain fully clothed in my presence, I'm still attracted to them on some level. Though *attraction* is often only defined as romantic or sexual, the feeling of being drawn to another person is so much richer and more dynamic than just the physical. And because means of attraction are myriad, they often get wrapped up in each other; they intersect, they intermingle, and they can be hard to tease out from one another. Sometimes, you can be so attracted to someone that you straight-up want to *be them*.

Queer people often ask ourselves a familiar question: *Do I want to* be *this person, or do I want to* fuck *this person?* Another way of asking that is *I know I'm attracted to this person, but* how *am I attracted to them?* Given the infinite ways in which a person can appeal to us, it's not always a simple question to answer, particularly when asked about people of our same gender. The answer can often depend on how we see ourselves now and on the kind of person we'd *like* to be. The question crops up a lot in adolescence, when our self-identity—not just our sexualities but our taste in friends and academics and art and movies and humor—is so in flux. Given how unclear it is, exactly, who we are, sussing out the manner in which we're attracted to someone is doubly difficult. Then factor in the object of your attraction sharing your same gender, and on top of *that* being closeted and/or unaware of your own queerness—what a fucking disaster.

Once I came out, I asked myself, *Do I want to be her or bang her?* quite literally and quite often. But why would I bother to interrogate my attraction at age thirteen, in what would be the throes of peak heterosexuality? I was making out in basements on the reg—why would I be anything but into boys? And yet I now see that even in the red dress, I didn't want to *be* Satine. I didn't want to be a tuberculosis-stricken damsel trapped in the clutches of a weasel duke. Maybe I wanted to be French and thin and a good singer, but that was where my idolization of Kidman's character ended. No, I just had a throbbing crush on Nicole Kidman.

I was fixated on the way Kidman's chest rose and fell, breathing deep to combat her corset, on her dazzle of red hair, on her so-aughts thin eyebrows, so strange and long, they nearly connected with her ears. I made the same mix-up with Scarlett Johansson in *Lost in Translation* (so cute she inspired me to rent *Ghost World* from Blockbuster), and then with Catherine Zeta-Jones in *Chicago*, and then with Blake Lively as a soccer star in *Sisterhood of the Traveling Pants*. I watched these movies over and over again, enamored by the leads. I became obsessed with early-aughts phenoms in middle school and, without the tools to figure out what, exactly, I was feeling, assumed my infatuation with hot, older women was a desire to *be* a hot, older woman. I was yearning for role models, and because I was a girl, mistook my teen horniness for female celebs as a desire to *be like them*. In truth, it was probably some mix of both.

I made the same mix-up with the guys, too. The other way around, though—with men, I assumed, thanks to compulsory heteronormativity, that my attraction to them *must* be romantic. When in reality, I just wanted to be them. Enter: a 2000s character archetype I like to call the Banter Boy.

The Banter Boy is clever. He's creative, though in his universe his wit goes woefully underutilized. He's not passionate about his daily life, be it school or work, but when he's lit up, he lights all the way up. His creativity bursts through in fits and spurts, in decorating for made-up family holidays, or penning punk rock songs, or, briefly free from his prison of boredom, creating an afternoon-long tournament of office games. The Banter Boy is quick with words, which really just means he's well written. He's a stand-in for the male writers of the film or TV show, or at least, it certainly feels that way. There's an overwhelming sense that the Banter Boy is destined for something great, greater than this rinky-dink town and greater than these small-minded people. Perhaps his most irritating quality is that he, too, seems to know this.

The Banter Boy is skinny with floppy hair, though he exists somewhere on the spectrum of alternative. He looks good in corduroy, and he can wear the shit out of a crewneck sweater. He's not all that athletic, or at least, his body doesn't scream athlete. He's approachable, maybe even explicitly uncool—he's good-looking because he's played by a good-looking actor, always, but is somehow deemed not so desirable in the context of his world. It's confusing. At times, the Banter Boy might even be reviled. He's not a full-on outcast, but the Banter Boy is certainly not in a position of power, nor does he generally want to be. Due to his lack of self-confidence regarding his looks and and inability to shut the fuck up, the Banter Boy is an excellent, excellent flirt.

Which brings us to the main thing about the Banter Boy. Above all else, he's a romantic. The Banter Boy always pines for someone out of his reach: the girl echelons more popular than he is, or who's literal property of a wealthy duke, or who's been engaged for three years. He's positioned as the underdog (again: written by male writers). He's spent years pining over this woman, whom he holds on a pedestal, whom he regards as ethereal and goddess-esque. Indeed, his crush borders on obsession and is so consuming that all the people around him know about it, except for her. But despite (because?) of the barriers, he pines. His feelings are unwavering and unquestionable, like he's merely following the instructions of something much greater and more powerful than he. His crush is so intense that it becomes integral to his self-identity; part of his character, the stuff of who he really is, is about someone else. He's only a full person in the context of a girl, yo-yoing back and forth between loneliness and wholehearted fulfillment.

———

If eighth grade was the straightest year of my life, my junior year of college might've been my gayest. I had yet to understand how queerness exists as an entity unto itself, and felt the only way to validate my existence was by having a girlfriend. The other larger and louder part of me really wanted to have sex on a regular basis. Whatever the impetus, I started my third year of college with Olympic levels of determination to make a girl fall in love with me.

I met Ella at a pre-Paris dinner. We were both doing our school's semester abroad program in the French capital, and at that dinner, I decided I wanted her to love me. I instantly had a crush: she was tall (my height, even!), a dancer, with big, brown doe eyes. She wore 90 percent ModCloth and studied English. Her French was very good. I could always spot her across campus in her bulky, green over-ear headphones, likely listening to the De-cemberists or Bright Eyes. This was the girl, I decided, who would teach me how to be in love. We bonded on a TGV to the Loire Valley in early January, over both knowing a large portion of Nicki Minaj's "Monster" verse. After a highly tactical footsie campaign I rolled out over the course of two weeks, magic happened: we got drunk and made out. It's strange, looking back, that I don't remember the first time we kissed.

We started kissing semiregularly (*not* on the métro). Ella hadn't been with a girl before, so we kept the whole thing under wraps. We'd stay out late at bars near the Bastille, then head back to our host families, and sneak up to her *chambre de bonne,* a little room on the seventh floor separate from her family's third floor apartment. But gayer than actually making out with a girl was the Gchatting. Neither of us had smartphones in France, and we had to pay for every text we sent, so we chatted on Gmail whenever our fingers found a keyboard. We'd start out making plans for what to do in Paris ("yo. assiette au fromage, rue mouffetard."), or about classwork, or what we missed about home ("ALL I WANT IS MEXICAN FOOD"). Then most conversations would slip into the stuff of newfangled, adolescent intimacy:

> it's like. you know when you realize your parents aren't superhumans? like, they're just people doing their best, but they suck sometimes. in the same way we suck sometimes. not sucking monumentally, just sucking the normal level. it's just that.

I was shocked she wanted to chat me back, but there she was, each night, chatting me back. A codependency was forged within a month, intimacy at warp speed, the rate at which all my college friendships seemed to move. Considering how little romantic experience I had, I was floored that a girl I'd found cute instantly upon meeting her wanted anything to do with me. That had never happened before. Because she dated me, she got to come out the way I'd wanted so badly to: with a girlfriend, *a thing* to point to, a reason for her queerness. It was a romance birthed, and that even thrived, on Gchat.

> i just . . . you know. you give a fuck about
> people and you use your brain. and god,
> you're so fucking earnest. this is so cheesy,
> but like, you've given me a tiny sliver of faith in
> humanity. i just like you.

Josh Schwartz couldn't write that.

~

For many, Seth Cohen defined mid-aughts teen culture. He was a fresh character who arguably made *The O.C.* stand out among other teen dramas of the era (like *One Tree Hill, Everwood,* and *Joan of Arcadia*) and, too, stand the test of time. As noted by a *Vulture* essay published around the show's ten-year anniversary, "even by the end of that very first episode, it was obvious that Seth Cohen was going to be the character people cared about—especially if you happened to identify as sensitive, Jewish, and dorky, and similarly inclined toward geeky pursuits."[1] *The O.C.* soundtrack, which I believe reflected Seth Cohen's personal taste in music, featured emo/hipster/indie bands like Death Cab for Cutie and Rooney and Aqualung, and shaped many a millennial musical sensibility (mine included). As *Pitchfork,* a publication Seth himself would devour, wrote in 2015, "For many teenagers, *Music from The O.C.*

paved an entry point into indie music." They added that the show itself gave indie bands their big break into TV and commercial placement "a decade before that became the new normal."[2]

Seth Cohen birthed a generation of witty sadboys. Boys who admired Cohen in high school had illustrious futures ahead of them, including curating mildly popular Tumblrs that paired newspaper headlines with iconic movie screenshots, perhaps dabbling in gif creation. Seth made indie music cool. He made blurting your hot take out of turn cool. He made skinny corduroys and sweaters and striped polo shirts cool. He even made liking comic books—well, maybe not cool, but acceptable. (Could he have even laid the groundwork for the Marvel mania of the 2010s?) And Seth made nerd culture cool, because he'd successfully used it to get hot chicks to want to fuck him—both Summer Roberts and teenage *O.C.* fans. His way didn't involve being athletic or suave or particularly masculine. One could just be, well, kind of annoying. Again, on *Vulture*: "At last, a certain subset of male viewers in their teens and [twenties] who felt uncomfortable in almost any social situation could feel that they were being represented on a major network television show."

Take Sam. Sam was not a TV character but a popular kid in my high school with a mop of Harry Potter black hair and Harry Potter bright-green eyes. He entered high school with kind of a stoner vibe, I think—I recall hemp bracelets, perhaps a puka shell necklace? Within a month or so, he pivoted to preppy, pink Lacoste polos for the remainder of freshman year. Sam drank beer in parks with the Lincoln Park boys and probably fingered girls? I don't know, good for him. Anyway, sophomore year, a curious thing happened: Sam started to listen to more indie music. Alexi Murdoch and Bloc Party and Belle and Sebastian. His pants got tighter, his sweater collection more robust, more patterned. Sam performatively pined—*pined*—over jarringly beautiful and funny and popular Ariel. Like Seth, he eventually won his dream girl over. Things got out of hand when Sam changed his voice mail greeting to seven simple words: "It's 2006, you know what to do." (Seth's had been in 2004, but, you get it.) Senior year, Sam would be a Kairos leader—a Catholic brainwashing retreat that, honestly, I don't have the energy to get into right now—and his contribution to the retreat mix CD was Patrick Park's "Life's a Song," which played in the final scene of *The O.C.*

It became an open joke that Ariel's boyfriend was actively trying to become Seth Cohen. He even had the same initials as the character! But unlike Seth, Sam wasn't an emo geek who became an insider. Rather, he did it the other way around: Sam went from preppy, popular kid to a Seth type. Maybe he admired or related to Seth. Or maybe he saw how many girls were head over heels for Adam Brody's character and rebranded accordingly. A midaughts survival-of-the-fittest tactic, really.

While boys wanted to *be* Seth, girls wanted to date him. There were two types of high school girls in 2004: those who had a crush on Ryan Atwood, and those who had a crush on Seth Cohen. There was no third option. Either you chose the sensitive beefcake and veritable bad boy who wore wife beaters to broadcast his bulging muscles; or you chose the annoying, hilarious, Death Cab–loving Jewish proto-hipster. Both were played by extremely handsome, cishet white actors in their midtwenties who gave teenagers of all genders wildly inaccurate expectations for how boys their age should look. Ultimately, the two weren't terribly different, but at least they were a bit more distinct from one another than the Backstreet Boys and *NSYNC had been. In any case, as a fourteen-year-old girl, your preferred *O.C.* boy spoke volumes about your fundamental human identity. If you liked Ryan, maybe you were into the wrong-side-of-the-tracks type, but mostly you valued traditional masculinity (the muscular bad boy who'll punch out a dumb jock for you). Or you liked Seth, which meant you were quirky and smart and interesting and a little neurotic and found those same qualities attractive in a boy.

I was team Seth and thus sought a real-life Seth Cohen to crush on, which was difficult, because everyone I knew was Catholic. I set my sights on Jimmy, a very tall, very lanky boy who played the keys in a garage band desperate to sound like Wilco. We were friends, and I hoped to morph that friendship into one that involved lots of kissing. My success was fleeting. At a party junior year, Unk's 2006 shout-jam "Walk It Out" came on. The lyrics go, *"Now walk it out (now walk it out) / Now walk it out (now walk it out) / Now walk it out (now walk it out) / Now walk it out."* A drunk Jimmy asked me, "Should we walk it out?" Very smooth. We went to the alley and kissed in the chilly March mist. That was the beginning and end of our romance. I continued to fling myself at him, relentlessly, like a bouncy ball at a brick wall, through senior year. All I wanted was a Seth Cohen boyfriend. It didn't work out.

The Office: another 2000s phenomenon-slash-Banter Boy propaganda. Unlike Seth, Jim is a grown-up Banter Boy. Which is to say, he's still not a *grown-up* grown-up. Untapped creativity is integral to the Banter Boy profile, and where Seth's comes out in illustrating comics and witty rapport, Jim's takes the form of pranks. Specifically, on his beet-farming deskmate, Dwight: Jim goes to work dressed as Dwight, faxes Dwight messages from "Future Dwight," puts all of Dwight's desk items in the break room vending machine, and incrementally adds nickels to Dwight's phone receiver and then, one day, removes them, prompting Dwight to thwack himself in the head. The unspoken conundrum of Jim Halpert is *If he's smart enough to come up with these ingenious pranks, why the hell is he working at Dunder Mifflin?* "My job is to speak to clients on the phone about quantities and type of copier paper. You know, whether we can supply it to them, whether they can pay for it," says

Jim in the pilot episode. "And, um . . . I'm boring myself just talking about this."

Other Banter Boys—like Seth Cohen and love interest Cliff Pantone in *Bring It On* and Dan Humphrey in *Gossip Girl*—also have greater things in store than their high schools. But they can't just up and leave—they're teenagers. Like Dan and Serena, and Seth and Summer, Jim is largely defined by his feelings for a girl: Pam Beesley. Loving Pam is a trait integral to his character, made clear in the show's pilot episode by the way Jim leans over her reception desk a little too far, by the way he only wants to go to team happy hour if she's going, too. I saw this and thought, *God, I want a Jim*, when really—well, you get it.

—

But long before that would happen, Ella dumped me. No, worse(!)—she told me she just wanted to be *friends*. It was a brisk and dreary February morning, the city clad in uniform peacoats, which every student abroad wore to appear as French as possible. Ella and I sat together on a bench just outside Montparnasse Cemetery, a stone's throw from Jean-Paul Sartre's and Simone de Beauvoir's graves. I was baffled by her rejection of me and confident that my life would never steep lower than that moment. She sobbed and told me she didn't want to drag me through her own self-discovery; I was sure I knew what I wanted—to be with her—and she just didn't know what she wanted. She said she needed space to figure it out. I decided it was my right as a sad person to reject that request.

What followed was a flurry of correspondences dripping in *Dawson's*-level earnestness and in Plath-level gravity: fraught twenty-one-year-old romantic confusion. I gave her a letter telling her that we could start from scratch, that we could go back to the beginning and take things slow. In a text, she thanked me for it—

she'd read the letter among the love lockets on the Pont des Arts, which even I found a bit on the nose—and I responded with something cold, an "Okay, have a good weekend." Perhaps I'd been *too much*, perhaps playing it cool and aloof would get her back. I found this new angle crushing to follow through with, and I abruptly bailed on it that night when I texted her and told her I'd do literally whatever she wanted to keep me in her life. She said she needed time to think. "I just reread your letter for like the twentieth time," she texted me on Sunday. "I think I'm going insane. And for some reason I think that me telling you I'm going insane will make me feel less insane." Emotional whiplash.

I pitied myself thoroughly. *Of course*, I thought. *Of course, something is finally going well, and it gets ripped out from under me.* (Excuse me? How *dare* you suggest I try to see outside myself.) But rereading our old Gchats, it's clear how confused Ella was about the whole thing. What I interpreted as her either a) being afraid of what people would think of her queerness, or b) actually thinking I'm a full-on lecherous troll was actually her wondering that same, familiar queer question: "I know I'm attracted to this person, but *how* am I attracted to her?" I was so busy feeling bad for myself, that my Falling in Love in Paris scheme had failed, that I couldn't see that she was going through a very normal gay process, albeit one I hadn't with her.

Ella and I didn't speak for about a week, which, to an infatuated baby gay like myself, felt like months. I continued to cry fat, teenage tears on the métro, to drag my feet through the Tuileries, to wander down Rue Mouffetard and think how much better the whole thing would be if a girl liked me back. I'd spent the past six weeks crafting my entire personality around having a crush on Ella; sadness emboldened that compulsion. Woe was, in fact, me.

And then my Banter Boy instincts kicked in. I'd put Ella on a pedestal and was having trouble getting her down from there.

Like Jim staring at the reception desk, we were still around each other, at classes, with the tiny group of friends we had in Paris. It was insufferable. So I settled for the distasteful runner-up to girlfriendship: friendship. "I just feel so much better being around her," I wrote to Devin on the record of love, Gchat. I announced my plan to immerse myself in the friendzone. And I did just that for the next few weeks of Parisian spring. It was friendship not born from an actual desire to be friends but instead from the optimistic (desperate) hope that maybe I'd be *such* a good friend that she'd want to continue to kiss me on the lips on a regular basis. Though thoroughly pitiful, I was actually in my most comfortable position. The Banter Boy is always the underdog, always the reject, always going for the girl on the pedestal who's out of his league.

—

When *The O.C.* premiered in summer 2003, lesbian representation on television was at a weird lull. *Buffy* ended in May of that year and had killed off Tara—one-half of network TV's first recurring lesbian couple—a year prior. That was pretty much it for queer girls on teen shows, though. Ellen changed the world when she declared, "Yep, I'm Gay" on the cover of *TIME* in 1997, but her sitcom was canceled in 1998; Carol and Susan cropped up every so often on *Friends,* almost strictly to emasculate Ross. *The L Word* would premiere on Showtime in 2004, but that content was far too adult (not to mention, way too fucking gay) for my presumed-straight fourteen-year-old self. There just weren't any lesbians on the TV I consumed. I didn't even have any tomboyish girls, like me, to idolize—straight or gay.

Without any gay girls (though a few tomboys—more on them later) on TV, I'd successfully convinced myself that Seth was my dream crush and ignored what he really was: at that point, the closest representation of myself I'd seen on TV. By high school, I'd outgrown my (alleged) desire to be like Satine and knew I wasn't anything like the waifish, glowing, feminine girls of Newport Beach and the Upper East Side. On paper, I was much more similar to the boys than I was to any of their objects of affection. They were smart and creative, and they fancied themselves better-than-you outsiders of the popular realm to varying degrees. They were tall and lanky, like I was. I often wore a blue sweater with a tugboat on it, with corduroys and checkered slip-on vans, an outfit Seth totally would've worn to the Harbor School. I was snarky like the boys, and I made mix CDs with Death Cab and Wilco and Rilo Kiley on them.

The Banter Boy isn't the most archetypically masculine guy. In season two of *The O.C.*, Summer starts dating a new guy, Zach, by whom Seth feels sufficiently one-upped. "That guy's like, Superman," says Cohen of the water-polo-playing son of a congressman. "He's a thoroughbred. I'm a monkey with cymbals." Seth's effeminate characteristics—his waifishness, passiveness, propensity for upbeat chitchat—get called out on the show all the time. Water polo guys shove Cohen aside, calling him a queer and a faggot. Cohen even read as queer to *The Washington Post*, which, in their scathing review of the 2003 pilot, described Seth as, "a neurotic adolescent who might be gay."[3] Indeed, Banter Boys are they kinds of guys who the (archetypically masculine) jocks rail on for being too feminine. As the Banter Boy thrived in the aughts, so, too, did casual homophobia.

Jim Halpert, too, endures being the butt of gay jokes. Todd Packer, Michael Scott's miserable homophobe of a bully/friend, constantly attempts to emasculate Jim publicly. "Halpert! Tall, queer, handsome as ever," says Packer, visiting Dunder Mifflin in season three. Then, in a high-pitched voice, says, "Hey everybody!

It's me, Jim!" When Karen (Rashida Jones) introduces herself to Packer as Jim's girlfriend, Packer spews disbelief: "Either this chick is a dude or Halpert got scared straight!"

Packer's joke goes totally unacknowledged by Jim and Karen, and that's what makes the Banter Boy appealing to queer audiences. It's not that they *seem* gay, really; their whole character is built around obsessing over a girl, after all. No, the appeal is that the Banter Boy doesn't seem to be particularly bothered by the gay jokes. In season two of *Gossip Girl*, Chuck Bass asks Dan "Lonely Boy" Humphrey, "Are you gay?" to which Dan replies, "That'd be out of my comfort zone, but no," and moves on with the conversation. Dan, like the other Banterers, is so secure in his sexuality because he's so secure in his obsession with Serena. When Michael Scott asks Jim who in the office he'd "do," Jim jokingly says he'd sleep with Kevin—"Yeah, I mean, he's got that teddy bear thing going on, and afterwards we could just watch bowling." He uses this to deflect from his honest answer, the girl who's then engaged to another guy, but he doesn't seem to care if Michael interprets his answer seriously. In late season one of *The O.C.*, Summer finally introduces Seth to her dad. Before their lunch at the club in late season one, Summer warns her boyfriend, "Order a steak—my dad says greens are effeminate."

"Celery's gay, got it," Seth replies.

I admired something in the Banter Boy's quiet self-confidence, despite him being a tad more waifish, a smidge androgynous compared with the rest of his cast. Perhaps because of it. It's like he had the wisdom and foresight to really understand that high school (or Dunder Mifflin) is temporary. They all have varying degrees of wealth and access, sure, but they're all cisgender white guys and thus have inherent privilege; the Banter Boy doesn't shatter any binaries. But I think, as a teenager, I lusted for how the Banter Boy let being called queer roll off his back. It took power away from whoever used the word. On some level, I wished I could thirst over girls with such confidence.

And that's the core characteristic of Banter Boys: the girls they love. They all pine for girls with boyfriends, who often don't even know of their existence. Seth Cohen's main thing is that he's obsessed with Summer, to the point of creepiness: I mean, he named his fucking boat after her before she even knew his name. Jim and Pam rose to sitcom will-they-won't-they hall of fame within two seasons of the show, and without them, *The Office* would've had about a tenth of the sentimental value. In the pilot of *Gossip Girl*, Dan Humphrey's little sister, Jenny, teases him for having been utterly infatuated with Serena van der Woodsen, a sixteen-year-old who all of New York weirdly wants to fuck, for years. Christian tells Satine he loves her the very first night they meet at the Moulin Rouge! Their crushes aren't circumstantial, they're not just there to advance a plot—no, they're full-blown personality traits. Love, to Banter Boys, is an independent force that must be adhered to and is ultimately unattainable unless shared with one particular person. Because drooling over their love interest is so utterly part of who they are, the Banter Boys all marry their dream girls in the end. Or, at least, their dream girls declare their reciprocal love while dying of tuberculosis in a Banter Boy's arms.

That's what appealed to me about Banter Boys as a queer kid. Not just the effeminateness or the fact that they liked watching movies alone more than hanging out with hordes of bros. It was the way they were defined by who they loved and how hard they loved them. As a teenager, I thought of queerness as something that just defined who you like, not a core essence that exists within you. Thus, I conceptualized my own sexuality as something that only existed within the context of someone else. Just like Seth wouldn't be Seth without Summer, and Jim, Pam, and Dan, Serena, I wouldn't be a fully realized human being with a sexuality—or a firm identity, really—out of the context of romance. I felt that without enough gay sexual and/or romantic experience, I didn't really count as gay. This could've come from all kinds of places: the "if you've never had sex with a guy, how do you know you're not into it?" rhetoric, knowing virtually zero openly gay adults, watching characters like Alex Kelly (Olivia Wilde) get toted into Newport Beach to give the show a lesbian kiss and ratings boom then get shipped back from whence she came, only existing in the context of another character. For whatever reason, by the time I came out, went to Paris, set my sights on Ella, and came *this close* to her falling in love with me, I was so inexperienced romantically that I felt like I couldn't really claim queerness yet.

What came first, the overeager collegiate dyke desperate for affection or the Banter Boy? Did the Banter Boy teach me to be a self-pitying romantic, or was this another piece of myself that I saw in him? Was I mirroring him or relating to him? Self-pitying, over-romantic lesbians have existed for eternity, and will continue to, but it's probably a bit of both.

⌒

It's Thanksgiving, and Seth and Summer are making out in the pool house. This isn't their first kiss. A week earlier, Summer grabbed Seth's face at a yacht party, to the young Cohen's utter bewilderment, kissed him hard, and growled, "Don't tell *anyone* this happened." But now, she's straight-up ditched her family on a national holiday, showed up at Seth's house, and demanded he kiss her again. And he does. As they kiss, Seth pulls back for a moment, touches her face, wearing a goofy look of unbridled glee: "This is happening." Like he needed to say it aloud to mark the moment's existence, to make it real. It's not romantic, it's just emo geeky.

Particularly in season one of *The O.C.*, Seth drips in absolute disbelief that any of what's happening to him is actually happening to him, beginning with the arrival of Ryan, his (unofficially) adoptive brother from Chino in the pilot. Seth had spent his entire life to that point as a lonely loser, an only child. And now, with Ryan's arrival, he has a friend—even a brother!—who's tough and fucks and, too, feels like an outsider. An unimaginable companion to Seth. With exactly one friend, Seth starts to go to parties with popular kids. He can't believe he's at those parties. He meets girls he can't believe actually want to talk to him. He finally kisses—and eventually charms into his pool house, then onto a coffee cart—his lifelong crush, Summer Roberts. *Is this really happening?* Going to parties, kissing girls, it's all fairly normal teen stuff in season one. But in Seth's eyes, it's completely wild that he could be so lucky.

So: a month of teeth-bared friendship. Ella and I continued to explore Paris together. We'd text. We'd Gchat. I clutched to the dregs of our intimacy for dear life. She'd tell me all the boring little things you really only tell your girlfriend: how little sleep she got last night, her favorite Oscar Wilde passages, how much she didn't want to write this French paper, the occasional, literal, "blah blah blah blah blah." We'd made it abundantly clear to one another that we liked each other best of all the people in our program, and considering there were only twenty of us total, well, we were stuck together. Oftentimes we'd converse in cartoon crab: we'd type V.v.V into the chat box, and Google would convert it into a claw-snapping, red crustacean. Pop it next to a boom box (with the "rock out" code: \m/), and it'd look like the crab was dancing. In that month, this was sex to me. We'd grown so comfortable with each other's names in the little chat box that even sending proto-emoji nonsense felt like some kind of relief. I'd be patient, I decided, and I would wear her down. I'd win her back not by naming my boat after her or writing a pop-punk love song or singing Elton John in her face but by waiting it out, assuming friendship, biding my time. It's not a strategy I would ever embark on again, but as a Banter Boy, the girl I liked was, essentially, the only person on the planet.

Springtime came in late March, which was new for me. I was shocked that Paris actually had spring, having only lived in Chicago and Boston to that point, where March comes in like a lion and out like a drunk lion. But March in Paris meant wearing only a sweater to bask in the eruption of cherry and magnolia blooms on the Haussmann streets, the whole thing so delightful, it felt like a joke. One afternoon, Ella and I went on a walk out of the city, in Neuilly-sur-Seine, to the Île de la Grande Jatte—the site of Georges Seurat's tableau of a Sunday afternoon, the one I'd seen hanging in the Art Institute since I was a kid. The slender, long island in the Seine was lined with tennis courts, with a one-lane path I'd sometimes run along, however gauche and American wearing athletic gear in public seemed to Parisians. We sat down on a bench. She had something to *say*. She danced around it for a while, nervous, her voice a little higher, her eyes darting toward everything that wasn't me. And then, finally:

"I think... I'm ready to try being more than friends again. Would you want that?"

It was not a grand declaration of love, nothing close to leaping on a coffee cart. But any/all conversations about feelings are elevated to High Romance when they take place in Paris. Her voice might've lifted at the end of her sentence, but it wasn't a question, really. It was in the category of questions like "Can I bring anything other than wine to the party?" or "Mind if I take the last fry?" Questions asked only out of politeness, whose answers, though obvious, are tacky to presume. It was as if the strings had swelled, as if I, the underdog, made sense narratively. I'd been so utterly barreled over when she initially broke up with me because, objectively, the first person to break your heart is the most cruel and incorrect person on the planet, and your heartbreak is worse than everyone else's, and your rejection lingers longer and is a referendum on your personhood in a way it couldn't possibly be for any of your friends. But all that was over now, because I'd been kind and patient and *deserved it, dammit.* I was the one who waited patiently for what seemed like eternity but was actually about one-sixth of a *Grey's Anatomy* season. We sat on the bench and kissed, sober, in the daylight, openly wanting each other. Finally, I got the over-the-top Parisian love story I'd craved since middle school. And finally, I wasn't Satine, but Christian.

This is happening, I thought. That's exactly how I felt every time I kissed a girl until I was about twenty-six. It took a while to get used to being out and gay. I felt that same Cohen awe when I drunkenly found myself in the girl's rugby suite with Kate on the last night of classes sophomore fall. And I felt it wandering through Washington Square Park after my first OkCupid date with a girl named Gillian. And I absolutely felt it whenever I got within inches of Ella. Absolute disbelief that somehow I had rigged the system to ensure a) I could kiss girls, and b) they would agree to—even be excited to!—kiss me back. What a scam. I wanted to hold each of their faces, Seth Cohen–style. *This is happening.*

DISNEY CHANNEL PRESENTS

SAPPHIC OVERTONES

I spent my childhood feverishly desperate for my brother's approval. Just eighteen months my senior (so, two grades ahead of me), Zach, to me, embodied the pinnacle of coolness and funniness from my earliest days through high school. When we were little, Zach played soccer, so I wanted to play soccer. Zach collected baseball cards, so I collected baseball cards. Zach played Pokémon, so I borrowed his Game Boy and played Pokémon after him—then stoked his ire by saving my own game and inadvertently erasing his, a memory that still wallops me with guilt. When Zach got into alt pop-rock bands like Weezer (*The Blue Album* and *Pinkerton* only, thank you) and blink-182 (all of it, frankly), I followed suit. Same goes for *The Simpsons* and Conan O'Brien and, in high school, *The Office* and, in college, *Summer Heights High*. I assumed Zach's taste in comedy was infallible and adopted it as my own.

I was a tomboy, sure. But when I was little-little—like, kindergarten age—my identity wasn't based on boys in the general sense. Rather, I gleefully based my whole sense of self on my big brother, who knew better than to bequeath unto me his love and approval, lest I get above my station. I'd try to hang out whenever Zach had friends over in the basement, but he'd give me the boot. This craving for Zach to validate my existence bled into our adolescence: when he drove me to high school my freshman and sophomore years in our family's green Volkswagen van, I could never touch the iPod. The soundtrack was always in Zach's hands and always included some Brand New. He laughed at *some* of my jokes, *sometimes*. Enough to keep me tap-dancing for him, trying to be cleverer, trying to win his laughter—the ultimate validation.

It might've been my literal desire to become my brother that spurred my infatuation with the Disney Channel Original Movie *Motocrossed* (2000).

Okay, so: meet the Carson family. They're your average, American, motocross-obsessed family. You know the type. The dad was an off-road motorcycle racing champion back in his heyday, and he's grooming his teenage son, Andy, to replace him as the Fastest Biker Boy. Andy's twin sister, Andi (note to parents seeking to avoid their twins swapping identities: give your children different names) is a cheerleader but desperately wants to be a motocrosser like the guys. But dad says no! Motocross is not for girls, it's for boys. "I want you to start concentrating on things that a thirteen-year-old girl should be concentrating on," says dad. "And that does *not* include motocross!"

But when Andy (the boy) gets injured and dad goes off to recruit another racer for their team, Andi (the girl) chops her hair off and races in (the boy) Andy's place. At first, their mother is horrified by Andi's dyke chop. "Just look at your beautiful hair!" she says, in the exact tone my own mother had upon viewing my foregone side-shave. But soon, Andi's mom is on board and takes her daughter to a motocross competition disguised as her son. There, hilarity ensues, including Andi developing a crush on a boy who thinks she's a boy. Apparently, *Motocrossed* is loosely based on *Twelfth Night*. Those adaptations sometimes work—*10 Things I Hate About You, Clueless,* and *She's the Man* are modern classics based on classic classics. Other times, you just get *Motocrossed*. In the end, Andi gets outed as a girl, but she wins over her crush nonetheless and wins a big motocross sponsorship. Girl power! As someone who spent the first ten years of her life trying to emulate her near-twin brother in every way, *Motocrossed* got me.

I'm sure I don't need to spell this out for you, as I just wrote *motocross* and *dyke chop* in the same paragraph, but the queer imagery in *Motocrossed* is, quite frankly, unrelenting. Andi, who looks like an *NSYNC member everybody forgot about—wait, no, that's Chris Kirkpatrick—spends 70 percent of the movie vrooming away on her hog, fretting that her real gender will be exposed. When she's not in head-to-toe motocross gear, she wears a baggy striped T-shirt with a flannel shirt layered on, spiky blond hair, khaki cargo shorts, and a faux-deep voice. In one scene, Andi and her crush, Dean Talon (my new drag king name), go on a motocross ride through backroads before stumbling upon a lake and taking a dip. Dunking and splashing is involved. As Dean thinks Andi's a boy, he does not know it's a date, but this is most certainly a date between two butch lesbians. Watching our heroine cross-dress is supposed to be a point of comedy, as it is in *Twelfth Night*, but, sorry to essentialize, any teen girl who yearns to mount a dirt bike is at *least* 30 percent queer. I was both enthralled with and terrified by Andi's boyishness, as I saw my own boyishness reflected in her. Upon rewatch, Andi's appearance isn't all that funny; rather, it's just a decently accurate depiction of a baby butch.

Six years later, *High School Musical* carried on the tradition of clearly-gay-but-actually-not-gay characters in DCOMs. *High School Musical* is a musical about auditioning for a musical. Two star-crossed heterosexuals, Troy (Zac Efron) and Gabriella (Vanessa Hudgens), discover their mutual crushes and singing talents and grapple with whether to try out for their school's new production. No one is more opposed to the duo's meteoric rise than Sharpay and Ryan Evans (Ashley Tisdale, Lucas Grabeel). The Evans twins rule the drama club and heretofore have happily scooped up leads in every school production for which they've auditioned.

The Evans twins are villains, both clearly sculpted by a gay man. Sharpay Evans's blown-out, cartoonish femininity makes one forget, momentarily, that they're watching a Disney movie and not *RuPaul's Drag Race*. But Ryan Evans is the one we really need to talk about. Ryan—I don't know how to put it any other way—is, well, very clearly a homosexual. Like Andi Carson simply *is* a baby butch, Ryan Evans just, like, *is* a gay boy. I say this with the utmost love: Ryan is a hip-swishing, jazz-square-dancing, eye-rolling, bitchy young man. He wears a different, neon-colored Kangol hat in every scene. "It's a crowd favorite," the allegedly straight character tells his twin sister/dance partner after their first audition for the musical. "Everybody loves a good jazz square!" I'm all for straight men embracing their femininity, but Ryan Evans is clearly played in the spirit of a gay musical theater terrorist, and arguing otherwise would feel insincere at best. To the point that, had Disney made Ryan openly gay, the character might've been panned as a gay cliché.

But they didn't. Ryan's sexuality isn't addressed at all until *High School Musical 3: Senior Year*, when he dates the composer for the drama club, Kelsi, who is in fact a girl. In 2016, Lucas Grabeel told *BuzzFeed News* he'd asked director Kenny Ortega about Ryan's sexuality right after reading the script.[1] "I know it's Disney Channel, so I'm not really gonna be gay, but I mean, yeah, right?" Grabeel paraphrased. Ortega apparently told him, "Well, think of it this way: you have the opportunity to play a character who's young, he's into theater, he's an artist, and let's go at it from that point of view." So Grabeel played Ryan as a peak theater twink and left it at that.

On the one hand, that's real. There was literally not one out gay person at my high school, but there were *plenty* of people who were just obviously queer. For Halloween one year, a fellow concert band flutist, Jonathan, went in full drag (heels, too) as a notoriously cruel popular girl, Hope Jameson (absolutely not her real name; I'm still terrified of her and fear she will hunt me down and pierce my heart with a stiletto if I publish her name). Particularly at a Catholic school with no Gay-Straight Alliance and teachers who told us God hated the sin of queerness, this was nothing short of rock-star behavior. It was hilarious and brave and perfect. Now, I don't know if Jonathan was out to his friends—we weren't friends, he was two years ahead of me and refused to speak to me despite sitting literally next to me in band—but he was someone who was just so plainly queer that he didn't have to *say* he was gay to be gay. It was just implied, it was understood. Jonathan was an extreme example, but there were a lot of teenage boys like Ryan Evans in the 2000s: effeminate, clearly uninterested in girls, but not explicitly out to their peers.

But *High School Musical* is a Disney movie, so "let's give gay teens an accurate depiction of their lives" probably wasn't a top-fifty priority for those executives.

As a culture, we do not like the idea that young children have sexual agency. We have a difficult time talking about kids playing doctor or masturbating or being curious or turned on in any way. It's weird, it's gross, it feels borderline predatory and pedophilic to even acknowledge that elementary schoolers have their own sexualities. Even writing about it, I feel a knee-jerk *yikes* on the topic. And it's because of that cringiness, I think, that I never talked about queerness with adults as a kid. It wasn't due to overt homophobia, per se; I don't think my parents and teachers and camp counselors explicitly *didn't* want me to know of or about gay people. Rather, queerness was deemed an inappropriate topic for kids to talk about. Gayness was sex, and sex was something for adults, and thus queerness simply wasn't in my purview as a Catholic nine-year-old.

It's this half-assed logic, I think, that creators like Disney used in the '90s and '00s (and continue to use) to omit queer characters from entertainment. Disney Channel Original Movies might've been about high schoolers, but they were made for elementary schoolers and thus devoid of any sexuality whatsoever. On the rarest occasion, characters engage in chaste, mouth-closed kissing (but nothing more); because straightness—though technically a form of sexuality—is seen as the default setting in our culture, boy-girl kisses are nonthreatening. And since culturally, we hadn't untied the Gay Community in popular society's mind from the image of hedonistic, meth-induced orgies in Berlin sex dungeons, there was no space for gay teenagers on Disney Channel. By merely existing, queerness is disruptive.

And yet, we talk about straightness *all the time* with little kids. Instagram bozos constantly joke about their two-year-old sons being "lady killers!" and preschool-aged boy/girl pairings get called "boyfriend and girlfriend" on the regular. Sure, these kinds of comments are typically facetious, but we're culturally quite comfortable with the notion that our three-foot-tall humans will grow into thriving heterosexuals. In the same sense, DCOM kisses might be rare and close-mouthed, but the movies almost always include a hetero romantic plotline. Even Jennifer and Kelly's *Cadet Kelly* rivalry, the beef that launched a thousand baby queers, is initially sparked over a boy. Andi Carson and Dean Talon don't make out at the end of *Motocrossed*, but the film ends on a freeze-frame of them both in midair on their bikes, flirtatiously racing around the Carsons' backyard motocross course, the Disney equivalent of hard-core pornography. Ryan Evans, the pink Kangol–wearing jazz-squarer, gets a *girlfriend*. In our real lives and on Disney

Channel, talking about sex itself might be cringey, but talking about heterosexuality on the whole is A-OK. All of this behavior teaches kids to perform straightness. And with that, for queer kids, comes massive confusion about how, exactly, to undo that performance.

—

I spent the day of my sister's eighth grade graduation in tears. I was in second grade and was a firm tomboy at this point: my preferred style included corduroys, crewneck sweaters, and the entirety of the Old Navy boys' athletic section. I picked blues and greens and grays over pinks and yellows and purples. Because Zach didn't want his little sister hanging around, I spent nearly every non-school hour with my neighbor, Nat, reading comic books, playing made-up sports (N+G Ball), and "running away from home" to a bush a hundred meters from his house for forty-five minutes, essentially Calvin and Hobbes cosplay (I was the tiger). We formed a band called the Rackets and put on air guitar concerts to the Beatles song "Savoy Truffle" (weird choice) for Nat's mom and Nat's mom alone. We orchestrated massive games of capture the flag with other kids on the block, which spanned four square city blocks and full afternoons. Each summer evening, I'd come home from Nat's sweating profusely and demanding a tall glass of cold milk. (Midwest.) While my parents were all for my boyishness, Rachel's graduation was a *special occasion*. I could wear all the cargo shorts I wanted most days, but when it came to holidays and church events, I had to "look nice," which meant wearing a dress. I'd accepted this, but such an event hadn't yet happened in school. So, for Rachel's graduation, my mother wrangled me into a dress, a little white jumper covered in red cherries. I'd worn a fluffy white gown and a flower crown for my First Communion just weeks earlier, so all things considered, May of 1998 was one of the more femme months of my life.

I recall absolutely nothing of the graduation ceremony or even the party. My heart thuds, though, whenever I think of the moment I entered my second-grade classroom that morning. We were all lining up to go downstairs to the graduation. I wasn't the only one dressed up—other classmates of mine, too, had siblings in eighth grade and were probably going out to lunch with their families afterward. But still, I stood out in my cherry dress. Upon seeing me, my then-friend Danielle, a tiny, blond ballet dancer, stopped dead in her tracks. She gasped, and she pointed at me. "OH. MY GOD." She had a flare for the dramatics. "You're in a *dress*!?" I erupted into tears and continued to heave heavy sobs the whole morning, humiliated not by the fact that I was in a dress but by the fact that my performing femininity was so rare and so note-worthy that it warranted Danielle's devastating point-and-shriek. It's extremely funny to me, in retrospect, how mortified Danielle's theatrics made me feel. This was the first time I recall realizing that other people perceived my gender performance in a certain way and had thoughts about whether or not it was acceptable. To me, this was a quintessentially gay experience.

Despite my mother occasionally forcing me into a dress for photo ops, my parents genuinely seemed to love the fact that I wasn't a girly girl. It was a point of bonding for me with both of them. Sports were always my way into a relationship with my dad, who coached my soccer teams, toted my ass around Chicagoland every weekend for tournaments, and then got extremely into track when I quit team sports and became a runner. My mom, one of the few women in her college journalism school, saw herself in my comfort around boys and in our mutual love for rock—though, ad-mittedly, I was more of a Tom DeLonge girl than she was. I do re-call one rage-filled morning in preschool when my teacher told me how pretty I looked in my dress—I *insisted* it was a big T-shirt and leggings—but my mom denies ever putting me in such a feminine outfit without my enthusiastic consent. I still suspect foul play.

Even with their support, it always felt implied that the tomboy identity was intended to be temporary, inherently juvenile. I remember aunts and parents' friends and friends' parents eyeing my knee-length athletic shorts and orange visor, smiling, and saying, "I was a tomboy when I was a girl, too." Their words were full of approval and support. The second half of that sentence—"but then I grew out of it"—was never actually spoken. It was felt, though. I heard it in the way they wore skirts and blouses and makeup and weren't wearing head-to-toe Cubs gear, like I was. Even those sporting short hair and pants wore makeup and heels and perfume, emitting a feminine aura I never dreamt attainable. Of course, the real problem was that I didn't know any butch women in my life. I got the message that being a girl who dressed masculine was okay as a kid, but wasn't okay as an adult. I learned that the gender expressions of kids and grown-ups were somehow inherently different, that one allowed space for boyishness and the other did not.

⸺

While character aesthetics make *Motocrossed* and *High School Musical* scream gay, it's a character dynamic that does so in *Cadet Kelly* (2002). The movie opens on Kelly (Hillary Duff) performing a ribbon dance at the New York Middle School of the Arts. She's artsy, she's a city kid, she's precocious. Her mom gets remarried, and her new stepfather (played by . . . Gary Cole??) quickly becomes the principal of a military academy upstate. Uh-oh! (It's worth noting that *Cadet Kelly* premiered in March 2002. It was cowritten by a former *Golden Girls* writer and a man who, in 2018, appeared on *Fox & Friends* to promote his book on "the struggle for the soul of the West."[2] Which is to say, it appears *Cadet Kelly* was a post-9/11 patriotism grab on the part of Disney Channel. I digress.)

The movie's central relationship involves not Kelly and a boy but Kelly and her superior officer, Jennifer Stone (Christy Carlson Romano, of Ren Stevens fame). Yes, the majority of female characters in *Cadet Kelly* sport low ponytails and bland, button-up military uniforms. But that's basically heterosexual compared to the Jen-Kelly relationship.

I wish I were being facetious when I write that Hillary Duff and Christy Carlson Romano's sapphic tension is nothing short of electrifying. Electrifying! Captain Stone and Kelly spend at least 50 percent of the film within six inches of each other's faces, lower lips trembling, both seething in adolescent passion. Captain Stone's nickname for Kelly is Maggot, as in, "You're on my list, Maggot." When Captain Stone notices Kelly's nonregulation rainbow blanket (ahem) on her bunk bed, she first steps on it then rips it to shreds. To retaliate, Kelly sneaks into Stone's barracks in the middle of the night and paints her hair rainbow (AHEM). In one particularly tense, wordless scene, the two engage in competitive drill routines, unspeakingly challenging each other to keep up, their eyes locked, intense, throughout. In the end, the two girls perform a special drill routine together, which involves both fake rifles and rainbow ribbons. From *Cadet Kelly*, I've learned that drill team is basically just masc ballroom dancing.

"That's when it hit me," Kelly says via voice-over while first watching the drill team perform, "this was like *Swan Lake*. Only instead of tutus, everyone was wearing uniforms. But still, they were so beautiful." Is this post-9/11 corporate-sponsored US military propaganda, or merely a young girl's quest to undo the compulsory femininity that binds her very soul? Again, I probably didn't think, *Wow, this is classic domme-sub dyke sexual tension!* as I watched *Cadet Kelly* as a sixth grader in the early days of the

War on Terror. But watching the TV movie now, said sapphic energy is impossible to ignore.

Of course, there's nothing explicitly gay about *Cadet Kelly*, nor *Motocrossed*. Like my meltdown over Danielle gawking at my cherry dress, these movies seem queer in hindsight, but at the time merely existed in the girl-power worldview. And these two are far from the only Disney Channel Original Movies that encourage young girls to take on traditionally masculine endeavors—which is to say, sports. *Double Teamed* (2002)—which, despite its title, is not pornography—tells the story of real-life twin sisters and WNBA stars Heidi and Heather Burge. *Go Figure* (2005) is about a (prissy) figure skating prodigy who's forced to join the rough-and-tumble girls' hockey team. *Rip Girls* (2000) is about a girl learning to surf. *Right On Track* (2003) follows two sisters (one of whom portrayed by a near-fetal Brie Larson) who conquer the boys' club of junior drag racing. In 2000s Disney Channel Original Movies, girls were more than allowed to break gender norms and get muddy. It appears that tomboy characters actually really worked for Disney, so much so that they kept cranking out the same formulaic movies over and over again. I mean, *Motocrossed* and *Right On Track* (two movies about girls breaking into motocross and drag racing, respectively) were released just two years apart.

I grew up in a moment when young girls adopting boyish interests—sports and alt-rock and hip-hop and video games and motocross racing, apparently—was completely acceptable. Championed, even! By the time *Motocrossed* premiered, we were hot off '90s Spice Girl mania and the GIRL POWER! the group championed. GIRL POWER! was probably more savvy branding than meaningful feminist messaging, and perhaps because of that, the idea stuck. While flouting girly norms was downright trendy on Disney Channel, the network hosted zero openly gay characters in the '00s. There was a complete disconnect between exhibiting boyishness and established, canonical queerness. With every tomboy character came a male love interest. Disney Channel Original Movies absolutely loved the idea that "Girls can do anything boys can do!" just as long as the "anything" wasn't "girls."

The straight tomboy phenomenon wasn't unique to Disney Channel. Think of Helga Pataki on Nickelodeon's *Hey, Arnold!*: a unibrow-sporting bully whose fists only unclenched for her crush, Arnold. Was Helga boyish? Oh, yes. But she was also aggressively straight, to the point of hiding a shrine to Arnold in her closet. Or there was Ashley Spinelli on *Recess,* a tough girl who wore a beanie and leather jackets, was mortified by her oh-so-feminine first name, and famously lusted for a boy, T.J. Lindsay Weir on *Freaks and Geeks* sported an iconic, non-girly, oversize green coat and made her way through the boys at William McKinley High School. Disney's Mulan is perhaps the ultimate gender-bending tomboy, and she ends up with her burly, mostly shirtless captain, Li Shang (whom the internet has deemed a bi icon).

Yes, I *know* that not all childhood tomboys turn out to be gay. Many outgrow that phase and master contouring makeup by seventh grade, which is a bummer for a whole host of reasons. Others retain their boyishness while also pursuing lifelong partnership with a man. This is fine, technically speaking. And on the other hand, there's a whole host of queer expression ranging from high femme to stone butch, and a million iterations and complications in between. Some absolute dykes played princess as kids; I get it. But it's disingenuous, at best, to completely ignore the relationship between gender expression and queerness, even in childhood. In the case of Disney Channel Original Movies, one could argue they co-opted gay aesthetics, Disneyfied them, and stripped characters of any identifiable, provable elements of their queerness. To believe that *no* masculine girls turn out queer requires active delusion, and turn-of-the-millennium kids' shows churned this narrative out relentlessly.

Disney Channel is far from the first to cherry-pick feminist ideas and abandon lesbians to appeal to a wider base. In fact, the feminist movement dealt with that same struggle internally in the 1960s and 1970s. In 1969, the *Feminine Mystique* author and mother of second-wave feminism, Betty Friedan, referred to the emerging lesbian visibility as the "lavender menace" to the feminist cause.[3] To Friedan, gay women posed a threat to the respectability of feminist politics. Feminism's survival, she argued, depended on distancing itself from the lesbian cause. The movement was fragile, and embracing women-loving women could make the whole feminist movement look like a joke.

Friedan publicly copped to her homophobia at the 1977 National Women's Conference, officially Embracing the Gays, but the damage was done. Friedan had already planted the seed that fighting for queer rights wasn't a requirement of mainstream feminism. We saw Betty Friedan's gay-free feminist agenda on the mass market. By 2000, second-wavers like my mom had families of their own, and the easiest, broadest kind of feminism—GIRL POWER!—had reached the mainstream. But Friedanism, too, had prevailed, and the kind of kid-friendly feminism that achieved Disney Channel status explicitly excluded any open queerness. So, thirty years later, here was Disney Channel, making Christy Carlson Romano engage in light verbal humiliation BDSM with Hillary Duff for middle schoolers' enjoyment, only to give them a mutual male love interest.

So, that's when I became a girl. At a time where gender-bending was encouraged and celebrated, but homophobia still reigned.

By the time I entered puberty, I had a whole slew of straight tomboy characters, and exactly zero gay characters, to admire/fantasize about befriending. These cool "I'm not like the other girls" straight girls of the early aughts hammered this notion into me that being a tomboy—your expression of your gender—had absolutely nothing to do with sexual preference. And to an extent, that's true. Over the past fifty years, feminism has allowed women to dress more androgynously, and such gender-bending isn't reserved for gay women. But my scared-to-be-gay teenage self took that idea a little too far.

That part of me thought—no, hoped—that being a tomboy actually *proved* my straightness. It was too obvious, I thought. It was too on the nose for someone who liked all the things that most boys like to like the gender that most boys like, too. This makes zero logical sense, but a) I was an adolescent, and b) this is what happens to developing brains when gender-bending is celebrated and queerness is frowned upon. (Every queer tween deserves a gold medal in mental gymnastics.) This, along with many internal and external logical cartwheels I've written about, kept my brain fortified against the reality that I was queer for quite some time. It kept me in the closet longer than any kid should be.

While Disney is not the only creator of children's entertainment, it's a massive one, and it continued to fail queer kids through the 2010s. Disney Channel wouldn't have an openly gay series regular until 2019—Cyrus, a tween boy on the show *Andi Mack*.[4] While much of pop culture got gayer throughout the 2010s, Disney didn't embrace the rainbow so much as it gave the rainbow a polite, forced handshake. In 2017, Disney touted an "exclusively gay moment" in its live-action reboot of *Beauty and the Beast;* that turned out to be approximately two seconds of Gaston's side-kick, LeFou, dancing with a man onto whom an enchanted wardrobe forced a dress. *Avengers: Endgame* (2019) featured a man in a support group grieving his husband's loss; he never comes back after that scene. Two women kiss at the Resistance's victory celebration at the end of *Star Wars: The Rise of Skywalker,* which you might miss if you blink. These characters all achieve the bare minimum in terms of representation.[5] Even in the 2020s, Disney is presumably more concerned with losing business in anti-LGBT markets—including ones that have censored and/or banned Disney films with "gay moments"—than with giving kids queer role models. In the 2020 Pixar film *Onward*, Lena Waithe voices a lesbian cyclops/cop (sure) who mentions her girlfriend and then disappears from the rest of the film, in classic Disney form, which got the movie banned in several Middle Eastern countries.[6] These little snippets of "representation" are so quick, so unessential to the plot, they seem tailor-made to be edited out for anti-LGBT markets.

I seemed *super* gay as a child. And it turns out, I'm super gay as an adult. Like Andi in *Motocrossed*, Ryan in *High School Musical*, and Jennifer and Kelly in *Cadet Kelly*, I just, well, *seemed real gay*. Sure, these TV movies had some wink-nudge gayness that a lot of millennial kids picked up on, were drawn to, exhilarated by. But ultimately, the facade that gender performance and sexuality have absolutely nothing to do with each other—the cherry-picked feminism of Disney Channel Original Movies—only pummeled me with further anxiety.

——

I lost my brother Zach to leukemia when he was thirty-one. "You lost your twin," my dad said to me in a big hug, in the first few minutes after he died. Conceding to my insufferable impulse to joke through tragedy, I asked if he was choosing that moment to tell me that Zach and I were in fact twins this whole time, that I was actually two years older than I'd thought this whole time, that we were in a reverse Michael and Lindsay Bluth situation—but no, dad clarified, we were not literally twins. It just felt that way, particularly when we were little.

In the week or so following Zach's death, I spent hours poring over old family photos. Until puberty, the two of us looked nearly identical—same blue/green eyes, same wide, brace-filled smiles, same long, thin noses. In one photo, we're visiting Santa, Zach on one knee and me on the other, both in dark corduroys and long-sleeve, patterned button-ups. (Speaking of "gay in hindsight.") In another, black-and-white, we pressed our foreheads together and smiled, big, at each other. Our physical similarities diverged a bit as we grew up, as did our interests and passions and senses of humor, but looking at those photos, all I could remember was how much I worshiped this guy. Maybe I could cut all my hair off and pass for him; maybe that would bring him back.

One of those long evenings before Zach's funeral, I found a photo of myself on the first day of seventh grade. I'm perched on the mosaic statue outside my grade school, a photo I'd taken every Wednesday after Labor Day for nine years. I'm wearing a look that can, frankly, only be described as Unregulated Baby Dyke Chic: knee-length cargo shorts meet knee-length blue soccer socks, which slide into American-flag Converse All-Stars I'd been trying to scuff up all summer. I'm wearing a tight, child-size T-shirt, which clings to my brand-new breasts. (I knew they were an asset, but I didn't know how to wield them. My best guess was to dig up a T-shirt from a 1995 Lincoln Park Zoo day camp.) It should be no surprise to you, at this point, that I have a messenger bag slung over my right shoulder. I'm smiling through braces, blissfully ignorant to any hairstyle option beyond my middle part and low ponytail. I thought myself very alternative at the time and felt this "punk" outfit reflected my music tastes (I already told you: Weezer) and the fact that, yes, I'd dabbled in skateboarding that very summer. Looking at this image now, it's clear that this thirteen-year-old would imminently harbor an unrelenting crush on someone named Jenny. A still life of a chaotic neutral baby gay.

This photo captures my exact transition from tomboy to someone trying to not be a tomboy any longer. I'd gotten my period
about a month prior. I was indifferent to it, honestly, neither embarrassed of nor particularly jazzed by my momentous step into
womanhood. I was more logistically concerned with the whole
thing, constantly darting my eyes at the clock and scrambling to
the bathroom the second another three hours had passed. I spent
my first period wrangling my bleeding vagina at Sima's family
friends' house in Wisconsin. I simply cannot tell you who owned
the house where I disposed of my first menstrual pads. I can tell
you, though, that Sima and I spent the whole weekend riding mini
dirt bikes through the wooded trails near the house. My general
attitude toward sexual maturity was "Well, here's something I
have to deal with for the next thirty years." And the obvious solu-
tion was, simply, to get on a dirt bike.

AMERICAN BITCH/
AMERICAN BUTCH

Type *butch/femme quiz* into Google and you'll find a smorgasbord of useless questionnaires. Each result takes you to an increasingly bunk website, and each website has a series of multiple-choice tests to determine, officially, your gender identity. One, absolutely littered with pop-up ads for dietary supplements, asked me hard-hitting questions like "Which animal do you relate to the most?" (dog) and "What is your favorite color?" (green, I guess) to discern my levels of butchness and femininity.[1] After eleven questions, I was informed that I'm a femme who takes time with her appearance and likes being chased. Another website, so janky that it caused my laptop to nearly iron my thighs, inquired about my hair and personal style, as well as my favorite color and music choices. That one told me, "You got DYKE!" and that I'm a lesbian who actually prefers to be called a guy. I do take delight in getting occasionally mistaken for a man—it happens whenever my shoulder-length hair is tucked into a beanie—but I had a feeling that one wasn't quite right, either. Yet another quiz on an HTML website asked in white text on a purple background:

When looking for a phone number you are more likely to:
- Call and ask a friend who has it
- Look it up in the phone book
- Look it up in your address book/rolladex [sic]

- Call information
- Skip calling all together [sic]

As you probably suspected, this particular quiz was posted in 1998. By some cosmic act it has eked its way onto the first page of Google search results. [2] Another question asks what piece of technology most intimidates you: the computer, stereo system, VCR, cellular phone, or video games. In fact, there are a hundred such questions, each as outdated and tedious as the last. And yes, I answered all of them. That one told me I'm an "androgyne," the true middle of the road, who has "absolutely no feeling of being femme or butch." I'd found my Goldilocks quiz. *Androgyne* isn't really used so much in queer circles anymore, and now its meaning is more akin to nonbinary or genderqueer than a specific lesbian expression. But I think what this particular, cursed website meant by androgyne is what the gay internet today would jokingly call "futch."

The Futch Scale was popularized on Tumblr in 2018. It's a meme, but like all good memes, it has a kernel of truth to it. The meme sections lesbian expression into categories, each a diamond, on a scale of one through ten. There are seven: high femme (1), femme (2–4), butchy femme (5), futch (5 ½), soft butch (6), butch (7–9), and stone butch (10). Each is a different shade of pink (for the femme side), blue (for the butch side), and purple (for futch). The game: pick a category and place each of its iterations in its corresponding place on the Futch Scale. There's a Winona Ryder futch scale with over twenty-seven thousand notes attached. *Beetlejuice* Winona is a butchy femme; *Girl Interrupted* is a soft butch. The Greek goddesses have been assigned butch/femme scale placements. Bill Hader, too, got the Futch Scale treatment (Stefan is a high femme). And then it gets more abstract and specific and esoteric, with categories that don't exhibit our conventional metrics—hair, voice, clothing—to assess gender identity. The phone charger futch scale puts the iPhone 4 charger into the femme category, where the iPhone 6-and-up charger is a high femme, and a good ol' USB is a butch.

Wow, visual memes are *deeply* unfunny in word form. Please, I beg you, go Google *futch scale* and get back to me.

Okay, thank you.

Anyway, to me, not only does the meme showcase these labels' goofiness, but it also proves that our conception and processing of gender expression is instinctive and often unexplainable. When it comes to pasta, I can't tell you *why* lasagna is a butchy femme and orecchiette is a high femme, but in my bones, that feels right. An espresso Frappuccino doesn't need to be wearing a three-piece suit, cracking its knuckles, and hopping on a motorcycle for me to understand that, in the context of Starbucks Frappuccinos, the espresso variety is a stone butch. *Obviously* a USB plug is a butch. Maybe it's its boxiness compared with the iPhone chargers' rounded edges, the comparative delicateness of Apple's Micro USB-B connector—I don't know, it's just *true*. Gender is often only identifiable in context, in relation to other phone chargers or Starbucks drinks.

Maybe I'm getting ahead of myself, assuming that the concepts of *butch* and *femme* and permutations therein are part of every reader's basic cultural lexicon, the way they are for me and all my queer friends. Even if you get the gist of them, these terms hold history: the dichotomy of butches and femmes refers to a specific subset of lesbian identities born out of working-class bar culture in the 1940s, '50s, and '60s.[3] The dynamic doesn't (and didn't) refer to all lesbian identities or relationships.

In many ways, in midcentury lesbian culture, butch/femme mirrored traditional gender roles: the butch was the breadwinner, the tough one, the emotional fortress. Their aesthetic could be (very generally) identified as white T-shirts, denim pants, work boots, leather jackets, gold chains, and, yes, motorcycles. James Dean and Marlon Brando are huge butch icons, their faces as smooth as their pickup lines. Bruce Springsteen has major butch lesbian energy, too. Butches didn't pass as men to femmes or other butches, but some presented masculinity to the point of passing as men to those outside of the lesbian community who held the reins of power (male employers). Butchness isn't just about clothes; it's a swagger, a confidence, a tough-kid attitude.

Butch and femme were (and are) both heightened expressions of masculine and feminine identities, almost camp, like traditional gender identity in a funhouse mirror. Where the butch was masculine, the femme takes the more traditionally feminine role: a domestic nurturer, more emotionally expressive and available, with sweetness where the butch has swagger. Femmes could more easily blend in with straight cultural aesthetics, but generally they sported long hair and makeup more done up than any straight girl. It was this heightened version of aesthetic femininity that tipped off other female queers that they were playing for the same team. Obviously, sex between a butch and a femme was focused entirely on female pleasure (they're lesbians), but the femme's orgasm took center stage. Instead of dressing to the nines to pleasure men, femmes were doing it up to get banged out. Wonderful.

Beyond feeling true to their internal gender, butches had plenty of valid reasons to present as butch: namely, to earn a living (whether they passed as men or were simply inviting their employers to treat them like men) and to protect themselves, their femmes, and their communities. They were tough, they were scrappy, they could win the respect of men of their class through brute strength. Indeed, in blue-collar pre-Stonewall America, having a butch partner might've been the only way to survive in a lesbian partnership.[4] It's been argued that the butch/femme dynamic made queer women visible and autonomous, paving the path to lesbian liberation;[5] it took lesbians out of the whispered, discreet upper-class femme-femme romance we see depicted in *Carol* (2015) and *Portrait of a Lady on Fire* (2019) and into public spaces.

The seminal novel *Stone Butch Blues* (1993) paints a vivid portrait of life as a butch around this time.[6] It's largely autobiographical, with narrator Jess's life of butchness and labor organizing in upstate New York closely mirroring author Leslie Feinberg's, and is heralded for documenting blue-collar lesbian life in the '60s and '70s. In it, the butch/femme dynamic is presented as comprising two inherently different archetypes: the butch wears work boots, the femme wears heels. The butch is an emotional rock, the femme coaxes her out of her shell. The butch drinks beer on the couch, the femme cooks dinner. The butch is the giver of sexual pleasure, the femme is the receiver. The relationship is played as a symbiotic one, too, where the butch protects the femme against the cops, assaulters, and rapists who always come swinging, and the femme nurses her butch back to health. (The word *tender* appears on what feels like every page of *Stone Butch Blues*.) Indeed, it's suggested that these two types are jigsaw pieces, that they complete each other. For much of the book, Jess is deeply entrenched in the butch/femme dynamic and is repulsed when a butch friend, Frankie, reveals she's in a relationship with another butch. Toward the end, Jess undoes her bias, suggesting that the author themself might not be all that married to the butch/femme dichotomy, either.

Then the '70s came, along with the institutionalization of women's studies and the rise of lesbian feminism. Central to the '70s and '80s feminist movement was a call for the end of traditional gender roles. But that didn't just apply to straight people—that meant lesbians, too. Influential lesbian theorists, including Adrienne Rich, critiqued the butch/femme dynamic, arguing it simply "role-plays" heteronormative relationships (and thus, misogynist power dynamics) and is, therefore, damaging to women.[7] As Feinberg documents in *Stone Butch Blues,* around this time the butch/femme dyke bar scene was diluted with college lesbians who fit neither archetype. Such college gays adopted a more androgynous presentation—what Tumblr would call "futch"—as part of the wider, rising feminist argument that performative femininity only exists to serve men. Butch culture, increasingly criticized for parroting patriarchal male culture, became devalued within the lesbian world. It wasn't until the late '80s and '90s that gender theorists argued the butch/femme dynamic, while mirroring male/female roles, was actually an inversion of patriarchal norms—as Gayle Rubin writes, "a deployment and manipulation of masculine gender codes"—and created economic sustainability for gay women, ultimately serving no men at all.[8]

The butch/femme dynamic is alive and well today; it just looks a bit different from how it did in the '50s. In April 2020, *T,* the *New York Times* style magazine, ran a cover story headlined, "The Butches and Studs Who've Defied the Male Gaze and Redefined Culture,"[9] which featured a photoshoot of notable butches looking sharp as hell: Eileen Myles in a thirty-five-hundred-dollar Gucci blazer, Lea DeLaria in an emerald jacket and a mohawk, Roxane Gay in a poof coif and a Cheshire Cat smile. The photo spread, to me, felt like a direct response to a question asked in op-eds throughout the 2010s: "Where have all the butches gone?" Those op-eds were usually written by what online queers call trans-exclusionary radical feminists, or TERFs. The general TERF argument is that the rise of trans visibility and rights somehow detracts from the rights of cis lesbians; more specifically, it's the backward thought that the existence of trans men somehow detracts from the butch community, that what they would cast as "becoming a man" is an act of treachery to womankind, ignoring the ways those '60s butches, too, grappled with questions of gender identity. But here the butches were in *T*, culture-defining butches across racial and gender boundaries, en masse, smiling and, most important, looking hot. As if to say, "Yes, hello, we're right here."

It's not that butches don't exist anymore; it's just that our gender vocabulary has widened. In midcentury queer culture, *butch* was a word that had a big umbrella and included people who identified as women, or "he-shes" (a self-identifier that has fallen out of fashion), or transgender men with full beards and thick biceps, or people who didn't feel they fell into any gender bucket at all. In the 1990s, we began to change how we talked about butches, as transgender studies emerged in academia and butch aesthetics became more visible in pop culture. Judith Butler's 1990 text, *Gender Trouble*, characterized gender as a performance, and butchness as one that subverted heteronormative expectations of womanhood.[10] *Stone Butch Blues* was published in 1993, and that same year, *Vanity Fair* ran a cover with (straight) supermodel Cindy Crawford giving butch musician k.d. lang a hot shave.[11] Ellen DeGeneres, soft butch of note, came out in '97. As the word *transgender* was popularized in the mid '90s, the *T* became attached to the LGB. Since then, we've given names to a lot of those gender identities that once fell under the large umbrella of *butch*. We now have more specific, more accurate names for gender identities. Butches of *Stone Butch Blues* might today elect descriptors like masculine-of-center, transmasculine, nonbinary, genderqueer, gender-nonconforming—though not all of those last three are necessarily butches. Look, no one said gender was *uncomplicated*. Today, some butches identify as women, and some don't, but they're very much here.

Since the '90s, too, the shades of expression we now see in the Futch Scale meme emerged. As more women of all sexualities dressed more androgynously, far more categories of expression in between butch and femme emerged. As I found on that janky internet quiz from 1998, the notion of butch/femme as a spectrum rather than a dichotomy had emerged by the turn of the millennium. A high femme or a stone butch would fall on the outermost ends of the scale, while the "soft" qualifier is a step closer to a total middle ground. For the record, *futch* appeared on that meme as a joke, which some Tumblr queers then adopted as a genuine identity label, as Tumblr queers are wont to do. Once, I went on a Tinder date with a girl whose profile read *futch4futch*. We both showed up in black jeans, a white tank/tee, white sneakers, and a denim jacket. We never spoke again, which is weird, because wasn't our matching exactly what she wanted?

Today, butch/femme exists as both a dichotomy *and* as a spectrum for millennials. Our generation has both embraced the dichotomy 1970s lesbian feminists sought to undo and also taken on a whole spectrum of queer identities, as evidenced by the Futch Scale. It's a smorgasbord of queer gender performance out there, and it seems like everyone around me knows exactly which smorgas they'd like from the bord. They declare themselves futch, they put it in their Tinder profile, and continue their lives as a confident futch living a futch life. The spectrum offers choice and so many choose definitively, whereas I feel no strong connection to any of those possible identifications. It's hard not to compare myself with those self-assured queers. And when I do, I'm riddled with an anxiety-provoking reprise: If I don't know where I fall on the gender spectrum, am I a bad queer?

———

I spent my youth opting for baggy athletic shorts over skirts. In fourth grade, I simply adored—*adored*—a pair of L.L.Bean jeans lined with flannel inside. I felt sports proved my self-worth (*clinks glass* hello, once again, I was on a *travel* soccer team). And I desperately—*desperately*—sought my older brother, Zach's approval, hence our wearing matching corduroys and flannel button-ups to see Santa in 1997. But I rarely saw adult women who dressed like me. Where, I wondered, were all the grown-up tomboys? I'd find an early answer to this in one of my all-time favorite movies, *Best in Show* (2000).

The Christopher Guest mockumentary follows five couples and their dogs as they compete in the fictional Mayflower Dog Show. It's pure Guest, a much-improvised fake doc with rich and ridiculous characters, like Parker Posey as a high-strung Weimaraner owner who verbally assaults a pet store owner; Cookie Fleck née Guggleman (Catherine O'Hara), who can't stop running into guys she's banged; and Fred Willard's Buck Laughlin, the clueless dog show announcer with perfect one-liners like "He went after her like she's made of ham!" Jack and I watched it constantly in middle school, the same era of our *Real World/Road Rules Challenge* obsession. Partially because we were simply addicted to dogs and the extended dog universe, but also because, similarly to *Mean Girls,* its humor was *just barely* in my intelligence range, and self-satisfaction makes everything funnier.

I think Jack and I, too, were drawn to *Best in Show* because of its two openly gay couples. First there's Scott and Stefan (John Michael Higgins and Michael McKean). Scott is a joyous gay troll, and Stefan, his adoring, albeit tamer, partner. In his opening scene at the butcher shop, Scott asks the meat guy for a pepperoni stick because, in his words, "I just wanna hold it." Later, sporting a red satin button-up and a *HELLO, I'M MARY* sticker, he introduces his partner to another couple, "This is my euphemism, Stefan." He's campy and kind of mean and seems to have genuine fun freaking straight people out; this was an important thing to see as a young queer. But more profound for me were Sherri Ann Cabot and

Christy Cummings (Jennifer Coolidge and Jane Lynch). In fact, *Best in Show* was my first substantial encounter with the butch/femme dichotomy.

Christy and Sherri Ann aren't technically a couple for most of the movie, but they function as such. They're not a *will-they-won't-they* but more of a *I-think-they-are-aren't-they?-oh-shit-they-are!* Christy handles Sherri Ann's prized poodle, Rhapsody in White, aka Butch (ahem), who's a two-time Mayflower winner and is going for blue ribbon number three. In looks and style, they're a classic butch/femme pairing. With short, spiky blond hair and an array of over-shoulder-padded sports coats, Christy is obviously the butch—one of the competition's announcers mistakes her for a man during the final round of judging. Her butchness isn't just in her style but in her masculine intensity. She runs and wrestles with Butch, pumps her fists, grins a boyish smirk, and laughs a low laugh. She's cocky not only because she handles a champion, but well, because she's butch. It's a role that could've been played more cartoonish in hands less deft than those of Jane Lynch, who is openly gay herself.

Sherri Ann, on the other hand, is a bisexual femme send-up of Anna Nicole Smith. Like the late supermodel, Sherri's married to a wealthy two-hundred-ish-year-old man named Leslie, who has zero lines in the movie. "We could not talk or talk for hours," Sherri says of her husband, "and still find things to not talk about." In every single scene, Sherri Ann is done up to the nines: big hair, bigger heels, bright colors, tight skirts, a French manicure, and a made-up face with big, sticky-looking, glossy lips. She's so feminine that it's campy, more like a drag queen than Princess Diana. Their dynamic is quintessentially butch/femme, too. In an opening talking head, the two women describe their "family," them and Butch: Sherri calls Christy, "Mr. Punishment" with Butch, while Sherri's role is to provide unconditional love and decorating abilities. "The heart and soul, you know? Which is what my mother did," Christy says of how Sherri provides for Butch. "And it worked for our family. Until my mom committed suicide in '81." Apart from that last bit, it's a butch/femme breakdown that could've been ripped straight from *Stone Butch Blues*. Christy Cummings is not so dark and sad and broken like Jess but of equal intensity, all of which is poured into handling Rhapsody in White.

Indeed, Christy and Sherri Ann are part of the decades-long tradition of butch/femme courtship. Their partnership is ostensibly over a poodle, but they flirt throughout, the femme's husband absolutely nowhere to be seen. Christy calls her boss "the epitome of glamor," and Sherri Ann insists on doing the handler's makeup for the dog show. Their romance goes unspoken and unconfirmed until Rhapsody in White wins the nonsporting group, getting the "family" one step closer to winning Best in Show. Christy, dressed "like a cocktail waitress on an oil rig," celebrates with an aggro fist-pump and a salute that would make the marines look like seamstresses. She rushes over to Sherri Ann, takes her in her arms, and ravenously makes out with her. "Rhapsody has two mommies," quips Scott in disbelief. Six months later the two are openly coupled, creating a magazine called *American Bitch: The Dog Magazine for Women and Their Dogs*. Christy describes it as "a focus on the issues of the lesbian purebred dog owner." Which is, in the film's final minutes, the first time the word *lesbian* is uttered.

Despite myself, I became obsessed with Christy and Sherri Ann, Christy in particular. Partially because they're both genius comedic actors—I've parroted Lynch's reading of *American Bitch* more times than there are numbers—but partially, well, you know why. Here was an adult who hadn't, like the other women in my life, grown out of her tomboy phase. It was exciting and also kind of frightening. I was captivated by her, but I definitely didn't want her to win, and I was definitely unclear on how and why Sherri Ann was drawn to her sexually. After all, Christy is the villain of *Best in Show*. Rhapsody in White, the two-time champion, is the agreed upon dog to beat, and Christy's overconfidence doesn't make her one to root for. After sweet Harlan Pepper from Pinenut, North Carolina, wins the hound group, she deliberately tries to psych him out. "I'm Christy Cummings. But you probably know that," she says through a sinister laugh. Associating gender-bending qualities with the Bad Guy didn't exactly inspire middle school me to want to carry on gender-bending. It felt like I was seeing a future version of myself, and it scared me.

Best in Show was a fairly niche film for a twelve-year-old to get into, and while I loved it, I'm not sure it paints a broad picture of where the Culture was at in the early aughts. *Saturday Night Live* can often help us place where liberal America's mind is at any given time, and the sketch "Queer Eye for the Straight Gal" can do just that for lesbiansism.[12] The initial run of the Bravo makeover show premiered in July 2003 and had apparently made enough of a splash to get the *SNL* treatment by that October. The sketch imagines an all-lesbian fab five—played by Amy Poehler, Rachel Dratch, Maya Rudolph, writer Paula Pell, and host Jack Black—making over helpless straight lady Tina Fey. They're all butch clichés: Mona Napoletano (Dratch) is a shredded leather jacket and bolo-tie-wearing "fashion expert" who suggests flannels for every occasion. Khabeira Jones (Rudolph), the culture expert, slams a djembe, tells Tina to forego pubic hair grooming, and performs slam poetry about the birth canal. Pam's (Poehler) specialty is simply softball. The sketch writers' take is summarized, as commercial parodies often are, in the fake review pull quotes: "Not as fun as the one with the guys," and "Untelegenic and weirdly humorless." These are women I grew up worshiping (sorry, Jack Black)—the women of Debbie Downer and "bitch is the new black!" and *Mean Girls*—so it's fair to say I took their assessment of gay women as gospel. It's a deep bummer to revisit, and yet, I can't help laughing at Tina Fey saying, "You guys would know something about tearing up carpet!" Like with *Mean Girls,* I find myself loving some comedy that doesn't quite love me back.

Somehow, butchness was simultaneously unseen on television *and* the prevailing, scary stereotype of how lesbians are. That idea permeated into my real life. It was the kind of queerness my friends and I grew up mocking. "I had to beg my mom not to get a dyke chop when she turned forty," a friend told me freshman year of high school. My college was rife with handsome cis gay guys, but visible queerness—butchness and transness—was limited, even a rarity. There was one long-haired skater butch who strictly fucked straight sorority girls, but beyond her, the hot, grown tomboys on campus felt hard to find.

Butchness was mocked in pop culture, and in that context butchness was synonymous with lesbianism, and so lesbianism was therefore being mocked. When it premiered in 2004, *The L Word* garnered uneven reviews—*The New Yorker* did, in fact, call portions of it "truly idiotic"—but where many critics agreed was that the show was doing some great service to queer women in not showing butches on-screen.[13] "All the women are beautiful," wrote the *New York Times* review, "which on the one hand works to dismiss the stereotype of lesbians as squat, plaid-shirted and mannish."[14] Here, beautiful and feminine are implied to be synonymous. "After years of living down our dumpy reputation, perhaps it behooves us to put our best, most made-up faces forward, for a change," wrote *New York* magazine in January 2004.[15] "I mean, how many 'anomalous' dykes does it take to prove to straights and gay boys that not all lesbians wear bolo ties and Birkenstocks? After *The L Word,* the answer will, one hopes, be zero." The relief that so many reviewers saw in *The L Word*'s all-femme cast was in itself a rebuke of butchness. Was that really any better than "Queer Eye for the Straight Gal"?

When I watched *Best in Show* as a tween and teen, I remember finding Christy predatory and cartoonish, but revisiting the film, that's really not true. Jane Lynch gives Christy some softness and realness that make the handler far more than a butch cliché. And it's not like Christy doggedly (har-har) pursues Sherri Ann without her consent; the femme is absolutely complicit in her affair with her employee. It's sad, then, that by the time I first saw *Best in Show* in sixth or seventh grade, I already had coupled butch presentation and the "lecherous lesbian" stereotype in my own mind. I went back to *Best in Show* thinking it'd be some root of my determination to lean away from butchness but found that it just represented something I'd previously internalized even as a tomboy, roughhousing with Nat from across the alley and donning head-to-toe boys' section athletic wear.

⌐

I spent high school as a lapsed tomboy. I finally fully shopped in girls' and women's sections, but never quite figured out dresses and makeup and, you know, the whole deal. Luckily, my high school's dress code included knee-length skirts and collared shirts, so no one was exactly the ideal of cool femininity in class. Sports remained core to my sense of self-worth, but I stayed out of trees and got a new gaggle of girls (and closeted gay dudes) with whom to gossip 24/7. I had virtually no close straight male friends, no one like Nat, which was fine and is still fine today. But I retained that sense that something within me needed to change. I still associated femininity with womanhood and tomboyishness with childhood. And therefore, I thought girliness was something I would inevitably grow into. Or, ideally, that a switch would flip within me, and one birthday, I'd understand how to properly apply blush.

That happened, in a way. The 2009 Grace Perry pivot to femme—known colloquially (in my head) as my Jenny Lewis-cosplay days—was a direct result of me coming out as queer. Suddenly, I wore dresses to class.

There were two reasons for the flip, both of which boil down to internalized homophobia, likely seeded by jokes like "Queer Eye for the Straight Gal." The first was that I'd finally identified the kind of person I wanted, and I suddenly craved girls' attention. Which is to say, I wanted to look *hot*. And I wanted other girls to think I was hot. And, without any real examples of sexy androgynous and/or butch women to go off of (see my next essay for thoughts on Shane McCutcheon's style choices), in my mind, hot = femme. I was mostly attracted to feminine girls, and because I lacked a sense of core self-awareness of my gender expression—though one could argue that from puberty on, my gender identity was "desperately crawling away from tomboyhood"—hotness meant femininity.

Secondly, visible couples like Ellen and Portia as well as Lindsay Lohan and Sam Ronson reinforced what I'd "learned" from *Best in Show*—that being gay meant I had to pick between butch and femme. As I didn't *really* feel like either, this was daunting and confusing to me. Sure, I'd been a tomboy as a kid, but I wasn't aggressively boyish in the same way now. Plus, I'd had so many examples thrust in my face of girly women who'd gone through their own "tomboy phase." And I'd internalized butchness as less of a valid identity than as the butt of *SNL* jokes. I sensed a butchness in myself but feared any association with masc-of-center-ness, or being "that kind of lesbian."

Post–women's movement, wearing pants and leather jackets and button-ups and sneakers is absolutely innocuous for women—as long as you're straight. (Bolo ties are still unforgivable for any non-Texan.) Yet when I came out, I suddenly became hyperaware of my clothing choices and overall gender presentation, far more than I had been when I was assumed straight—and I was pissed about it. I resented the fact that my gender presentation wasn't even something I had to consider whatsoever until I became visibly gay.

Consider the flannel. I went to a New England liberal arts college where nearly half the school was in mountain club. This meant every girl on campus owned a flannel shirt, myself included. I simply didn't think anything about flannel before I came out. But suddenly, with my queerness elevated from *suspected* to *confirmed*, I wasn't just a girl in a flannel shirt anymore; I was a lesbian in a flannel shirt. I'd gone (in my mind, at least) from innocuous to cliché. Now when I opened my shirt drawer, I saw Rachel Dratch in a bolo tie telling me my plaid button-up would be a great choice for my sister's wedding or my meeting with the adoption agency.

I noticed that straight girls could dress as boyish as they pleased without representing their entire identity group. No one's looking through a Madewell catalog like "Wow, a whole booklet of masculine women!" even though they pretty much sell traditionally male clothing for women. This is in part because femininity isn't just about what clothes you're wearing but about your hair and your makeup and your vocal timbre and the way you carry your body. It's about being a boxy USB cable of a person. But still, the swath of what women are "allowed" to wear, when compared to men, is quite vast. Everyone from Blake Lively to Halle Berry to Amy Poehler have worn suits on the red carpet in recent years—albeit, with makeup and jewelry and feminine cuts. (The spectrum of acceptable clothing choices for men has been widening in recent years, thanks in part to the femme red carpet stylings of entertainers like Billy Porter and Harry Styles.) Skating around the butch/femme spectrum stylistically has become so routine for straight women that they don't even consider it an identity marker.

But for college-aged gay me, the boyishness I'd exuded as a straight girl suddenly read as butch, which scared me. That fear fueled my pivot away from the gender expression that I truly felt drawn to. I gave myself just one option: be femme.

And so, for a few years in there, I "got into dresses." I flatironed my hair and penciled on (unfortunate) eyeliner before going to the library. When I wasn't in track clothes (spandex), I was put together and smelled like lilac and maybe, *maybe* wore a headband? (Forgive me, *Gossip Girl* was in its third season.) Heels were attempted, albeit infrequently and with little success after forty-five minutes. It was the first time in my life I spent more than fifteen minutes getting ready for my day. I'd made a decision: I might be a queer girl, but dammit, I was going to be a *girly* queer girl. (I'm certain, now, that the whole aesthetic did not come off as particularly effortless.)

You think it'd be the other way around—that I'd femme myself up to stay in the closet—and I think, for a lot of queers, it is. But instead, openly gay, I felt a presumption of masculinity looming closer. So, I spent one frigid Boston winter wearing skirts and tights up and down the hill, sacrificing feeling my thighs in hopes of avoiding my certain fate. In a way, I envied, and still envy, straight women for their sheer unawareness of the butch/femme spectrum, their lack of self-awareness of where their gender expression falls on a scale of one to ten, the way flannel makes them appear "chill" and not "scathingly gay."

My pivot to femme petered out by the end of college. Frankly, I just got tired of putting the effort in and also never really mastered heels. I've learned I read as extremely gay to queer women, but sometimes I have to tip gay guys and straights off to it. (I mentioned this to a bisexual friend recently, and she choked on her orange wine, utterly baffled by a human not reading my aesthetic as gay.) I spent much of my twenties feeling like I was too femme to be butch and too butch to be femme. Then I embraced the power of the funky-patterned, short-sleeved button-up: a surefire signal of queerness that felt true to my middle school tomboy self. I started to feel like myself, and yet, I still felt no strong sense placement on the Futch Scale.

Around the same time the Futch Scale meme blew up in 2018, so, too, did Personals. Personals was an Instagram page, and a precursor to the dating app Lex. Both are lo-fi ways for queer women, trans people, intersex people, asexual women, and gender non-conforming people to connect. Basically, it's a dating app that's not for straight and/or cis men. I became aware of Personals when a date mentioned it to me offhand. My unfamiliarity with the hot new way to get laid made me feel decrepit, so I followed the account, hoping to stave off my inevitable aging/mortality. Instagram users would submit a one-hundred-character bio (and five dollars) to Personals, along with a catchy headline and their Instagram handle. Here's a template for 90 percent of Personals posts I'd see:

[FOUR VAGUE/DISCONNECTED WORDS]
[age] [race] [placement on the futch scale] [gender identity]
[sexual identity] witchy [zodiac sun sign] [fat if applicable]
[zodiac rising sign] [zodiac moon sign]. ISO [top/bottom/
switch] to my [top/bottom/switch]. [more kink terminology I
don't fully understand]. Cuddles required. Looking to move
west.
[Instagram handle]
[location]

"27-year-old femme switch bottom, Gemini with Taurean tendencies." Or, "Soft butch ISO femme top of my dreams. Scorpio sun, dreamy Piscean moon. Be tender with me." It was glaringly obviously obvious that labels, while not particularly important to my own sense of sexual identity, are crucial to many others, or at least to lots of Personals posters. I yearned for some kind of mystical amulet to decode it all. I was twenty-eight and felt old. I questioned whether the barrage of identity labels reflected a poster's attachment to them, or if we were all just falling in line with the formula others presented, thinking the information mattered to potential suitors. Posts rarely offered any sense of the submitter's personality, and I would usually just scroll through their Instagram profile and make a split-second assessment of their attractiveness. Was this really any different from a photo-forward dating app?

But I was single, already sick of apps, and intrigued by the options of lo-fi dating, so I thought to give it a whirl. Six Mondays straight, I jotted down the same to-do on my weekly list: WRITE PERSONALS AD. I must've written twenty drafts of my Personals post, each of them more embarrassing to me than the last. My existential crisis was real: *Am I a top or bottom? Butch or femme? But wait—soft butch? Hard femme? Stone butch? High femme? Futch? Would a self-deprecating dig make me sound more approachable or genuinely self-destructive? Am I even queer enough to post a Personals ad? Is a string of buzzwords + expressing a desire to cook omelets while holding hands any more authentic than just a photo of my big, dumb face? I can totally encapsulate something as vast and malleable and adaptable as human sexuality to a hundred-character post, right?*

As I tried to draft my Personals post, I kept trying to find my place on that goddamn Futch Scale meme. And when I couldn't, I felt sad that there was some supposedly core sense of my own identity that I didn't have a handle on. As millennials have embraced both the butch/femme dichotomy *and* the butch/femme spectrum, that means there are seemingly infinite permutations of gender expression, all of which are complicated by the butch/femme scale placement of our partners at any given time. With all that, for me, comes a whole heap of anxiety.

A lot of people get a lot of strength from these identities, these words. There's power to the fact that butch aesthetics are esoteric, that they aren't *for* cis/straight people. There's power in subverting the world's expectations for how we look and dress, the cars we drive and the timbre of our voices, who we fuck. Not like, a theoretical, nose-in-*Gender-Trouble,* Women's Studies power—*actual* power, personal and intimate and soul-affirming and confidence-raising. Dressing femme to the nines and then hanging on the arm of another woman all night—a fuck-you to straight men—can feel electrifying. And butch confidence, the grit to invert every traditional way a woman is supposed to look, is wholly contagious. Gender labels of all kinds can mean freedom: they can help us define our communities, bring us comfort, and make us feel like our true selves, whatever that means. They're very often fought for—especially for trans and gender nonconforming people—and the strength they offer is deemed worth the struggle. But I do think our obsession with identity labels implies such things are stagnant, perhaps even permanent, which is both incorrect and, like most bad ideas, limiting.

It's not that I'm completely ignorant of my gender presentation or that I don't consider it constantly in the way most queer people do. Ultimately, my gender identity is "probably somewhere around futch, but is that even a real thing, I don't know, whatever" (and just getting to identify/shirk identification like that is an enormous, albeit brainless-sounding, privilege). It's similar, and probably related, to my indifference to identifying as gay or queer or a lesbian. But beyond that, my Futch Scale placement is fluid and often contradicts itself. How I dress and act and react depends so much on who I'm with on that day or how I feel that week or what

I happen to have in my childhood closet to wear to my family's Christmas Eve party. If I'm the one dyke at the bachelorette party, sure, I'll wear a ridiculous short dress. But bright suiting has become my wedding outfit of choice. I love short shorts. If I had my way, I would never remove my chunky white Reeboks. Lacing up Doc Martens gives me a cocky self-assurance; a lacy bra makes me feel the same way. Once, a girlfriend and I both wore baseball caps to a party. The host, a bi girl, roasted both of us. "You can't *both* be the one in the flat-brim!" she said, a little drunk. I half-heartedly defended our choices of headwear but removed mine, blaming the Chicago August heat and the packed apartment.

Being queer is complicated for many reasons, not least of which is that I can't write a dating app profile without falling into a gender identity existential black hole. What I really wanted was to post nine different Personals ads: one for me on first dates, one for me in long-term relationships, one for me around girls butcher than me, one for me around femmes, one for when I'm in bed watching *Grey's Anatomy* and playing Candy Crush, one for me in five years if my five-year career plan works out, one for me when my five-year plan inevitably fails, one for how people on Twitter see me, and one for me ordering at a coffee shop, disassociating and spiraling into automated midwestern polite mode, rattled with anxiety but outwardly kind. I found the thought of nailing my personality down into one, knowable, static lump overwhelming and tragic, and the notion that this is where queer dating was going whether I liked it or not was a particular anxiety-stoker.

I agonized over my Personals post for much of the summer of 2018 and finally landed on an ad I liked: "LET'S MAKE OUT!" Simple, elegant, no horoscope signs or markers of identification other than a desire to kiss. But I never submitted it. I'd become

TALKING / LAUGHING / LOVING / BREATHING

About ninety seconds after I came out to one person, I decided the time had come for me to watch *The L Word*.

More accurately, I decided I could allow myself to watch women having sex with each other, and thus, that I needed to watch *The L Word*. During one fateful lunch hour, alone in my dorm room, I embarked on an odyssey of which Homer could never dream: streaming an off-air TV show in a pre-Netflix world. I plugged my MacBook into the Ethernet and searched, with some shame, *L Word season one watch online*. I found it on a now-defunct website that featured a URL with at least twelve periods, copy written in broken English, and an assault of pop-ups I deemed worth it to see Jennifer Beals in (only) a bra. The potential of losing my entire semester of coursework to a devastating computer virus was no match for my queer, virginal curiosity. My thirst could weather all buffering. And so, with my roommate safely in class, I watched Jenny Schecter's lesbian awakening, bit by bit, alone in my dorm room.

The main thing about sex on *The L Word*: there is, objectively, far too much of it. Ilene Chaiken's seminal series is an embarrassment of orgasms. They are, frankly, unrelenting. Soulful sex to Tracy Chapman in marital beds. Fingerbanging in the pool. Fingerbanging in the coffee shop bathroom. Oral in the writing studio daybed. Whipped cream licked off bodies on the kitchen floor. Strap-on sex in a glamping tent. There is at least one, and typically more like three, sex scenes per episode, the vast majority of which, as you'd expect, are girl-on-girl, so at least there's that. The onslaught of frottage is well documented in reviews of the pilot episode, and critics were quick to question who all that sex was really for. The *New York Times* review of the series premiere in 2004, titled "Women Having Sex, Hoping Men Tune In," was a thousand-word eye roll published in the paper of record.[1] Of the "steamy scenes of women making love," the review reads, "While ostensibly celebrating the lesbian life, the two-hour pilot is in such a rush to pander to male viewers that at times it seems less like an American television show than a hastily dubbed Swedish 'art' film."

The *Times* was far from alone in making that observation. "Perhaps Showtime hopes the sex, explicit and frequent, will help [keep viewership]," wrote *TIME*.[2] "Some advance buzz has even hailed the show's well-coiffed, model-perfect cast for breaking lesbian stereotypes of buzz cuts and Birkenstocks. But anyone who thinks that improbably beautiful women who get it on under flattering light are not lesbian stereotypes has not watched much straight-male porn." *The L Word* was applauded for erasing butch stereotypes, as if butchness were a destructive myth concocted to tarnish the concept of lesbianism on the whole.

But nineteen-year-old me wasn't a TV critic, just a kid desperate for some sexual guidance. Though the series had just concluded a few months before I started my viewing, I'd never seen it, as it's riddled with the aforementioned sex. (I told myself I'd get in trouble if my parents saw me watching it, a fear that mysteriously didn't keep me from devouring *Sex and the City*.) For new viewers, the sexual deluge is the partial delight of season one, particularly of watching it as a baby gay, particularly a baby gay who lived in near-literal fear of pornography, like myself. I hadn't watched any porn at that point. Outwardly, I'd adopted an Andrea Dworin–

esque "all pornography is bad" feminist ethos, which was a convenient way of blanketing my own sexual uncertainty-cum-Catholic guilt. But in my late teens, I had the nagging suspicion that lesbian porn might actually be good for one specific woman: me. In those days, I saw *The L Word* as a Rosetta Stone of the world of lesbian sex.

None of my friends knew I was watching *The L Word*—I was too embarrassed to tell them. Though I'd befriended lots of gay guys, I lacked queer girl friends to watch it with. But now, watching *The L Word*, I felt like I knew some lesbians. I got to see gay women with perfect, flat stomachs and perky breasts of proportional smallness fight and fuck and fall in love and, in one particularly cursed plotline, kill an old dog to get another woman's attention. I saw Jenny Schecter get lured out of the closet by a European sexpot the show promptly discards after season one. I was envious of Jenny and wondered why my coming out process felt absolutely nothing like hers. I allowed myself, with detached caution, to explore queer blogs like Autostraddle and AfterEllen, and got to witness writers demand Shane McCutcheon bulldoze them. I wondered what the Shane appeal was, and why all these internet lesbians unabashedly thirsted for a woman who, as *The New Yorker* published in 2004, "has the worst-looking, most unkempt hair in the history of television."[3]

The women in *The L Word* weren't anything like me. They were adults with jobs and flawless bodies, who were trying to have babies and wore T-shirts over button-up blouses and paperboy hats. The thing we had in common was, you know, that big thing. And then, right as Marina pushed Jenny up against the bathroom wall in pulp frenzy, I'd hear my roommate fiddle with our doorknob, snap my laptop shup, and pretend to pore over a bio textbook, creating a Potemkin village of heterosexuality for my dear, sweet, so-straight-she-married-her-college-boyfriend buddy.

Whether you like it or not, *The L Word* is iconic gay television. But it's not iconic because of its cinematic and/or storytelling prowess. I repeat: *The New Yorker* deemed portions of the show, and I quote, "truly idiotic." Watching the mid-aughts show now in the golden age of television—in a post–*Mad Men*, post-*Fleabag* world—*The L Word* is an absolute mess. It feels like an impression of prestige television created by someone who'd only half-heard of prestige television as a concept. Seasons one and two look like they're filmed entirely in an undiluted Instagram filter from 2012 (Crema). The tone shifts give the viewer whiplash, alternating from a charming, banter-driven comedy to pulpy, oversaturated soap opera–style drama that would make *General Hospital* look like Scorsese.

Plot-wise, the show doesn't exactly flow seamlessly. Much of the whole setup fails to make any sense whatsoever: How are all of these women of disparate economic levels friends with each other again? And why are they still friends, considering how few moments of genuine camaraderie they seem to share? How did Shane and Jenny, a hairdresser and a broke writer, live next door to Bette, a high-power art dyke? How did they all manage to spend the first four hours of each day gathered at the Planet to talk shit about each other? From what faucet did this endless surge of single, hot lesbians emerge? How on earth are we to believe that Shane, with Kate Moennig's flawless, stubble-less face, was to pass as a gay male sex worker? And why, *why* was Alice meticulously tracking all of her friends' and acquaintances' sex lives? And if she had to have a chart of who they'd all slept with, did it have to be written on her living room wall?

And of course, there's the theme song. Introduced in season two, it's perhaps the show's most iconic element strictly *because* it's terrible. *The L Word* theme song—titled "*The L Word* Theme"—is an (admittedly) catchy, pop-rock song with late-'90s shimmery guitar by the band Betty. The song describes an ostensibly lesbian lifestyle: "*Girls in tight dresses who drag in mustaches / Chicks driving fast, ingénues with long lashes.*" But the true chaotic evil comes in the breakdown. A cascade of fifteen gerunds barked in less than six seconds:

TALKING / LAUGHING / LOVING / BREATHING
FIGHTING / FUCKING / CRYING / DRINKING
RIDING / WINNING / LOSING / CHEATING
KISSING / THINKING / DREAMING

It's as if to say, "This show has multidimensional female characters!" in the most hammer-headed and irritating fashion possible.

Nor is *The L Word* iconic because it accurately depicts the rich, multifaceted experiences of queer people. The show utterly failed to give space for the breadth and diversity of the queer experience. It's rife with lesbians, obviously, but that's about it for well-rounded representation. Alice Pieszecki kicks the series off as proudly bisexual, to the incredulousness of her friends: "When are you going to make up your mind between dick and pussy?" Dana asks in season one. At first, Alice defends her bisexuality, explaining she's looking for the same thing in men and women. But by season three, as Dana is dying in the hospital, Alice sees Tina dressed up for a date with her then-boyfriend. "You're right," Alice quips to Dana. "Bisexuality is gross. I see it now." There's no arc dissecting her shift in identity, and her bisexuality isn't mentioned again for the rest of the series.

The inter-LGBT biases don't stop with Alice. Max, the show's one transgender series regular, utterly fails the trans community. Not only do most of the lesbian characters misgender and snicker at Max as he's transitioning—which is unfortunately realistic, to be fair—but the show's writers depict him as a petri dish of gender confusion rather than a whole, real person. Max's body is treated as a freak show. He ends the series (unexpectedly) pregnant, serving only as shock and awe rather than any realistic (or optimistic) vision of a trans person. The mistreatment of Max was obviously on writers' minds in *The L Word: Generation Q*, the show's 2019 reboot, for which they crafted more dynamic trans characters.

The show doesn't stand the test of time regarding assault and consent, either. In season one, desperate to get pregnant, Bette and Tina coerce a straight man into having an unprotected threesome with them while shielding their true baby-crazy motives—not exactly an open and consensual situation. The next season, Shane and Jenny's filmmaker roommate, Mark, secretly films the women going about their daily lives, including having sex. When the girls find out, they're mad, but they still let him live with them? Which I'm going to go ahead and deem an underreaction to such a breach of trust. And then there's the time Jenny adopted an old dog and immediately put him down to get back at a writer who gave her book a bad review. That doesn't super have to do with assault and consent—it's more emotional abuse—I just feel like we all need to reckon with this batshit plotline in some way or another.

No, *The L Word* is not iconic for being a good television show. *The L Word* is iconic simply because it was *there*. It's like—you know how before 1990, cable was barely a thing, and so everyone just watched the same three broadcast networks? Which meant more people watched the same shows, consumed the same content, which resulted in 106 million people watching the *M*A*S*H** series finale in 1983, because it was pretty good but mostly because it was, well, there?[4] *The L Word* didn't weasel its way into the lesbian lexicon because it was such a great show or because it really connected with great swaths of the queer experience. Sure, *The L Word* was revolutionary in that nearly all its series regular characters were queer people. Yes, they were dynamic, multidimensional female characters who only interacted with men when absolutely necessary (or when Alan Cumming was a regular, c. S3). But *The L Word*'s place in the annals of gay television history is mostly to do with lesbian millennial thirst for content. *The L Word* was all we had.

Well, okay, that's not literally true. Lesbian and bisexual characters cropped up all over 2000s TV. HBO's *Deadwood,* NBC's *Friday Night Lights,* and FX's *Nip/Tuck* all featured queer women in otherwise straight worlds, here and there. And yes, of course, there was *Buffy,* a series I was too closeted to seek out as a teenager, in the early aughts. But with lesbian appearances on TV came cringey tropes: the lesbian kiss for sweeps week, which is never spoken of after the ratings come in, the depraved and insatiable bisexual, the homoerotic dream sequences that give viewers a titillating peek at queer sex but deliberately sidestep developing queer characters. Gay men were a tad better represented than women were: *Will & Grace* and *Queer Eye for the Straight Guy* were both very gay shows starring gay actors and characters, and *Queer as Folk* was *The L Word*'s partner in gay-sex-on-cable crime, though all those shows broadcast wealthy white cis men as the queer standard. But if one were to pick up the channel changer intent on watching queer women do queer women things (including, but not limited to, talking, laughing, loving, and breathing), there was just one show to watch.

My experience watching *The L Word* alone in my dorm room is far from novel. In fact, it's an extremely normal one for millennial queer women. One friend of mine, suspecting she might be queer but never having kissed a girl before, rented the Showtime series from her college library for "research" (translation: *if I'm into this, I'm probably gay*). As a teenager, another friend of mine would sneak in episodes at her grandparents' house (they had cable, she didn't). Another friend started college the year *The L Word* debuted.

As a wide-eyed freshman on a Division I soccer team rampant with sapphic energy, the upperclassmen made her watch it with them. ("Obviously, I was the Jenny in that scenario," she told me.) Lots of my queer friends have told me they first watched *L Word* sex-scene supercuts on YouTube before finagling a way to watch the real deal. Multiple friends of mine rented it on DVD at Blockbuster, then watched it piecemeal in the basement after their parents went to sleep. Scores of women say they first watched the whole series, in earnest, with their first girlfriends. "You *have* to watch it," their girlfriends said, as if you're not officially gay until you've binged six seasons of melodramatic soft-core porn with light dustings of cohesive plotlines here and there.

All these first-time experiences have one commonality: they occurred in the throes of self-discovery. Indeed, watching *The L Word* has become a sort of rite of passage for queer millennials. If we're identifying Gen Y as those born from 1981–1996, as Google dot com tells me to do, my cohort was between ages 8–23 when the show premiered. (I was fourteen.) Elder millennials watched it as college kids, while the rest of us watched on janky, virus-spreading websites like I did or once it began streaming on Netflix in the early 2010s. The cult of *The L Word* only strengthened in the following decade, lingering low in our collective consciousness. It's still perceived as the Lesbian Show, enough for Showtime to reboot the series in 2019. Watching *The L Word*, be it on TV or streaming, for many millennials, is tied to the advent of our own queerness.

Whether or not we were out going into our viewings, *The L Word* forced some curious girls to confront their same-sex attraction, or affirmed others' then-shaky identities, or piqued some sapphic curiosity that had, until then, lain dormant. For some, the show allowed us to envision a life out of the closet, and perhaps even gave us a boost of courage. Some girls watched it in secret, and others partook with their girlfriends, and some already had gay friends when they came out, a reality I'll forever envy. But for so many queer millennial women, the *L Word* watch-through served, in retrospect, as the beginning of something.

Once out of the closet, I longed for two things: a) someone to kiss, and b) a queer community I felt genuinely connected to. I wouldn't openly admit the second one—I felt like saying that meant I wasn't happy with my straight friends, which I was—but I wanted my queerness to feel understood and accepted. Being in the closet is an isolating experience. So it's natural that when we come out, we crave community. The act of coming out to our friends and family and acquaintances and to CollegeACB is, in itself, an act of asking for community. It's an admission that we want to be seen and known; or, at the very least, it's an admission that we'd like to get laid. Both are valid experiences of human connection. And in both cases, openly claiming queer identity is a declaration that we want some form of queer communion with others.

With that in mind, it makes total sense why baby gays are so drawn to *The L Word*: it provides, in its own weird way, a sense of community.

That sense is twofold. First, there's the show itself, a peek into what a gay lifestyle for women could look like. As is the whole theme of this book, there simply weren't many other lesbian stories and characters on television beyond *The L Word*. The sheer dearth of other gay girl shows made Ilene Chaiken's opus the assumed authority on aughts lesbian culture, however flawed and inaccurate and harmful the show's messaging might be. So, *The L Word* gave us a group of friends. It gave viewers that feeling of connecting with real people, that the characters are real friends of yours, a vaguely unsettling yet comforting byproduct of sticking with any long-running TV show. It gave us a fictional sense of community with this chaotic platoon of comingling queers. And with that came the dream that our gaggles were out there, somewhere, waiting to be assembled.

But then—and much more important—there's the *real* sense of community cultivated around *The L Word*: a baseline of common references, of characters, plotlines, and the (untrue) concept of "nipple confidence." It provided us with queer archetypes: saying someone has Bette Porter vibes probably means they're a high-powered, (rich) butchy femme who, if necessary, is hot enough to pull off fashion suspenders. Calling someone a Shane means they're an unaffected boyish type who has a lot of sex. Saying they're a Tina probably means they're boring and addicted to ponchos, I think? I don't hang out with many Tinas.

The particular timing of *The L Word*'s run certainly contributed to its ravenous fandom. The show coincided with the rise of the blogosphere, including Autostraddle and AfterEllen and a whole slew of Tumblr blogs dedicated to Jenny Schecter's escapades. When baby gays like me dared to explore the annals of the nonpornographic lesbian internet, we were all but guaranteed to encounter *L Word* content. Not all *L Word* fans were online lesbians, but it sure seemed like all online lesbians were *L Word* fans. The jokes were all right there, on the internet, at the tip of my fingers, and I didn't get them. I wanted to get them. I wanted to become a part of the community, and understanding the community's esoteric *L Word* zingers was, I felt, a step closer to achieving connection. Ultimately, *The L Word* gave me endless fodder with which to bond to other queer women, which is a special thing.

From that common set of *L Word* references, inside jokes form, and inside jokes are integral to intimacy. They're cliquey in the best way. Inside jokes let us harbor joy within a small group of people, bottling it up, tight. When my high school friends and I said, "Jan says 'hi,'" to each other in the hallways, we harkened back to Labor Day weekend in southwest Michigan, where we drove around desperate for a gas station to sell us Mike's Hard Lemonade. Keeping jokes on the inside isn't selfish—rather, it's key to keeping them funny, to bottling the joy. Explaining inside jokes is a famously unfunny endeavor. When uttered to someone who wasn't in Michigan over Labor Day 2007, the humor is ripped from "Jan says 'hi,'" leaving it a dry husk of a once-pure joke. That joke I just made about Tina Kennard's poncho addiction is only funny (or, at least, of note) if you've watched *The L Word*. And if you haven't, I don't really care to explain it to you.

When referencing shows or books or movies, it's generally considerate to determine whether the other person's seen/read/heard it. "Are you a *30 Rock* person?" I'll ask quickly, before making a joke about Mickey Rourke's sex grill. Some art has permeated society so deeply that you shouldn't have to ask someone if they get it. You don't have to be a *Star Wars* fan to get someone speaking in a Yoda voice. You don't have to have seen all forty-odd seasons of *Survivor* to know what "getting voted off the island" implies. You don't have to have purchased and viewed a bootleg DVD of the film *Troy* to know how a Trojan horse works. (Okay, fine, *that* was the last time I'll mention *Troy*.) And, duh, the phenomenon of having jokes about a TV show is obviously not unique to *The L Word*. Sharing a common set of references and jokes and theories about a show or book or film series is the entire point of fandom. Whenever someone makes a deep-cut *30 Rock* reference, I perk up and feel instantly connected to them, as though watching Tina Fey's seminal sitcom fifty times over means we are, on some level, the same.

But what makes *The L Word* fandom unique is its synonymy with a niche subsect of people. The Venn diagram of *The L Word* fandom and queer millennial women, while not a complete circle, is much closer to a circle than other show/identity group crossovers. Some guy friends of mine have dabbled in the American adaptation of *Queer as Folk* (2000–2005), but the *Queer as Folk* fandom isn't synonymous with gay men quite like *The L Word*'s is with lesbians. *In Living Color* and *The Cosby Show* were huge for Black Americans in the '80s and '90s, but they wouldn't get the streaming rewatches for two decades after they went off the air. The '90s nostalgia industrial complex would lead you to believe that every millennial has seen every episode of *Rugrats*, *Guts*, and *Lizzie McGuire*, but "millennial children" is a massive population and a lot of us didn't have cable as kids. The rise of streaming coincided with the end of *The L Word*; thanks(?) to that (and the *Generation Q* reboot), it's like the show never went off the air. The rite of passage of watching *The L Word* kept churning on from 2003 through the 2010s, as it lived online.

For queer millennial women, *The L Word* is our *Star Wars*. It's not that everyone's a fan, but it's just assumed that, when talking thirtysomething dyke to thirtysomething dyke, they'll get what "The Chart" means. I can't count the number of internet dates I've been on where, with literally nothing in common, an oblique *L Word* reference—"So is this place like, your Planet?"—leads to an extended conversation about our favorite and most reviled *L Word* characters. We joke about Bette Porter's jail cell sex with her carpenter sidepiece, the jokes forge connection, connection gets muddled with intimacy, and then (sometimes, occasionally, maybe) things get physical. It's a social lubricant. I can ask for any queer girl's take on *The L Word: Generation Q* and, whether they've seen it or not, they'll have something to say about it. It's the lingua franca of the millennial queer girl community.

If I went into *The L Word* looking for a sexual how-to, I can firmly say I didn't get it. Watching dozens of male-gazey sex scenes did not teach me anything about sex. I studied cunnilingus like it was theory, pouring over deeply cursed "how to please women" blog posts written by straight men. But that, too, only got me so far. I'd end up feeling about *The L Word* and how-to blogs as I did about academia on the whole: that praxis was the only way to really learn. And the sex in *The L Word* gets old, fast. Repetition is boring, even when topless women are involved. Plus, by the time I eventually watched the whole series through in my early twenties, I'd begun having sex, and watching overproduced sex scenes wasn't interesting to me any longer. So at every whiff of Sade and mood lighting—which I felt cropped up every other scene—I'd roll my eyes, whip out my phone, and play a round of solitaire. Within my card game, I'd play another game: see if I make those playing cards fly before the sex scene ended. When I heard two jacked femmes start to come in perfect unison, I knew I needed a red four or I'd be toast. I usually won, which is a testament to both my phone game prowess and the sheer tediousness of *L Word* love scenes. No, instead *The L Word* gave me a bottomless well of lesbian fodder, which is probably more useful for making friends than sex instruction is, anyway.

In March 2020, *The L Word* left Netflix US. Perhaps this marks the end of an era of *The L Word* as lesbian baptism, but frankly, I have a hard time understanding how Gen Zers would be into the oh-so-aughts show. I can't imagine people who've been graced with empathetic representations of bisexual and transgender characters as teens wouldn't circle back to these chaotic WeHo lesbians and wonder, *How the fuck did this get made? Who approved this? Were there any adults working at Showtime between 2004 and 2009?* With shows like *Glee* and *The Fosters* and *Pretty Little Liars* and *Skins* and *Euphoria*, younger generations of queer women had

TAYLOR SWIFT MADE ME A U-HAUL DYKE

I remember two lesbian jokes strongly from my early life. The first came about in seventh grade, from a kid we called RJ, who wore Dead Kennedys shirts and salivated constantly. It went like this:

Q: What did the one lesbian vampire say to the other?

A: See you next month.

I went through the classic stages of gay jokes with this one, in subsequent tellings: 1) laugh along at the joke, wholly unclear on its meaning, so straight boys would like me, 2) finally get the joke, continue to laugh along so straight boys would like me, 3) perform offense at the joke on behalf of gay women, with whom I did not identify, and finally, about ten years later, 4) now identifying as gay, genuinely laugh at the joke because it's so utterly brainless.

Hearing this joke in seventh grade was one of the first times I considered how lesbians expressed themselves sexually. For several years afterward, I thought of cunnilingus as strictly something that happened between two women; it didn't even occur to me that men would perform it on women, too. The same goes for period sex. Also, do the lesbian vampires only feed once a month? Or does this one vampire go from one menstruating vampire to the other? Also, do vampires get their periods? Can they reproduce the way humans do? If a woman is "turned" during her reproductive years, does she really have to live doubled over in bed with cramps once a month for the rest of eternity? That seems cruel for anyone to undergo, even an immortal being who feasts on human fluids. I can't believe I still have these questions after watching (nearly) all of *True Blood*.

I didn't hear the second joke until high school, I don't think, though it had been around for decades.

Q: What did the lesbian bring to a second date?

A: A U-Haul truck.

Comedian and butch-about-town Lea DeLaria wrote it in 1988.[1] Again, I didn't get this one right away, because I was looking for some sexual innuendo in it—those were the only kinds of lesbian jokes I'd heard before. But eventually I, a genius, figured it out. The joke is that lesbians fall into immediate, monogamous (read: boring) relationships, and within weeks, will settle down and adopt a cat and spend once-fun weekends knitting sweaters and talking around plans to cook a big soup. It's a gay stereotype that totters precariously atop the gender stereotype that all women lust for stable, long-term relationships—perhaps, too, folded into the notion that women are jealous and/or don't desire sexual freedom. The joke has become such a cliché that two women rushing into a relationship is used as a verb: U-Hauling.

Like many stereotypes, this one comes from a nugget of truth that's been blown out of proportion or has been prevented from evolving. An *Atlantic* piece from 2013 attributes the "urge to merge" cliché to the 1950s and '60s, when gay people couldn't date freely or openly, and monogamy meant safety.[2] The cliché has long existed as more or less fact in the public consciousness, or at least it's given straight people and gay men a vague idea of how queer women operate romantically. It crops up in media made by lesbians and straight people alike: *The L Word* makes light of the trope with Dana and Tonya in season one, who seemingly instantly get engaged and share wardrobes. The specific moving-truck brand is even referenced in the lesbian cult novel *Stone Butch Blues* (1993); Theresa and Jess use one to move in together after a few short weeks of dating. Even in the cursed *O.C.* season two bisexual plotline, Marissa (as a high school junior) moves in with her new girlfriend, Alex, after two episodes of dating.

But, also like most stereotypes, the lesbian U-Hauling trope isn't really true. A 2018 study out of Stanford University surveyed three thousand couples and found that the average couple moves in after about eighteen months of dating.[3] Some groups move in more quickly than others—older couples do, and so do those where at least one person is an evangelical Christian—but queer female couples aren't one of them. "Contrary to popular conceptions of lesbians as eager to commit," the study's abstract reads, "our results indicate that after controlling for couple age, there are no significant differences in relative rates of cohabitation among couple types."

The truth is, some couples move in quickly, others don't. I've always thought of the sub-twelve-month move-in as a kiss of death, that no two people could possibly know what they want so quickly, but that's not always the case. And while I've never lived with a partner, I've been known to dive headfirst into relationships. I told Ella I loved her like, a month into dating her. I decided to date someone long-distance after we'd been hooking up for about five weeks. I once drove to western Wisconsin to spend a weekend with a girl I'd met one (1) time a month earlier. My last week of college, a sophomore left a scrap of paper with her number on it on my laptop keyboard, and I toyed semi-seriously with the idea of getting a graduate degree just to see where this would go. I can think of five people I told my friends, over the course of my twenties, were someone I was certain I'd marry one day. I get swept up in early romance, in early infatuation, in the rush of being liked back. The full-body physical buzz of those first days of texting back and forth with fewer and fewer pauses, of getting dressed up for dates, of a new shampoo smell and new bed feel and new lip taste—new, new, new. So many times, I've mistaken that newness for some cosmic sign of being *meant for* someone. Only after ten years of dating women could I finally spot my own emotional gullibility before I could break my own heart. But that was only after I'd successfully done so again, and again, and again.

Though I've never technically rented the truck, I spiritually, emotionally, and begrudgingly have to admit: I'm a bit of a U-Haul dyke. And I'm going to go ahead and blame that on Taylor Swift.

———

Taylor Alison Swift was born on December 13, 1989, in Reading, Pennsylvania, which is not Nashville. Her date of birth isn't actually important, but it's important to me, because she came into the world just seven weeks after me. So many of my close friends were, too, born in the fall of 1989. Years before I'd irritate every partygoer I'd encounter with a boozed-up explanation of their birth charts, I've felt a sort of cosmic, superstitious connection to fall '89 babies. I shrieked when I learned US Representative Alexandria Ocasio-Cortez is an October '89 baby, like me, and I feel a bizarre closeness to Dakota Johnson and Brie Larson for the same reason: that we're similar because we've seen almost the exact same amount of time pass on Earth. I'm sure they feel the same way about me, too.

Because of our closeness in age, I've long felt connected to Taylor Swift—sometimes like she *gets* me, but truthfully, it's more like the connection between Lupita Nyong'o and her underground-dweller double in *Us*. We—Taylor and I—were both eighteen when I first heard her pre-*Fearless* single "Our Song." She was five-foot-ten and slender, lanky like so many of my distance runner pals.

She felt familiar to me, and I was certain that, had we gone to high school together, we'd be friends. Over a decade out, the way I follow Swift looks less like fandom and more like keeping close tabs on a weird girl you went to high school with who annoyingly got hot and is now worth three hundred and sixty million dollars (according to Google), about whom my cunty group thread of high school friends would text constantly.

Fearless came out on November 8, 2008, in the blip of time when I was nineteen and Taylor was still eighteen. She was full-blown country then—she'd remain firmly Nashville until *Red* (2012), an album equal parts country and pop, before going and remaining utterly pop with *1989* (2014). Though it was her second record, *Fearless* was the world's big introduction to Taylor Swift. It spent eleven nonconsecutive weeks at number one on the *billboard* charts.[4] It was the best-selling album of 2009 in the US[5] and got solid critical reception, to boot: *Rolling Stone* even called Swift a "songwriting savant."[6]

A friend in my dorm got ahold of *Fearless* and burned copies for all the girls on my floor. I wore that album out. Well, first I uploaded it to my iTunes library, then I downloaded it back onto my red iPod Nano, and *then* I wore that album out. My whole floor did. About eight of us would, each night that November, sit in Lauren and Rachel's room across the hall and just listen to *Fearless*. We were absolutely *mind-blown* by the fact that she wrote all her own songs. We'd collectively swoon over chorus lead-ins like *"You're just so cool, run your hands through your hair / Absent-mindedly making me want you."* I didn't know if Lauren or Rachel or the rest of my floor had more romantic experience than I did, if the music hit them differently, but I was smitten. The thought of record-listening parties feels so quaint, born of a time when records were so cumbersome and expensive that listening en masse was born from necessity. Perhaps we were driven by the collegiate impression that experiencing anything solo is humiliation worthy of dropping out, but I think we just wanted to catch each other's smiles at our favorite lines, sing along poorly, and procrastinate on our midterms.

At this point, I was in the Deep Closet and had so thoroughly detached my conscious mind from my physical desires that you'd think I'd been guillotined. I was Marie Antoinette, if all those French tabloid lesbian rumors were real, and not just designed to make her a monster in the eyes of the Third Estate. I was taking Intro to European History (can you tell?) and calculus and a child development seminar. I was not dating anyone, nor had I kissed anyone in college to this point. This, despite being thoroughly entrenching in the (at times, too intense) subculture of my Division III cross-country team, which included much intermingling between the men's and women's teams. My college track teammates and I devoured *Fearless* as a collective, just like my freshman hall did. Runners, like Swift, spend a lot of time alone in our heads; I wonder if that's why we were so drawn to the album.

Runners also talk a lot about visualization. My high school coaches told me about it first: in the days leading up to a race, you're supposed to visualize, visualize, visualize. Visualize the first chaotic moments of the race, the burst of two-hundred-odd girls leaping off the starting line, speeding beyond your goal pace to get a good position, then funneling into the wooded path in a quarter mile. Imagine the excitement and adrenaline coursing through you. Imagine the clock at the first mile mark and seeing your goal pace in red, clicking digits. Imagine your lungs straining and your legs flushed with lactic acid. Prepare yourself for your limbs going numb, your brain blurring, your body clicking into a movement and a pace you've stuck to in all your workouts. Imagine digging into the deep, deep, deep of you to unearth a last burst of energy, and use it to pick off those last, lagging girls limping into the finish chute.

The theory of visualizing is, basically, that the more you mentally prepare yourself for a race, the less surprised you'll be during it, the more capable you'll be of overcoming your pain and hitting your goal time. That the more you've imagined your ideal outcome, the more likely it is to come true. It's *The Secret* for jocks. I did this before every cross-country and track race in high school and college, and then I started doing it for my own love life. Not even admitting to myself that I was gay, I spent my freshman year of college concocting elaborate fantasies about kissing nice indie boys on a crisp New England night. It was as if I thought "visualizing" heterosexuality would make it more achievable, more conquerable when I at last encountered a boy who wanted to kiss me.

My dream boyfriend at that time wasn't any boy in particular, but just: Boy. This, in itself, should have been a sign. Anyway, Boy is skinny and scrappy and has a big smile. We meet at the Rez, the student-run coffee shop, where I'd frequently sit and study until they started handing out eight-hundred-calorie muffins. Boy and I know each other from around campus, but not well. Boy asks if he could sit with me. I survey the café: a few tables sit empty across the small room. Boy could sit anywhere, and yet, he stands above me, bright-eyed, nervous, waiting for my response. I say yes. We sit across from each other, catching eyes with increased frequency. Boy breaks the silence to ask a question about his Calc I worksheet. I know the answer, because it's 2008 and my brain has not yet drop-kicked its ability to calculate anything beyond a 20 percent tip.

We talk, eyes locked, until the Rez closes. (I forego my muffin tonight.) We're both smiling so big, so goofy. We're young enough to remember that feeling of just having our braces removed: slimy, seductive, freeing, adult. Boy offers to walk me the thirty seconds back to my dorm. It's out of his way, but he doesn't mind. It's chilly out, yet we linger outside anyway, clinging to this fledgling connection. I tease him for asking that easy calculus question—*"You seriously can't calculate a limit?"* Boy admits he knew the answer, that he just wanted to talk to me. A pause. Locked eyes. And in the quiet New England November night, I kiss Boy, quietly, for too long. I drape my hands over his shoulders, because that's what girls do in movies. We want to go inside, but we don't, not tonight. We let the kiss be what it is. He squeezes my hand goodbye and heads uphill, back to his own XL twin bed, where he thinks about me.

Good God, this is a deeply uninteresting fantasy. This is the tragic brain of a young woman trying to convince herself she's straight, a brain so shrouded in shame it's lost its knack for imagination.

Looking back, the fact that I was subconsciously going through the same preparatory paces in my brain for both falling in love with a man and dragging my body through 3.1 miles of sheer hell should have been, uh, a red flag. Not to mention the fact that my visualizing heterosexuality never went beyond kissing. But in any case, I found comfort in concocting fantasies and running them on a loop in my head. I so clearly ripped this one from rom-coms and teen TV—it feels so stale, so false, so phony. It feels so clearly written by someone who's never experienced a romantic connection with a boy before.

Over a decade later, Taylor Swift is now notorious—infamous, even!—for writing her real love life into her song lyrics. *Fearless* hosts the first quintessentially Swiftian move that would come to define her career: writing break-up songs about famous dudes.

While promoting the album on *Ellen,* Taylor dropped the bomb that the track, "Forever and Always" was about Joe Jonas breaking up with her *over the phone*.[7] Naturally, that got people interested, and playfully shit-talking Jonas became Taylor's hook. It was juicy—hearing celebrities speak on (seemingly) real, emotional terms about their heartbreak is rare and irresistible to many, especially when dumped in such a rude way. Taylor was funny and charming and seemed in on the whole joke of it, too.

And while that's all fun to gossip about, the Jonas tea isn't what made me fall for *Fearless*. I wasn't even really clear on which Jonas Brother was Joe, being *just* too old for them when the trio burst onto the teen scene in the mid aughts. It's ironic, to me, that Taylor has become synonymous with break-up songs about famous exes, because I'm not convinced a single thing Taylor Swift sings about on *Fearless* actually happened to her. What drew me to *Fearless* was how Taylor was, to me, so clearly singing about fantasies, that she had just as little experience in love and heartbreak as I did. I felt connected to *Fearless* because the whole thing sounds so utterly made-up.

Fearless begins with the snap of a snare drum and the weepy twang of an electric six-string. This is the album's titular song. From its first few frames, the album bleeds optimism. An infectious kind, the teenage kind, the kind that can only come from a person peering eagerly over the precipice of adulthood. "Fearless" captures the unbridled optimism and faith in love—the, ahem, *fearlessness*—that defines the album on the whole. On *Fearless, innocence* isn't a euphemism for *naiveté;* rather, it's a tool, a power. Swift assures us that when bottled just right, innocence can propel us into the adulthood we've always dreamt of but never really lived. Literally. On a 2008 blog post for Big Machine Records, who produced *Fearless*, Taylor wrote of the album's first track: "This song is about the best first date I haven't had yet."[8]

That perfectly summarizes the entire album: it's a record where big feelings are *imagined*, wrapped up in a digestible narrative, and repackaged in catchy twang. And no song exemplifies this theory better than "Love Story." In the country-pop retelling of *Romeo and Juliet,* Swift casts herself as the romantic heroine: she even uses those names for herself and her lover, hurling any subtlety out the window. In the song, Swift and a boy meet at a ball, his dad says they can't be together, they sneak out to a garden for a moment.

Unlike Shakespeare's tragedy, the two end up happily engaged and, most important, alive, concluding with a joyous, celebratory key change.

But like "Fearless," Swift never actually lived this experience. In a 2009 interview with *TIME*, Swift said "Love Story" was inspired by a guy who was never really her boyfriend, and of whom her parents weren't the biggest fan, and who kind of just fell off the map.[9] Way less romantic than *Romeo and Juliet*. And so, Swift blew this extremely mundane, albeit relatable teenage experience— "My parents don't like the guy I like!"—up into a fairy tale, hyper-removed from her mid-aughts Rustbelt reality. To me, "Love Story" speaks to Swift's broad tendency to slip between reality and fantasy in her lyrics, her impulse to situate herself as the lead in her own romantic dramas. It's a very teenage impulse. After all, every eighteen-year-old is the star of their own screenplay.

Where "Love Story" was at least based on Taylor's life, the story behind "You Belong with Me" is even further removed the songwriter. In that same Big Machine blog post, Taylor explains the song's inspiration: she overheard a male friend apologizing profusely, over the phone, to his girlfriend for God knows what, and Taylor felt bad for him. She imagined being in love with him and being the girl who *gets him*, whom he doesn't need to apologize to. The girl next door vs. popular girl plot was spun from there, and "You Belong with Me" stretches a non-romance into a teen rom-com of the *She's All That* variety. Indeed, the only song on the album whose lyrics sound like a real, lived experience is "Fifteen," and that's a story about her best friend, not about Taylor herself.

The biggest hint to me that *Fearless* was written by a complete and total virgin, though, was the rain thing. Something you must know about early Taylor Swift: she was simply addicted to the idea of kissing and/or dancing in the rain, much like I was addicted to the image of a chaste kiss on a blustery autumn night.

She sings about it all over *Fearless*. The thing about kissing in the rain, though, is that it sucks. Unless you're in like, a super warm Deep South summer downpour (reminder: Taylor Swift is from Pennsylvania), rain is cold and unpleasant and typically accompanied by wind. Kissing inside a warm house after escaping a deluge? Delightful. Kissing in a car while sheets of rain thump down on the windshield? Apart from the awkwardness of leaning across the gear shift console, fun. Actually making out in a thunderstorm gets old, quick, as nagging discomforts and oncoming hypothermia can overtake even the truest of loves. The only reason any couple would tongue through a downpour is not roaring love but a quiet hope that someone will see them and think, *Wow, those people are in* love. Kissing in the rain is romantic only if one's idea of romance is fulfilling a predisposed notion of what romance is. That is, it's only romantic to a teenage songwriter who has experienced next to nothing.

I'm not going full Sarah Koenig right now—Taylor has long admitted she draws from media and her friends for inspiration. In her 2019 appearance on NPR's Tiny Desk, Taylor took a good chunk of monologue time to explain that she gets lyrical inspiration from book characters and movies. And it's all totally normal! Songwriters sing from the perspectives of friends and exes and fictional characters alike. Even eleven years after *Fearless*, with a heap of ex-lovers in her wake and a frankly puzzling mania for Joe Alwyn, she wrote songs outside of her then-present experience. On *Lover* (2019), Swift uses media to channel feelings she's already had; on *Fearless*, she uses media to fill in the blanks of a life she hasn't lived yet. But her lyrical sorcery has been constant.

And that's precisely what I identified in Taylor Swift on *Fearless*. It wasn't "game recognize game," but "inexperienced-teen-who-craves-love recognize inexperienced-teen-who-craves-love." I saw another girl who wanted so fucking badly to experience joyous, cinematic affection, the kind where rain machines follow your every move and your own feelings are clear and obvious as if you, yourself, are the viewer. I saw someone else who, for whatever reason, didn't get a full chance to live before age eighteen. And like Taylor Swift, I thus saw every minute interaction with a boy as something to be stretched thin like Silly Putty to fill in predetermined romantic expectations. But my loneliness and inexperience came from being closeted, and Taylor's inexperience came from, it appears, being gawky and transferring high schools to become a country star.

In college, I'd eventually learn on an emotional level, not just an intellectual one, that real-life love doesn't follow the Hero's Journey screenplay structure. But still, for years into my twenties, I wanted to kiss in the rain—metaphorically I mean, I've made my thoughts on rain makeouts clear—and wanted love at first sight, something magical and undeniable and all-consuming. Like Carrie Bradshaw in the *Sex and the City* finale, but gay, struggling to hold together my collection of funky patterned button-up shirts instead of my pearl necklace. Taylor Swift kept me fantasizing about that kind of love. And in doing so, Taylor Swift turned me into a U-Haul dyke.

I ditched the chaste heterosexual smooch fantasy after coming out, but I continued to "visualize" relationships with my crushes well into my twenties. Some fantasies were sexual, but most were just so fucking gay. They'd always play out in the thick of a white-hot crush.

In college, I fantasized about my then-girlfriend and I breaking up then meeting again in San Francisco (a place I have never lived nor have ever wanted to live outside the realm of this one daydream) years later, only to realize we were each other's *ones* all along. I picked out, on Google Maps, the exact spot on the Île de la Cité were I'd propose to my friends' friend that I'd met IRL just one (1) time.

I'd play the fantasy on repeat in my head in quiet moments—while commuting to work or before bed—until I lost interest in the crush or bored of the fantasy, forced to concoct a new one. Once, in 2012, I chatted with a girl on OkCupid, stalked her on Facebook, discovered her family had a vacation home in Maine, then basked in a blissful delusion of our romantic getaway to Kennebunkport, filled with ice cream and lobster and tide pools, only for her to blow off our first date and never contact me again. I recognize this is objectively deranged behavior, but it's not like I ever *told* anyone about my gay little daydreams, or that I auditioned nearly every cute girl I met for the role of soul mate in my lonely idle mind. But, let's get real—to those girls, my U-Haul energy was unmissable.

When I was twenty-four, Gillian sent me a message on OkCupid. When I received it, I was on the fifteenth floor of Northwestern Memorial Hospital, in a northeast-facing corner room that overlooked the Museum of Contemporary Art and the glittering blue lakefront. It was late April and Zach was getting a stem cell transplant. He'd been diagnosed with leukemia about four months prior and would turn twenty-six in a few days. A stem cell transplant is only as invasive as a blood transfusion, but the stakes still felt high. Before the infusion, a hospital chaplain led my family in a blessing of the stem cells. I, my parents, sister, and Zach's girlfriend, Molly, held hands around Zach's bed, where he sat alert and calm and bald, as the chaplain laid hands on the sack of the anonymous donor's fluid. That was the first time I saw my dad cry; my sister and I made fleeting *holy shit!* eye contact. The infusion went smoothly, and Zach would be home to recover in a couple weeks, with an immune system strong enough to venture forth from the sterile oncology floor and several more healthy years to live. Open and vulnerable, I messaged Gillian back. That she had messaged me at such a critical moment in my life felt Swiftian in its cosmic implications.

A week later, we were at a wine bar off Washington Square

Park. She was whip-smart (starting an MD-PhD in the fall), gorgeous (wore Madewell, drank beer), and hilarious (laughed at all my jokes). She suggested one drink more than we should've had on a weeknight, with work in just a few hours. Around midnight, we ended up wandering into the park, stopping to make out against a tree for a while. It remains one of my all-time best first dates. Gillian adored New York, a place I'd been struggling to fall for but badly wanted to, and her love for the city was contagious. We met again a few days later, at an East Village bar where I spilled a cocktail in her lap before kissing more on the F Train platform. She said she loved this time of year in New York, when the night air was still cool and the warm rush of air from the subway would engulf her upon descent. We clicked—it was going well, and I had the strong suspicion she would be my girlfriend, if not a crusade to make her so. In other words: I wanted to U-Haul.

Then Gillian went to Portugal. Not abruptly or anything, this has been the plan. Three weeks completely solo, in a small town at the country's most southwestern non-island point, learning to surf, a sort of last-time-I'll-ever-have-fun-again-before-med-school-starts self-indulgence. That she was taking this trip made her even more attractive to me. The whole thing felt like a Taylor Swift song. It was love at first sight! And then, suddenly, we were an ocean away! And it was springtime! In New York! Where everyone falls in love on-screen! I recognized a real-life Swift bop and acted accordingly. It was as if by listening to *Fearless* on loop for years, I'd given myself permission to heave my whole body into this nascent romance. Remember when Taylor bought a house on Cape Cod next to that Kennedy she dated for like, a month? That's the energy I brought to the next three weeks.

And so, as millennial lovers flung an ocean apart are wont to do, Gillian and I texted. Constantly. She sent me photos from the beach, with great crags erupting in the Portuguese surf. I responded with my own updates on Meowmeowers, a nightmare cat my roommates and I had drunkenly offered to look after while our downstairs neighbor was in India. I saw our relationship stretched out before us: I imagined us loafing in Prospect Park, taking a get-away upstate, sauntering through art galleries and getting day drunk because, fuck it, what else was there to do than be together? I spent parties wishing I could show her off and afternoons on my roof awaiting her return, when we could start our blissful summer romance in earnest. She kept texting me, all the way from Europe, which could only mean she'd written out the same future for us, too. For Memorial Day, I went to Austin with some friends. And when I flew back into LaGuardia, I felt, for the first time, the sensation that I was returning home.

Finally, June arrived, and Gillian was back in New York. Once she'd recovered from the jet lag, we made post-work plans to meet in Washington Square Park then visit some Chelsea galleries Gillian knew would be serving free wine. But we never made it out of the park, because she sat me down on a bench and told me, in the most gentle way she could, that she didn't want to date me. Once again, I was getting dumped on a park bench, an item I had already ticked off on my "sad baby lesbian experiences" scavenger hunt.

I made her explain and re-explain that to me for about an hour, and then I cried for days. Days! *Days.* But I wasn't mourning what we'd had; I mourned what we didn't have. Gillian and I went on a total of three (3) dates, and yet, this was the most acutely painful breakup of my twenties. Not because of some mythic connection between us but because of the extravagant expectations I'd placed on our future together. I'd hyped it up so much that I had to take a wrecking ball to the life I'd frantically erected for us in my mind.

I'd decided that, because of my brother's illness and the stress it put on my family, the universe was throwing me a bone. That an extremely good thing *must* follow an objectively frightening one. How fortuitous was it that Gillian had come into my life right now? Surely it *meant something* that she'd messaged me during my brother's life-saving procedure. No, it couldn't possibly have been that she worked at a lab and had swaths of time to kill during experiments and had hopped on OkCupid out of boredom. Then I'd mistaken us getting along as some kind of cosmic sign. Then I'd decided her texting me over her trip was unfettered desire, when really, it was probably the loneliness of solo travel getting to her. (I also hadn't been dumped before, really, especially not by someone who seemed to like my personality (my jokes) a lot.)

Lost potential can hurt so much more than a relationship that's tried and failed. When a long-term relationship ends, the evidence for why two people don't work is usually right in front of you; you've given it an honest shot, and it didn't work. But lost potential felt like a referendum on what I'd admitted I wanted and why I didn't deserve it. There was miscommunication on both ends, but really, I'd stretched the courtship out to fit my own idea of what My New York Girlfriend would be like. I know now how holding such expectations was a) deeply unfair to Gillian, as I filled in the blanks of her personality and desire for my own self-satisfaction, and b) probably way, *way* less subtle than I thought, which likely prompted her to dump me on a pleasant summer evening in Washington Square Park.

⌒

Ahead of her 2019 album, *Lover,* gossip buzzed around media circles, and then leaked onto Twitter, that Taylor Swift was going to publicly come out as bisexual on her forthcoming album. Such rumors had been flying around for years—specifically, that her very public friendship with Karlie Kloss was in fact a romantic one, a theory meticulously detailed on Tumblr, mostly via gifs. In the grand tradition of Sherlocking which song is about who on each record, fans theorized which Taylor tunes were actually about Kloss, either reading the gay innuendo or bringing their own romantic experience to the text. In April, she donated a hundred and thirteen thousand dollars to the Tennessee Equality Project, a pro-LGBTQ organization, which hopeful tweeters saw as a breadcrumb to her coming out.[10] Were Swift to publicly identify as bi, she'd be all but confirming that the two leggy blondes had been in love. As someone who's lost years of my life to the #Kaylor internet hole, I was eager to accept those rumors as fact, to say the least. It would've affirmed all my feelings about *Fearless* being a queer album; it would've tied my whole journey with her music together in such a neat, Swift-esque narrative.

And then, "You Need to Calm Down" happened. The video for the second single off of *Lover* came out in mid-June, Pride Month, and featured a barrage of cameos from famous gays: Ellen DeGeneres, Billy Porter, Laverne Cox, RuPaul, the *Queer Eye* squad, and dozens more. It's an onslaught of queers clad in rainbow, in a candy-colored trailer park performing what seems like a straight white girl's interpretation of camp, all in the face of (a pretty classist portrayal of) anti-gay protestors. In a roundtable of *New York Times* culture writers headlined, "For Taylor Swift, is ego stronger than pride?" critic-at-large Wesley Morris called it, "as much a music video as it is a detonated rainbow-flag piñata."[11] He went on to write, "all of that flamboyant Willy Wonkaness is meant to signal to the viewer—louder and more shablamingly than the song itself—that Swift supports and loves each letter of the queer community." In other words, it felt to many gays like a wokeness parade, a grab at what had become the cachet of queerness in pop culture. I felt so, too. The music video's cluelessness was all the confirmation I needed that Taylor wasn't queer, but two months later, she bravely came out as straight to *Vogue*. I felt a little let down and used, but mostly, I felt like rolling my eyes. *Classic fucking Taylor*, I thought, like she was some girl I'd gone to high school with.

Ultimately, Taylor's own sexual identity doesn't matter. Whether or not she's queer doesn't change the fact that *Fearless* guided my ascent into adulthood, that it carved out the kind of queer woman I'd grow up to be. It doesn't change that I felt like her songs were ripped directly from my diary or that her teenage fantasies felt like mirror images of my own. Did I tell everyone I've ever met that I was 98 percent confident the pop star was going to come out as bisexual? Sure. Was I wrong? Well, okay, apparently.

For me—and I'm going to go ahead and project myself onto Taylor, too—I floored it in relationships because I craved self-worth. I spent much of my adolescence waiting for my life to start and thought that falling in love was the starting gun of real life. So much of my high school and college gossip was about who was dating whom, who had hooked up with whom last night, how far they'd gone, who had said "I love you," and who'd broken up. Friends and acquaintances alike became defined partially by their sexual partners; the hotter the person they got with, the more social points. In thinking this way about others, I implicitly defined my own self-worth by the same metric. I might have been witty and smart and a solid friend, but to myself, I was not a person yet, because I had not been the subject of *the big thing* yet: love, or sex, or even *like* plus making out. Because the Claire Thing was so under wraps, to me, it didn't count. Not that I hadn't had feelings, but no one had had feelings for me, and therefore I was undesirable. I had no right to claim the human condition as mine, because what the fuck did I know about anything? That loneliness, that sense of disconnect, can happen to young people of any identity, but the closet sure makes it a common feeling for queer kids.

Taylor Swift might not have made me a romantic, but she absolutely fueled my tendency to over-romanticize. After spending high school listening to indie albums my cool New Yorker sister had recommended, I felt seen and understood by a pop country album. *Fearless* told me it was okay to be a mushy, over-expectant fangirl of romance and perhaps let me linger in my own adolescent dreaminess longer than I otherwise would have. I really wanted to be in a singular, unquestioned kind of love, with my feelings as white-hot at ages twenty-one and ninety-one. Leaning into that urge proved to be my own worst enemy over and over again; Gillian wasn't the only person I scared off with my expectations of grandeur after three dates. After gathering enough real-life dating experience, I found that living in a *Fearless*-esque fantasy wouldn't lead me to a real, sustained, long-term romance. It was, however, a tool I needed as a lonely baby gay, and one that made me optimistic about—even excited for—queer adulthood.

THE *GLEE* BUBBLE

There is teen television before *Glee*, and then there is teen television after *Glee*. Allow me to take a cartoonishly large breath.

Okay. Ready.

Glee is a musical television dramedy about show choir kids at (the fictional) William McKinley High School in Lima, Ohio (a real place, apparently). The cast evolved throughout its six seasons, but for the first two (what we'll call, cautiously, "good *Glee*"), here's what we've got: a nerd who uses a wheelchair; an Asian American girl with a stutter; one (1) Black girl who, don't worry, compares herself to Beyoncé before the pilot episode's over; a twink; a pregnant cheerleader; a type-A, Broadway-bound overachiever; ambiguously gay cheerleaders who are later confirmed bi/lesbian; and a sensitive quarterback who *finds himself through the music* and yep, you guessed it, falls in love with the Broadway nerd. The club is championed by a youngish teacher, Mr. Schuester, the Earth's most earnest man, who falls in love with a guidance counselor who wears medical gloves while eating lunch. Watching *Glee* was the first time I recall an ensemble show feeling truly contrived—like each character was ticking a box of sexual and/or racial minority. Today, I'd call it performative wokeness. Then, I just called it, "how the fuck are all these kids friends?" The answer, *Glee* posits: the power of music. Okay.

Glee is a show of contradictions. It is at once Kidz Bop and a sexy *GQ* centerfold (Kidz Bop for horny teens, a happy medium indeed). It's simultaneously both sarcastic and sincere; both self-aware and painstakingly naive; both peppered with pithy one-liners making fun of deaf kids and drenched in sappy monologues imploring teens to be themselves. It's a show that demands mammoth suspensions of disbelief from its viewers. Not just in the way musicals always do but, for instance, Mr. Schuester's wife fakes a pregnancy and keeps up the charade for six entire months? The great expanse of *Glee* is a slog to endure. And then, one of these show choir cornballs will say something that feels so true to your sixteen-year-old self, you'll feel an overpowering urge to journal. *Glee* is both sort of good and, well, mostly bad. Some argue *Glee* is a send-up of teen dramas of yore, like *Election* (1999) or Ryan Murphy's first show, *Popular* (1999). (*Yore* meaning 1999.) I say it still falls squarely into the genre, just with some solid zingers peppered in. As Rachel Berry shrieks in the pilot episode, "*There is nothing ironic about show choir!*"

Glee brings me more secondhand embarrassment and rage than I'm comfortable putting to ink. The bubblegum color scheme and the adult white guy rapping to "Gold Digger" with a bunch of teens and the tedious football player/theater nerd romance we're painstakingly forced to endure—no. And yet, I watched seasons two through four in real time, every week. I'm not better than *Glee*. And, as annoying as it feels to admit, *Glee* changed the representation game for queer kids on TV, which, in turn, changed the real-life game for queer kids off TV.

Whether you love or hate or fully ignored the cultural phenomenon of *Glee*, there's no denying it was a very gay television show. I mean, it was a series about show choir kids learning to be themselves—how could it not be? From its pilot, McKinley High School's glee club is mocked, in an oh-so-aughts way, for being, like, so fucking gay: the football guys call it "homo explosion," cheerleader Quinn Fabray calls Rachel Berry "RuPaul," and the former club supervisor, Sandy Ryerson, drapes pastel sweaters over his shoulders and *swears* he has a long-distance girlfriend in Cleveland. "People think you're gay now, Finn," Quinn tells her boyfriend, the quarterback, in episode two. "And you know what that makes me? Your big, gay beard." Though the pilot positions three straight people (Rachel, Finn, and Mr. Schuester) as the leads, it, too, sets the show in a world where gayness is present and talked about, if not always in the most pleasant terms.

With time, Mr. Schue's plotlines fade from the main stage, and sidekicks like Kurt, Santana, Mercedes, and Puck share screen time with Rachel and Finn. Ryan Murphy, once a closeted Catholic midwestern kid, pins his longtime rejection in Hollywood on being, well, too gay. "I only wrote or created shows that I really wanted to watch, so they inevitably had gay characters and trans characters and minorities," Murphy told *The Guardian* in 2019.[1] "And I made them the leads instead of the sidekicks, because that is what I did in my own life." With *Glee*, Murphy weaseled his way onto network TV with straight leads, made a smash hit, then put the gay story lines into the spotlight.

Glee was Ryan Murphy's third show. First was *Popular*, a biting teen dramedy that, like *Glee*, found conflict from upending the established high school social hierarchy. Unlike *Glee*, *Popular* wasn't really made for teenagers. One of the show's regulars, Leslie Grossman, once characterized it as "by gay men in their thirties, for gay men in their thirties."[2] Perhaps that's why the show only lasted two seasons on the WB. Murphy's next series, *Nip/Tuck* (2003–2010), was a hit, making it to one hundred episodes on FX. The dark dramedy/medical drama followed the staff of a private plastic surgery clinic in Miami (and then Los Angeles), and it is quintessentially Murphy: glamorous and grotesque, shimmery and pulpy, fun as hell. Even in 2020, after a decade of groundbreaking smashes like *Pose* and *American Horror Story* and *American Crime Story, Vulture* argued *Nip/Tuck* "is still the ultimate Ryan Murphy show."[3] But with *Glee,* a queasily genuine, feel-good show, Murphy departed from his adult-centric content, embraced corniness, and became a household name.

Given the comparative wealth of LGBTQ+ stories told on TV and film now, it's easy to take for granted how much attention *Glee* paid its gay kids. We watch a gay character, Kurt, come out to a loving and supportive working-class dad. We watch as he and Blaine get crushes and fall in love and have their first kiss and lose their virginity to each other—the stuff we've seen straight kids do for decades on *The Wonder Years* and *Dawson's Creek* and *Friday Night Lights*. We watch girls go from casually hooking up to sorting out their muddled feelings to being girlfriends. We watch the full arc of gay bullying to the bully coming out as gay, a short-sighted cliché but, in the midst of the "It Gets Better" campaign of 2010, interesting to see play out on-screen. Those first couple seasons earned *Glee* GLAAD Awards for Outstanding Comedy Series, validating the show's ongoing quest to make network television gayer. Perhaps more validating than all the world's GLAAD Awards was the predictable outrage over same-gender teenagers kissing. After the season three Lady Gaga–themed (read: extremely pro-LGBTQ+) episode, "Born This Way," conservative media critic Dan Gainor on ABC News called it, "Ryan Murphy's latest depraved initiative to promote his gay agenda," and the fictional William McKinley High School, "the gayest high school in the history of mankind."[4] Gorgeous.

Glee's gayness even earned the show the academic treatment. In the intro to *Queer in the Choir Room: Essays on Gender and Sexuality in* Glee (2014), Dr. Michelle Parke asserts up front that the show "confronts issues of gender and sexuality alongside and against subjects such as race, religion, disability, education and, of course, music. And, among current quality and complex television shows, it is certainly one of the queerest."[5] Scores of legitimate criticisms of the kind of gay it was have been leveled (many in said academic essay collection): that it often presented bisexuality as confusion or a phase, that most attention was given to the white gays, that gender identity narratives were mishandled. But the fact that this prime time show so explicitly examined queer adolescence, however insufficient it might've been in hindsight, was in itself a breath of fresh air.

But *Glee*'s sheer gayness isn't what changed the game; its lucrativeness did. *Glee* was a smash hit from the get-go: the pilot roped in 9.62 million viewers, and episodes averaged about the same through the whole first season.[6] The show snagged eleven Primetime Emmy nominations in 2010 and had three winners: Jane Lynch, Ryan Murphy, and guest star Neil Patrick Harris. Gleek fandom permeated every corner of the internet. A *Hollywood Reporter* cover story, "Inside the Hot Business of *Glee*," (January 2011), wrote that the show's brand, "through its inventive packaging of music and mall-ready charisma of its stars, has redefined how big a TV business can be."[7] There were chart-topping soundtrack albums. An international *"Glee* live!" arena tour. A spin-off reality show. *Glee*-branded Sephora nail polish. A number one iPad app. And, of course, there was the old-fashioned way of making money: three hundred thousand dollars per thirty seconds of ad time. *Glee* was such a moneymaker from the start, FOX inked a twenty-four-million-dollar overall deal with *Glee* after its very first season.[8] Hollywood took note: stories about queer kids and outsiders could print cash. As Ryan Murphy told the *New Yorker*, "Against all odds, the quote-unquote 'fag musical' became a billion-dollar brand."[9]

Technically, *Glee* swooped in at the very end of the aughts.

But it felt more like the beginning of something than the end of it. *Glee* ushered in a decade of LGBTQ+ progress that, relative to other social movements, happened at warp speed. In 2010, "Don't Ask, Don't Tell" was repealed. In 2011, New York legalized gay marriage, and then-Secretary of State Hillary Clinton told the United Nations, "Gay rights are human rights, and human rights are gay rights." Thousands of "It Gets Better" videos flooded the internet, a viral attempt to save bullied queer teens from suicide. The next year, Barack Obama became the first US president to voice his support of gay marriage, and Wisconsin elected the first openly gay senator, Tammy Baldwin. The Defense of Marriage Act fell in 2013, paving the path to the Supreme Court for *Obergefell v. Hodges,* eventually legalizing gay marriage in 2015. Laverne Cox and Caitlyn Jenner posed on magazine covers, pushing transgender issues into the realm of public discourse. A May 2009 Gallup poll found 40 percent of Americans thought gay marriage should be illegal, a number that fell to 26 percent over a decade.[10] (A whopping 60 percent of Americans opposed it in 2004—thanks for nothing, *Will & Grace.*) California passed a law banning conversion therapy in 2012, as did another eighteen states, DC, and Puerto Rico by 2019.[11]

TV, too, got way gayer in the 2010s. In 2009, GLAAD found 3 percent of scripted prime time broadcast regulars were LGB (zero were transgender, zero were Black, only three weren't white).[12] In 2019, the same annual report found 10.2 percent of regulars were LGBTQ, ninety in total, six of whom were trans.[13] Beyond broadcast, the shifting nature of how we watched gave way for more niche storytelling. The rise of streaming giants like Netflix and Hulu and Amazon shifted the industry from broadcast to the internet, from weekly sit-downs to weekend binges. Shows no longer had to try to appeal to everyone but to appeal very strongly to smaller, more loyal groups. Following *Glee* came an onslaught of shows about gay teens: The UK's *Skins* had sweet gay Maxxie in its first generation (2007–09) but went all-in on the (at first) clandestine romance between Naomi and Emily in its second, 2009–2010. *Pretty Little Liars* made Emily Fields's coming out narrative a core plot of season one and kept her romances with lesbian and bisexual girls coming all seven seasons (including a visit to a raucous, suburban Pennsylvania dyke bar. Sure, babe). *Once Upon a Time, Teen Wolf, Arrow, The Carrie Diaries, The Fosters, Faking It, The Flash, Jane the Virgin, Crazy Ex-Girlfriend*—those are just a few of the 2010s shows geared toward younger people with fully realized, fleshed out gay characters and plotlines. In 2018, coming-of-age rom-com *Love, Simon* grossed $66.3 million at the box office worldwide.[14] *Euphoria* and *Sex Education* and the 2017 *One Day at a Time* reboot capped the decade with queer, confident teens on streaming services.

It makes absolute sense to be putting LGBTQ+ characters front and center for Gen Zers—a 2016 study found less than half of that generation identifies as "exclusively heterosexual."[15] But there's a bit of a chicken-or-egg situation there, too. More kids come out when they see versions of themselves, or even gay role models, in stories on-screen; the audience for LGBTQ+ stories gets bigger; gay stories thus become more profitable; more gay stories get told. What *Glee* meant for those queer middle and high schoolers was clear to me from the start. They were just a few years younger than me—I was nineteen when *Glee* premiered—and I was jealous of them. The sheer existence of *Glee* made me realize I'd been exposed to so few gay people, real or fictional, that I'd barely been confronted with a single opportunity to consider my own queerness. I felt angry that I'd been stripped of an opportunity to see funny, fully realized gay kids come out and fall in love and be supported by their friends and families. I was incensed that I'd never gotten to watch Santana invite Brittany over for "sweet lady kisses" as a kid. Sure, maybe I would've purposefully hidden from *Glee,* afraid it might force me to confront something uncomfortable about myself. But as *Glee* fever swept teen America, I envied the fourteen-year-old who, swooning over Blaine's "Teenage Dream" serenade, could only think: *Fuck. Fuck. Fuck. Fuck. Fuck. I'm gay, aren't I? Oh, fuck.* I envy tweens who felt a panic I didn't feel in earnest until college.

It's tough to find another issue where public opinion—and with that, laws—has shifted so rapidly as it has on gay rights. According to Harvard psychology professor Mahzarin Banaji, cognitive dissonance plays a big role in LGBTQ+ acceptance.[16] It's very difficult for, say, a parent to love their gay son and revile queer people on the whole, especially when they've established love for their child long before he was identifiable as gay. So as the rate of coming out increases, so, too, does the rate of acceptance. Of course, same-sex marriage certainly isn't the be-all and end-all of LGBTQ+ rights, and swiftness does not equal permanence. By the end of the 2010s, President Trump had rolled back a number of transgender protections, despite posing with rainbow flags while campaigning. The 2018 Supreme Court case *Masterpiece Cakeshop, Ltd. v. Colorado Civil Rights Commission* ruled in favor of a baker who argued making wedding cakes for same-sex couples violated his religious freedoms. And that quarter of Americans against marriage equality hasn't budged since *Obergefell.* But the 2010s were a significant decade for queer Americans, and *Glee* came into the decade guns blazing.

It's impossible to draw a complete cause-and-effect between the rise of queer characters on TV and the sweeping pro-gay wave of the 2010s. But seeing LGBTQ+ characters regularly on television makes us feel like we "know" them, and it's clear that personal connection to gay people makes straight people more tolerant. In 2012, a *Hollywood Reporter* poll found both Democratic and Republican voters were more likely to support gay marriage after watching *Glee* and/ or *Modern Family*.[17] That same year, then-Vice President Joe Biden chalked the change of public opinion on gay marriage to TV, too. "I think *Will & Grace* probably did more to educate the American public than almost anything anybody's ever done so far," he said on *Meet the Press*, while publicly announcing his support for marriage equality. "People fear that which is different. Now they're beginning to understand."[18] It's impossible to gauge how much one television show Changed Things, but *Glee*'s season one, precariously teetering on the edge of the 2010s, is symbolic of what was to come. *Glee*'s timing isn't insignificant.

I admit, *Glee*'s cosmic timeliness felt particular to me, as the show's first season corresponded perfectly with my year of coming out. The show premiered at the end of my freshman year of college, the same month I (finally) befriended a handful of out gay guys on a summer abroad program. Weeks later, two of my best friends from high school came out. When I went back to college for sophomore year, *Glee*'s first season picked back up, and I internally admitted I was queer. As I came out to friends one by one over the course of those two semesters, being gay became all I could think about. I agonized over my gender presentation, I pined for someone to kiss, and I worried whether my friends would treat me differently. On *Glee*, the blond cheerleader's belly got bigger, the Regionals got closer, the gaps between Finn and Rachel's longing gazes grew shorter, and the jokes about gay teens just kept coming.

Simply put, from my perspective, the whole world suddenly got a lot gayer. I wasn't actually watching *Glee* at that time—I didn't pick it up until season two, when the lesbian plots cropped up— but it felt very present, very talked about on campus and online. I was at a liberal arts college full of thirsty gay ex-theater kids, after all. By the end of my sophomore year, I'd told all my college friends I was gay. They were supportive, if fairly unsurprised. I'd (what felt like *finally*) started hooking up with a girl, Kate. I'd signed up for a bunch of feminist theory classes for the following fall. I'd amassed gay friends I felt like I could really *talk to*. I was totally comfortable with the thought that people might gossip about me. I was out! I was finally starting to like myself, to be proud of myself, to see myself as a sexual being other people might, maybe, be attracted to. There was one whole piece of the puzzle missing, and that was telling Claire.

We met at Athenian Room, the Greek diner my friends and I haunted in high school. I was back in Chicago for a few weeks, post-finals, pre-summer job back on the East Coast. Claire and I had maintained a platonic friendship at the beginning of college, but by now, it had faded into scattered, stilted catch-ups over breaks. We didn't text anymore, we didn't have phone calls. I didn't realize it at the time, but in all practicality, we'd broken up. I ordered a gyros sandwich, shredded meat packed on a pita, wrapped in tinfoil. We caught up. It was fine, you know, considering. The check came, and I intentionally lingered, knowing I had to spit this whole thing out. "Well," I started.

I futzed with the edges of my customer's receipt. My hands were clammy. They always got all cold and wet when I was nervous— they still do. In high school, I'd vomit before every cross-country race. We'd be in the middle of doing our pre-race strides on the starting line, minutes before the gun went off. I'd prance off, find a trash can, boot into it, then saunter back to the line to start the 5K. The person who would've held my hand and calmed me down, were we still in high school, was now sitting across the dinky table from me, the source of my pre-race jitters.

"I wanted to let you know that I've been coming out to people," I said.

What a strange way to phrase that. Despite having kissed her, I'd never actually, verbally told Claire I was gay before. I'd never said, "I might be gay," or "maybe I'm bisexual?" or "I'm definitely into girls," or just "I'm into you," or "I'd like to kiss you." The whole relationship had been nonverbal. It just happened. But now, for the first time, I was presenting my sexual preferences as a known fact between the two of us, as if we'd previously discussed it. "Per my last email, I'm a dyke," was the energy I brought to the Athenian Room table.

"Okay," she said. She might have added a congratulations or an "I'm happy for you," but those have blurred from my mind. There was a pause. Her *okay* had the tone of "What does this have to do with me?" Which I suspected she was using to cloak her nerves.

"Well, I wanted to give you a heads-up, because people are going to ask questions," I said steadily then added, "about us."

"Has anybody?"

"No," I assured her, lying. Several people had. No less than forty-five seconds after telling Jack I was queer, he asked if there was anything going on between me and Claire. I'd lied then, too. "But I won't be surprised if they do," I added to her. "And I want to know what you want me to say." I've had a long habit of burying my own needs in relationships, assuming others' needs are more important than mine. It's resulted in some dissatisfying circumstances.

Claire took a moment to think. Her eyes fluttered down to the paper place mat, where blue ink depicted the birth of Athena via Zeus's head. I curled my customer receipt into what looked like an infant's attempt at an origami crane.

"It's my business, too," she concluded. "So I'd appreciate it if you left me out of the story."

I was heartbroken, not because I still had feelings for her but by her flat-out rejection of a connection that once existed. I felt like she was ashamed of me. I felt, to use a contemporary cliché, gaslighted. But I also pitied her. I'd become so comfortable in the

Glee bubble and assumed we—"the culture," etc.—were all on the same page. But really, I was just at a liberal arts college, in a liberal family, and she was at Catholic school with a family that, I imagined, would be less welcoming of her sexuality. I was so certain she was having a similar experience grappling with her sexual identity as I was; perhaps she was, at a different pace or on a different track. But in that moment, I felt I'd done something very wrong. That seeking my own happiness had caused pain to others, to someone I cared about a lot, once. But mostly, I felt like stuffing the whole thing away. It was a disheartening cap to a very confusing chapter of my life, one that clashed starkly with the changing world around me. Just like that, I felt closeted again. I walked home from lunch full of shredded rotisserie meats and self-loathing.

〜

Post–2016 election, we began to talk a lot about bubbles. The left's shock at Trump's election, many argued, was the result of our living in political bubbles: only consuming liberal-leaning media and news, only talking to our blue-state friends, and having a geographic political separation with equally distinct spheres on social media. Liberal arts college is the most quintessential liberal bubble. It's in the name, after all. Claire's rejection of me—of us—highlighted the razor-thin sliver of the LGBTQ+ experience I'd known. The media I consumed, the news I read, the shows I watched, those were all feeding me this narrative that everyone was pro-gay now, that everyone was coming out on my personal timeline. I'd been duped into thinking what I saw in the media was a one-to-one reflection of the real world.

All narrative television is fantasy, to a degree. Some of that fantasy involves dragons and direwolves and incest; others are gritty depictions of working-class British teens constantly on MDMA.

Glee, certainly, is a fantasy. A world where the gay kids are on top and everyone has Broadway-caliber timbres and a backing track is obvious fantasy, by design. Fantasies are critical, yes, and mass-marketed stories have the power to move the needle forward on social issues, to change the conversation, to shape culture. They give us hope and perspective and friends we might not otherwise get the chance to know. But the moments when those fantasies collide with our disappointing realities are reliably painful.

Thus is the defining characteristic of gay millennials: we strad-dle the pre-*Glee* and post-*Glee* worlds. We went to high school when *faggot* wasn't even considered an F-word, when being a lesbian meant boys just didn't want you, when being nonbinary wasn't even a remote option. We grew up without queer charac-ters in our cartoons or Nickelodeon or Disney or TGIF sitcoms. We were raised in homophobia, came of age as the world changed around us, and are raising children in an age where it's never been easier to be same-sex parents. We're both lucky and jealous. As the state of gay evolved culturally and politically, we were old enough to see it and process it and not take it for granted—old enough to know what the world was like without it. Despite the success of *Drag Race,* the existence of lesbian Christmas rom-coms, and openly transgender Oscar nominees, we haven't moved on from the trauma of growing up in a culture that hates us. We don't *move on* from trauma, really. We can't really leave it in the past. It be-comes a part of us, and we move forward with it.

For LGBTQ+ millennials, our pride is couched in painful memories of a culture repulsed and frightened by queerness. That makes us skittish. It makes us loud. It makes us fear that all this progress, all this tolerance, all of Billy Porter's red carpet looks can vanish as quickly as it all appeared. It makes us frustrated by those who won't evolve on other social issues—health care, income inequality, climate change—as quickly as we witnessed them flip their attitudes on gayness. It makes us optimistic or greedy, depending on who you ask. We're hungry, impatient, and wanting. It makes gay millennials deeply fucking annoying to a lot of people. We have a particular superiority over the bullies and bigots of our youths. We *won,* after all, we're on the right side of history. Though that voice lingers, lurking, a parasite in our minds, piping up on rare occasions to ask: *What if those assholes were right, though?*

I don't think this position means queer millennials are stronger than future generations or inherently more progressive than older ones. Despite my Catholic upbringing, I don't believe pain holds any essential moral value. But our dual existence gives us a unique vantage point. That lunch at the Athenian Room with Claire, I felt my childhood and adulthood clashing. I'd come off a year of school where I felt the world changing around me, I felt the ushering in of a new chapter for myself. And then, the rainbow rug was ripped out from underneath me. That's the thing about being a queer millennial: it's not about things getting better in any linear fashion but holding a painful past and an optimistic future together, one in each hand, at the same time. It's a challenging balancing act, and perhaps because of our relative luckiness, one others rarely even notice.

That gyros lunch marked the end of Claire and me keeping in any kind of touch. I agreed to keep her privacy. When people asked if anything had been going on between us in high school, I laughed and changed the subject. We'd broken up in practicality at the end of senior year, and it took another two years, my coming out, seeing other people, and telling her as such for me to realize this had been a relationship. But I was still connected to the closet mentality, so I valued her shame over my pride, her regret of the past over my optimism for the future. At least for a while. Then I got out of the bubble.

ACKNOWLEDGMENTS

Thank you, thank you, *thank you*, to everyone at St. Martin's Griffin who brought *The 2000s Made Me Gay* to life. Thanks especially to my editor, Sylvan Creekmore, for believing in this project so hard from the very start, and for geeking out over gay TV as hard as I do. And to Jonathan Bush, for designing the cover art, which, in my opinion, absolutely slaps.

Thanks to my agent, Tim Wojcik, for his infectious good-naturedness and his ability to massage this book idea out of my brain. Without him, this collection would probably still be a vague podcast idea that I'd never get around to producing.

Thank you to my early readers, for telling me when my writing has ceased to make sense: Margaret Delaney, Jack Glascott, Ryan Willison, Catie Disabato, and Erin Sullivan. And to my writers group, which has miraculously stayed intact through the Zoom era, by some kind of sorcery.

To my family: Mom and Dad, for not thinking my writing full-time was such an outrageous idea; Rachel, for introducing me to Rilo Kiley and leading by example; Molly, for unmatched empathy, and for single-handedly keeping the USPS operational; and Zach, for always upping the bar for jokes, IMDb-based trivia recitation, and public transit map mastery. My brain would be mush if I'd never known you.

To my queer friends: I shudder to think how boring I'd be without you. And to Sophie, the best, best, best.

And finally thank you to Laura, my third-grade teacher, for casting me as Eleanor Roosevelt in our class play. I'm sorry I cried when you announced our roles; I had just never heard of Eleanor Roosevelt.

NOTES

Real-World Gays and *Real World* Gays

1   Kleine, Ted, "Reality Bites," *Chicago Reader*, August 2, 2001, https://www.chicagoreader.com/chicago/reality-bites/Content?oid=906087.

2   Bowen, Sesali, "A lot has changed since Aneesa became reality TV's first bi black woman," *Nylon*, June 26, 2019, https://www.nylon.com/aneesa-ferreira-interview.

3   Carter, Chelsea J. and Alan Duke, "Sean Sasser, whose ceremony with partner on 'Real World' was TV first, dies," *CNN*, August 8, 2013, https://www.cnn.com/2013/08/08/showbiz/sean-sasser-death/index.html.

Harry Potter and the Half-Assed Gay Character

1   Smith, David, "Dumbledore was gay, JK tells amazed fans," *The Guardian*, October 21, 2007, https://www.theguardian.com/uk/2007/oct/21/film.books.

2   Rothstein, Edward, "Is Dumbledore Gay? Depends on Definitions of 'Is' and 'Gay,'" *The New York Times*, October 29, 2007, https://www.nytimes.com/2007/10/29/arts/29conn.html.

3   Harris, Mark, "Dumbledore's outing: Why it matters," *Entertainment Weekly*, October 30, 2007, https://ew.com/article/2007/10/30/dumbledores-outing-why-it-matters/.

4   Warner Bros. Entertainment, "A Conversation between JK Rowling and Daniel Radcliffe," YouTube Video, 53:03, September 22, 2013, https://www.youtube.com/watch?v=7BdVHWz1DPU&t=1729s.

5   Desta, Yohana, "J.K. Rowling Has More to Say About the 'Sexual

Dimension' of Dumbledore and Grindelwald," *Vanity Fair,* March 14, 2019, https://www.vanityfair.com/hollywood/2019/03/jk-rowling -dumbledore-grindelwald-relationship.

6   Abidor, Jen, "21 Massive Things J.K. Rowling Has Revealed About 'Harry Potter' On Twitter," *BuzzFeed,* February 7, 2019, https://www .buzzfeed.com/jenniferabidor/huge-harry-potter-reveals-jk-rowling -has-made-on-twitter.

7   Malloy, Antonia, "JK Rowling: 'Of course' the entirely fictional Hog-warts would be a safe place for LGBT students," *The Independent,* December 18, 2014, https://www.independent.co.uk/news/people /jk-rowling-of-course-hogwarts-would-be-a-safe-place-for-lgbt -students-9932810.html.

8   Haysom, Sam, "17 key 'Harry Potter' secrets J.K. Rowling has re-vealed since the books finished," Mashable.com, June 4, 2016, https:// mashable.com/2016/06/04/j-k-rowling-harry-potter-secrets.

9   Couch, Dustin (@Dustinkcouch), "waiter: anything to drink? JK Rowling: the sorting hat can fuck but chooses not to," Twit-ter, January 21, 2019, https://twitter.com/dustinkcouch/status /1087385268695588865.

10   Whitehurst, Rachel (@RachLWhitehurst), "me: [blank] jk rowling: buckbeak is into light choking but hasn't found the right partner," Twitter, January 26, 2019, https://twitter.com/rachlwhitehurst /status/1089089149473218560.

11   Flood, Alison, "JK Rowling under fire for writing about 'Native American wizards,'" *The Guardian,* March 9, 2016, https://www .theguardian.com/books/2016/mar/09/jk-rowling-under-fire-for -appropriating-navajo-tradition-history-of-magic-in-north-america -pottermore.

12   Rowling, J. K., "Grindelwald casting," J. K. Rowling website, December 7, 2017, https://www.jkrowling.com/opinions/grindelwald-casting/.

13   Freeman, Hadley, "JK Rowling has defended Johnny Depp's casting in Fantastic Beasts. Is it time we moved on?" *The Guardian,* Decem-ber 16, 2017, https://www.theguardian.com/society/2017/dec/16/jk -rowling-johnny-depp-fantastic-beasts.

14   Shakeri, Sima, "Outrage Ensues After Claudia Kim Cast as Nagini in

'Fantastic Beasts: The Crimes of Grindelwald," *HuffPost Canada*, September 29, 2018, https://www.huffingtonpost.ca/2018/09/29/claudia
-kim-cast-as-nagini-in-fantastic-beasts-the-crimes-of-grindelwald
_a_23545795/.

15 Stack, Liam, "J.K. Rowling Criticized After Tweeting Support for Anti-Transgender Researcher," *The New York Times*, December 19, 2019 https://www.nytimes.com/2019/12/19/world/europe/jk
-rowling-maya-forstater-transgender.html.

16 Rowling, J. K., "J.K. Rowling Writes about Her Reasons for Speaking out on Sex and Gender Issues," J. K. Rowling website, June 10, 2020, https://www.jkrowling.com/opinions/j-k-rowling-writes-about-her
-reasons-for-speaking-out-on-sex-and-gender-issues.

17 Gonella, Catalina, "Survey: 20 Percent of Millennials Identify as LGBTQ," *NBC News*, March 31, 2017, https://www.nbcnews.com
/feature/nbc-out/survey-20-percent-millennials-identify-lgbtq
-n740791.

18 Lewis, Mary Grace, "Study Says Only Two Thirds of Gen Z Is Straight," *The Advocate*, July 6, 2018, https://www.advocate.com/youth/2018/7
/06/study-says-only-two-thirds-gen-z-straight.

19 "Fact Sheet: Attitudes on Same-Sex Marriage," Pew Research Center, May 14, 2019, https://www.pewforum.org/fact-sheet/changing
-attitudes-on-gay-marriage.

20 Bendix, Trish, "'Faking It' Finale Proves MTV Does Not Know Lesbian Sexuality," *The Hollywood Reporter*, June 10, 2014, https://www
.hollywoodreporter.com/live-feed/faking-finale-proves-mtv-does
-710958.

The Gospel According to *Mean Girls*

1 Augustine, Saint and Maria Boulding. *The Confessions*. New York: Vintage, 1998.

2 Tauber, Michelle, "Under Pressure," *People*, December 20, 2004, https://
people.com/archive/cover-story-under-pressure-vol-62-no-25/.

3 Styles, Jennifer, "Lohan's father arrested for unpaid bill," *CNN*, June 30, 2004, https://www.cnn.com/2004/SHOWBIZ/Movies/06/30
/lohans.father/.

4   Williams, Greg, "Hell Hath No Fury Like a Showbiz Father Scorned," *New York*, February 18, 2005, https://nymag.com/nymetro/news /people/features/11159/.

5   Dale, Austin, "What Really Happened to Lindsay Lohan, Part 2: The Ingenue," *IndieWire*, November 20, 2012, https://www.indiewire .com/2012/11/what-really-happened-to-lindsay-lohan-part-2-the -ingenue-172226/.

6   Tauber, Michelle, "Under Pressure."

7   Peretz, Evgenia, "Confessions of a Teenage Movie Queen," *Vanity Fair*, February 2006, https://archive.vanityfair.com/article/2006/2 /confessions-of-a-teenage-movie-queen.

8   Errico, Marcus, "Lohan Busted for DUI, 'Contraband,'" *E! Online*, May 26, 2007, https://www.eonline.com/news/55252/lohan-busted-for -dui-contraband.

9   Associated Press, "Lohan completes jail time in 84 minutes," *The Hollywood Reporter*, November 16, 2007, https://www.hollywoodreporter .com/news/lohan-completes-jail-time-84-155188.

10 Resnick, Brian and National Journal, "No, Rick Perry, Being Gay is Not Like Alcoholism," *The Atlantic*, June 12, 2004, https://www .theatlantic.com/politics/archive/2014/06/no-rick-perry-being-gay -is-not-like-alcoholism/453657/.

11 Heyman, Marshall, "Lindsay Lohan: Myth vs. Reality," *Harper's Bazaar*, December 2008, https://web.archive.org/web/20081218230936 /http://www.harpersbazaar.com/magazine/cover/lindsay-lohan -cover-story-1208.

12 Aurthur, Kate, "It's bigger than both of them," *Los Angeles Times*, July 20, 2008, https://www.latimes.com/archives/la-xpm-2008-jul-20-ca -lindsaylohan20-story.html.

13 Hilton, Perez, "saMAN Wasn't LezLo's First!" PerezHilton.com, July 20, 2008, https://perezhilton.com/saman-wasnt-lezlos-first/.

14 *Us Weekly* Staff, "Lindsay Lohan: Samantha Is the 'Only Woman I've Been Attracted To,'" *Us Weekly*, February 23, 2010, https://www .usmagazine.com/celebrity-body/news/lindsay-lohan-samantha-is -only-woman-ive-been-attracted-to-2010232/.

15 Morgan, Piers, "'Seeing Mum's face as I turned myself in to jail was the worst moment of my life. I cried for four days': Lindsay Lohan talks drugs, sex and rehab with Piers Morgan," *Daily Mail*, May 4, 2013, https://www.dailymail.co.uk/home/event/article-2318388/Lindsay-Lohan-interview-Piers-Morgan-Seeing-Mums-face-I-turned-jail-worst-moment-life.html.

16 Williams, Wendy, "Exclusive: Lindsay Lohan," YouTube Video, 17:22, January 12, 2018, https://www.youtube.com/watch?v=sF3H48pN4Ao.

Cherry ChapStick

1 Azzopardi, Chris, "10 Years Later: Katy Perry's Queer Touchstone 'I Kissed a Girl' Opened the Door For Sexual Fluidity, But Not Without Criticism," *billboard*, April 27, 2018, https://www.billboard.com/articles/news/pride/8348403/katy-perry-i-kissed-a-girl-10-years-later.

2 Brown, Mark, "Chart-topping lesbian love song divides gay community," *The Guardian*, August 7, 2008, https://www.theguardian.com/music/2008/aug/08/popandrock.gayrights.

3 Gresehover, Ehren, "Six Reasons Katy Perry's 'I Kissed a Girl' Isn't the Song of the Summer," *Vulture*, August 11, 2008, https://www.vulture.com/2008/08/katy_perrys_i_kissed_a_girl_st.html.

4 Tyrangiel, Josh, "Katy Perry's I Kissed a Girl," *TIME*, August 27, 2008, http://content.time.com/time/specials/packages/article/0,28804,1834301_1834300_1834283,00.html.

5 Carpenter, Ellen, "Why I Hate Katy Perry," *SPIN*, November 12, 2008, https://www.spin.com/2008/11/why-i-hate-katy-perry/.

6 Garratt, Sheryl, "Kiss me, Katy," *The Guardian*, August 9, 2008, https://www.theguardian.com/music/2008/aug/10/music.popandrock.

7 Jean M. Twenge, Ryne A. Sherman, Brooke E. Wells, "Changes in American Adults' Reported Same-Sex Sexual Experiences and Attitudes, 1973–2014," *Archives of Sexual Behavior*, June 1, 2016, https://link.springer.com/article/10.1007/s10508-016-0769-4.

8 Rosa, Christopher, "Katy Perry Says She'd Probably Rewrite 'I Kissed a Girl' If It Came Out Now," *Glamour*, February 6, 2018, https://www.glamour.com/story/katy-perry-would-rewrite-i-kissed-a-girl-video.

9   Kim, Michelle, "Hayley Kiyoko: Rita Ora, Charli XCX's 'Girls' 'Does More Harm Than Good for the LGBTQ+ Community,'" *Pitchfork*, May 11, 2018, https://pitchfork.com/news/hayley-kiyoko-rita-ora-charli-xcxs-girls-does-more-harm-than-good-for-the-lgbtq-community/.

Be the PR Team You Wish to See in the World

1   Heaney, Katie, "The Reign of King Princess," *The Cut*, July 18, 2020, https://www.thecut.com/2018/07/the-reign-of-king-princess.html.

2   Bennett, Willa, "King Princess: Free to Be," *them.*, June 21, 2019, https://www.them.us/story/king-princess-free-to-be.

3   Chauncey, George. *Gay New York: Gender, Urban Culture, and the Making of the Gay Male World*. New York: Basic Books, 2008, 6–7.

4   Kennedy, Hubert C, "The 'Third Sex' Theory of Karl Heinrich Ulrichs," in *The Gay Past: A Collection of Historical Essays*, ed. Salvatore Licata, Robert P. Petersen (New York, New York: Harrington Park Press, 2013), 103–106.

5   Stern, Keith. *Queers in History: The Comprehensive Encyclopedia of Historical Gays, Lesbians and Bisexuals*. Dallas, Texas: BenBella Books, 2009, 460.

6   Jarnot, Lisa. *Robert Duncan, The Ambassador From Venus*. Berkeley, California: University of California Press, 2012, 90.

7   Ibid., 79.

8   Sawyer, Diane, "Ellen Degeneres," *20/20*, ABC News, April 25, 1997, https://www.youtube.com/watch?v=jPMthYke01g.

9   Winfrey, Oprah, "Ellen Degeneres," *The Oprah Winfrey Show*, Harpo Studios, April 30 1997, https://www.youtube.com/watch?v=o3Y1rIr5Vo8.

10 Green, Sylvia, "How Working On Ellen's 'Puppy Episode' Changed My Life," *HuffPost*, April 28, 2017, https://www.huffpost.com/entry/how-working-on-ellens-puppy-episode-changed-my-life_b_58fa809ee4b06b9cb916ffc9.

11 Aviles, Gwen, "Laura Dern said she lost work, needed 'Security De-

tail' after 'Ellen' coming-out episode," *NBC News,* December 3, 2019, https://www.nbcnews.com/feature/nbc-out/laura-dern-said-she -lost-work-needed-security-detail-after-n1094946.

12 Smith, Austin, "Rosie's Comedy Club Confession . . . OK! I'm Gay," *New York Post,* March 1, 2002, https://nypost.com/2002/03/01/rosies -comedy-club-confession-ok-im-gay.

13 Sullivan, Emmet, "Wanda Sykes Proclaims, 'I'm Proud to Be Gay,'" *People,* November 17, 2008, https://people.com/celebrity/wanda -sykes-proclaims-im-proud-to-be-gay.

14 *People* Staff, "EXCLUSIVE: Neil Patrick Harris Tells PEOPLE He Is Gay," *People,* November 3, 2006, https://people.com/celebrity /exclusive-neil-patrick-harris-tells-people-he-is-gay.

15 Associated Press, "George Takei, 'Mr. Sulu,' says he's gay," *Today,* October 27, 2005, https://www.today.com/popculture/george-takei-mr -sulu-says-hes-gay-2D80555905.

16 Laudadio, Marisa, "Lance Bass 'I'm Gay,'" *People,* August 7, 2006, https:// people.com/archive/cover-story-lance-bass-im-gay-vol-66-no-6.

17 BBC News, "Barack Obama 'chokes up' giving Ellen DeGeneres 'Medal of Freedom," YouTube Video, 1:58, November 23, 2016, https:// www.youtube.com/watch?v=4ZQaayjVPZs.

18 NBC, "Kate McKinnon's Tribute to Ellen DeGeneres—2020 Golden Globes," YouTube Video, 2:45, January 5, 2020, https://www.youtube .com/watch?v=1owY3QPg4Bc.

19 Weaver, Hilary, "Ellen DeGeneres's Groundbreaking Coming Out: 20 Years Later," *Vanity Fair,* April 28, 2017, https://www.vanityfair.com /style/2017/04/20th-anniversary-of-ellen-degeneres-coming-out.

20 Stromberg, Joseph, "Coming Out of the Closet May Be Good For Your Health," *Smithsonian Magazine,* January 29, 2013, https://www .smithsonianmag.com/science-nature/coming-out-of-the-closet -may-be-good-for-your-health-7400182.

21 Lee, Esther, "Michelle Rodriguez, Cara Delevingne Cuddle at Knicks Game: See Pictures of Their Bizarre Behavior!" *Us Weekly,* January 8, 2014, https://www.usmagazine.com/celebrity-news/news/michelle -rodriguez-cara-delevingne-knicks-game-pictures-bizarre-behavior -201481/.

22 *Saturday Night Live*, "Kristen Stewart Monologue—SNL," YouTube Video, 4:51, February 5, 2017, https://www.youtube.com/watch?v=Qc4ahnZzVM4.

23 Brooks, Xan, "Kristen Stewart: 'It's not confusing if you're bisexual. For me, it's the opposite,'" *The Guardian*, March 9, 2017, https://www.theguardian.com/film/2017/mar/09/kristen-stewart-bisexual-personal-shopper-trump-tweets.

24 Spanos, Brittany, "Janelle Monáe Frees Herself," *Rolling Stone*, April 26, 2018, https://www.rollingstone.com/music/music-features/janelle-monae-frees-herself-629204/.

25 Mulkerrins, Jane, "Break The Mold with Tessa Thompson," *Porter*, June 29, 2018, https://www.net-a-porter.com/en-us/porter/article-502e16f70e0351fa?cm_mmc=LinkshareUS-_-TnL5HPStwNw-_-Custom-_-LinkBuilder&ranMID=24449&ranEAID=TnL5HPStwNw&ranSiteID=TnL5HPStwNw-MCACM9sEVLn3bMJmAHFSSw&siteID=TnL5HPStwNw-MCACM9sEVLn3bMJmAHFSSw.

26 *Observer* Staff, "Destroying Reputations: as easy as ACB," *Tufts Observer*, February 28, 2011, http://tuftsobserver.org/destroying-reputations-as-easy-as-acb.

27 Clifton, Derrick, "Sam Smith's they/them pronoun backlash highlights an ongoing cultural disconnect," *NBC News*, September 19, 2019, https://www.nbcnews.com/think/opinion/sam-smith-s-they-them-pronoun-backlash-highlights-ongoing-cultural-ncna1056136.

28 Spanos, Brittany, "#20gayteen: The Year of Hayley Kiyoko," *Rolling Stone*, July 20, 2018, https://www.rollingstone.com/music/music-features/how-hayley-kiyoko-became-lesbian-jesus-695667.

Blair Waldorf Has Notes on My Sex Life

1   "A Survey of LGBT Americans," Pew Research Center, June 13, 2013, https://www.pewsocialtrends.org/2013/06/13/a-survey-of-lgbt-americans.

Banter Boys

1   Diamond, Jason, "Seth Cohen Is My Spirit Animal," *Vulture*, August 9, 2013, https://www.vulture.com/2013/08/seth-cohen-is-my-spirit-animal.html.

2 Stubbins, Sinead, "Death Cab for Cutie, Seth Cohen and the Indie Influence of the Teen TV Soundtrack," *Pitchfork*, May 11, 2015, https://pitchfork.com/thepitch/763-death-cab-for-cutie-seth-cohen-and-the-indie-influence-of-the-teen-tv-soundtrack.

3 Shales, Tom, "'The O.C.': Land of The Brooding Teen," *The Washington Post*, August 5, 2003, https://www.washingtonpost.com/archive/lifestyle/2003/08/05/the-oc-land-of-the-brooding-teen/c7c18c5c-b01c-4d76-9d6d-b808d133ae6c.

Disney Channel Presents: Sapphic Overtones

1 Etkin, Jamie, "The 'High School Musical' Cast Reveals Facts You Probably Didn't Know," *BuzzFeed News*, January 20, 2016, https://www.buzzfeed.com/jaimieetkin/still-in-this-together.

2 "Michael Walsh," Internet Movie Database, https://www.imdb.com/name/nm1047701.

3 Fetters, Ashley, "4 Big Problems With *The Feminine Mystique*," *The Atlantic*, February 12, 2013, https://www.theatlantic.com/sexes/archive/2013/02/4-big-problems-with-the-feminine-mystique/273069.

4 Ellison, Briana R., "Trending: Disney Channel just made a huge leap forward in LGBT representation," *The Washington Post*, February 10, 2019, https://www.washingtonpost.com/express/2019/02/11/trending-disney-channel-just-made-huge-leap-forward-lgbt-representation.

5 Brown, Tracy, "With 'Onward,' Disney continues its token LGBT representation. We're ready for more," *Los Angeles Times*, March 10, 2020, https://www.latimes.com/entertainment-arts/movies/story/2020-03-10/onward-lgbtq-representation-disney-pixar.

6 McNary, Dave, "'Onward' Banned in Several Middle East Countries Due to Lesbian Reference," *Variety*, March 6, 2020, https://variety.com/2020/film/news/onward-banned-lesbian-kuwait-oman-qatar-saudi-arabia-1203526359.

American Bitch/American Butch

1 McCormick, Joseph, "QUIZ: Which queer female subtype fits you best?" *PinkNews*, May 21, 2016, https://www.pinknews.co.uk/2016/05/21/quiz-which-queer-female-subtype-fits-you-best.

2   Jade and Rebel, "Butch? Or Femme?" *Women's Voices,* 1998, http://members.tripod.com/~womens_voices/BF100/BF100.html?.

3   Goodloe, Amy, "Lesbian Identity and the Politics of Butch-Femme," 1993, http://amygoodloe.com/papers/lesbian-identity-and-the-politics-of-butch-femme.

4   Ibid.

5   Nestle, Joan, "Butch-Fem Relationships: Sexual Courage in the 1950s," *HERESIES: A Feminist Publication on Art and Politics,* bol. 5, no. 4, iss. 12, The Sex Issue, (1981).

6   Feinberg, Leslie, *Stone Butch Blues.* New York, New York: Alison Books, 2003.

7   Rich, Adrienne, "Compulsory Heterosexuality and Lesbian Existence," *Signs,* vol. 5, no. 4, Women: Sex and Sexuality. (Summer 1980), 631–660.

8   Rubin, Gayle, "Of Catamites and Kings: Reflections on Butch, Gender, and Boundaries," *The Transgender Studies Reader,* ed. Susan Stryker and Stephen White (New York, New York: Routledge, 2006), 472–481.

9   Manders, Kerry, "The Renegades," *T: The New York Times Style Magazine,* April 13, 2020, https://www.nytimes.com/interactive/2020/04/13/t-magazine/butch-stud-lesbian.html.

10 Butler, Judith, *Gender Trouble.* New York, New York: Routledge, 2010.

11 Bennetts, Leslie, "k.d. lang cuts it close," *Vanity Fair,* August 1993, https://www.google.com/search?q=vanity+fair+kd+lang+cover&oq=vanity+fair+kd+lang+cover&aqs=chrome.0.0j69i57.3041j0j4&sourceid=chrome&ie=UTF-8.

12 Tina Fey Is Awesome, "Queer Eye for the Straight Gal," Tumblr, April 17, 2011, https://tinafeyisawesome.tumblr.com/post/4688666130/queer-eye-for-the-straight-gal-you-know-what-i.

13 Franklin, Nancy, "L.A. Love," *The New Yorker,* January 26, 2004, https://www.newyorker.com/magazine/2004/02/02/l-a-love.

14 Stanley, Alessandra, "TV WEEKEND; Women Having Sex, Hoping Men Tune In," *The New York Times,* January 16, 2004, https://www

.nytimes.com/2004/01/16/movies/tv-weekend-women-having-sex
-hoping-men-tune-in.html.

15   Bolonik, Kera, "Not Your Mother's Lesbians," *New York,* January 2,
2004, https://nymag.com/nymetro/news/features/n_9708.

TALKING / LAUGHING / LOVING / BREATHING

1   Stanley, Alessandra, "TV WEEKEND; Women Having Sex, Hoping
Men Tune In," *The New York Times,* January 16, 2004, https://www
.nytimes.com/2004/01/16/movies/tv-weekend-women-having-sex
-hoping-men-tune-in.html.

2   Poniewozik, James, "Television: Less Than Letter Perfect," *TIME,*
January 26, 2004, http://content.time.com/time/subscriber/article
/0,33009,993195,00.html.

3   Franklin, Nancy, "L.A. Love," *The New Yorker,* January 26, 2004,
https://www.newyorker.com/magazine/2004/02/02/l-a-love.

4   Andrews, Travis M, "106 million people watched the 'M.A.S.H.' finale
35 years ago. No scripted show since has come close," *The Washington Post,* February 28, 2018, https://www.washingtonpost.com/news
/morning-mix/wp/2018/02/28/106-million-people-watched-mash
-finale-35-years-ago-no-scripted-show-has-come-close-since/.

Taylor Swift Made Me a U-Haul Dyke

1   DeLaria, Lea (@realleadelaria), "I wrote this joke in 1988 and I am still
not a @uhaul brand ambassador!" Twitter, March 2, 2020, 12:46 p.m.
https://twitter.com/realleadelaria/status/1234580814635003904.

2   Miller, Shauna, "Beyond the U-Haul: How Lesbian Relationships
Are Changing," *The Atlantic,* July 3, 2013, https://www.theatlantic
.com/sexes/archive/2013/07/beyond-the-u-haul-how-lesbian
-relationships-are-changing/277495.

3   Orth, Taylor and Michael Rosenfeld, "Commitment Timing in Same-
Sex and Different-Sex Relationships," *Population Review* 57, no. 1
(2018), https://muse.jhu.edu/article/682834.

4   "Taylor Swift Chart History," *billboard,* accessed August 9, 2020,
https://www.billboard.com/music/taylor-swift/chart-history
/billboard-200/song/597828.

5   Caulfield, Keith, "Taylor Swift Edges Susan Boyle For 2009's Top-Selling Album," *billboard*, January 6, 2010, https://www.billboard.com/articles/news/960801/taylor-swift-edges-susan-boyle-for-2009s-top-selling-album.

6   Rosen, Jody, "Fearless album review," *Rolling Stone*, November 13, 2008, https://www.rollingstone.com/music/music-album-reviews/fearless-252671.

7   DeGeneres, Ellen, "Memorable Moment: Taylor Swift on Joe Jonas," *The Ellen Show*, YouTube Video, 4:13, uploaded July 10 2012, https://www.youtube.com/watch?v=amh859mNeKI.

8   Swift, Taylor, "Cut by Cut," Big Machine Records blog, accessed August 9, 2020, https://web.archive.org/web/20100725202904/http:/www.bigmachinerecords.com/taylorswift/index.cfm?id=110.

9   Swift, Taylor, "10 Questions for Taylor Swift," *TIME*, April 23, 2009, http://content.time.com/time/magazine/article/0,9171,1893502,00.html.

10 Hudak, Joseph, "Taylor Swift Supports Tennessee Advocacy Group With $113,000 Donation," *Rolling Stone*, April 9, 2019, https://www.rollingstone.com/music/music-country/taylor-swift-donation-lgbtq-tennessee-819987.

11 Caramanica, Jon, Caryn Ganz and Wesley Morris, "For Taylor Swift, Is Ego Stronger Than Pride?" *The New York Times*, June 18, 2019, https://www.nytimes.com/2019/06/18/arts/music/taylor-swift-you-need-to-calm-down-video.html.

The *Glee* Bubble

1   Mulkerrins, Jane, "I made gay sidekicks the leads: how Ryan Murphy changed TV for ever," *The Guardian*, October 26, 2019, https://www.theguardian.com/tv-and-radio/2019/oct/26/ryan-murphy-american-horror-story-pose-politician-glee-nip-tuck.

2   Nussbaum, Emily, "How Ryan Murphy Became The Most Powerful Man In TV," *The New Yorker*, May 14, 2018, https://www.newyorker.com/magazine/2018/05/14/how-ryan-murphy-became-the-most-powerful-man-in-tv.

3   James, Becca, "Nip/Tuck Is Still the Ultimate Ryan Murphy Show,"

Vulture, March 11, 2020, https://www.vulture.com/2020/03/nip-tuck
-ultimate-ryan-murphy-show.html.

4   Fisher, Luchina, "'Glee:' 'Born This Way' Episode Has Sparks Flying,"
     ABC News, April 25, 2011, https://abcnews.go.com/Entertainment
     /glee-lady-gagas-born-episode/story?id=13451313.

5   Parke, Michelle, "Introduction," *Queer in the Choir Room: Essays on
     Gender and Sexuality in* Glee. North Carolina: McFarland & Com-
     pany, Inc., Publishers, 2014, 1.

6   Seidman, Robert, "Top Fox Primetime Shows, May 18–24, 2009,"
     TV by the Numbers, May 27, 2009, https://web.archive.org/web
     /20100426123807/http://tvbythenumbers.com/2009/05/27/top-fox
     -primetime-shows-may-18-24-2009/19470.

7   Halperin, Shirley, "EXCLUSIVE: Inside the Hot Business of 'Glee,'" *The
     Hollywood Reporter,* January 25, 2011, https://www.hollywoodreporter
     .com/news/hot-business-glee-75593.

8   Andreeva, Nellie, "'Glee' Co-Creator Ryan Murphy Signs Giant New
     Deal With 20th Century Fox TV," *Deadline,* July 19, 2010, https://
     deadline.com/2010/07/glee-co-creator-ryan-murphy-signs-gigantic
     -new-deal-with-20th-century-fox-tv-54606.

9   Nussbaum, Emily, "How Ryan Murphy Became The Most Powerful
     Man In TV."

10   Gallup Poll, "In Depth: Topics A to Z, Gay and Lesbian Rights,"
     Gallup News, accessed August 9, 2020, https://news.gallup.com/poll
     /1651/gay-lesbian-rights.aspx.

11   The Movement Advancement Project, "LGBT Police Spotlight: Con-
     version Therapy Bans," LGBT MAP, July 2017, https://www.lgbtmap
     .org/file/policy-spotlight-conversion-therapy-bans.pdf.

12   Gay & Lesbian Alliance Against Defamation, "Where We Are On
     TV: GLAAD's 14th Annual Diversity Study Previews The 2009-2010
     Primetime Television Season," GLAAD, October 1, 2009, https://
     www.glaad.org/sites/default/files/whereweareontv2009-2010.pdf.

13   Gay & Lesbian Alliance Against Defamation, "Where We Are on TV,"
     GLAAD, November 7, 2019, https://www.glaad.org/sites/default/files
     /GLAAD%20WHERE%20WE%20ARE%20ON%20TV%202019%20
     2020.pdf.

14 Box Office Mojo, "Love, Simon (2018)," IMDb Pro, accessed August 9, 2020, https://www.boxofficemojo.com/title/tt5164432/?ref_=bo_se _r_1.

15 Tsjeng, Zing, "Teens These Days Are Queer AF, New Study Says," *Vice*, March 10, 2016, https://www.vice.com/en_us/article/kb4dvz /teens-these-days-are-queer-af-new-study-says.

16 Schmidt, Samantha, "Americans' views flipped on gay rights. How did minds change so quickly?" *The Washington Post*, June 7, 2019, https://www.washingtonpost.com/local/social-issues/americans -views-flipped-on-gay-rights-how-did-minds-change-so-quickly /2019/06/07/ae256016-8720-11e9-98c1-e945ae5db8fb_story.html.

17 Appelo, Tim, "THR Poll: 'Glee' and 'Modern Family' Drive Voters to Favor Gay Marriage—Even Many Romney Voters," *The Hollywood Reporter*, November 3, 2012, https://www.hollywoodreporter.com /news/thr-poll-glee-modern-family-386225.

18 NBC News, "FLASHBACK: May 6th, 2012, Joe Biden Endorsed Same-Sex Marriage | Meet the Press | NBC News," YouTube Video, 3:03, uploaded May 6, 2012, https://www.youtube.com/watch?v =vyjYg3ZYFfQ.

ABOUT THE AUTHOR

Kort Havens

GRACE PERRY's work has been published in a variety of outlets, including *The New Yorker, New York* magazine's *The Cut, BuzzFeed, Outside,* and *Eater.* She's also written for *The Onion* and the feminist satire site *Reductress.* Most of her work, comedy and journalism alike, interrogates the intersection of queerness, pop culture, and the internet. She lives in Los Angeles.